To the Project for Excellence in Journalism

THE NIGHTLY NEWS NIGHTMARE

THE NIGHTLY NEWS NIGHTMARE

Media Coverage of U.S. Presidential Elections, 1988–2008

THIRD EDITION

Stephen J. Farnsworth and S. Robert Lichter

ROWMAN & LITTLEFIELD PUBLISHERS, INC.
Lanham • Boulder • New York • Toronto • Plymouth, UK

Published by Rowman & Littlefield Publishers, Inc.
A wholly owned subsidary of The Rowman & Littlefield Publishing Group, Inc.
4501 Forbes Boulevard, Suite 200, Lanham, Maryland 20706
http://www.rowmanlittlefield.com

Estover Road, Plymouth PL6 7PY, United Kingdom

British Library Cataloguing in Publication Information Available

Library of Congress Cataloging-in-Publication Data

Farnsworth, Stephen J., 1961-
   The nightly news nightmare : media coverage of the U.S. presidential elections / Stephen J. Farnsworth and S. Robert Lichter. — 3rd ed.
      p. cm.
   Includes bibliographical references and index.
   ISBN 978-1-4422-0067-8 (cloth : alk. paper) — ISBN 978-1-4422-0068-5 (pbk. : alk. paper) — ISBN 978-1-4422-0069-2 (electronic)
   1. Press and politics—United States. 2. Television broadcasting of news—United States. 3. Political campaigns—United States—Press coverage—United States. 4. Presidents—United States—Election—History—20th century. I. Lichter, S. Robert. II. Title.
   PN4888.P6F37 2011
   070.4'49324973—dc22   2010014853

Printed in the United States of America

Contents

Tables

Preface to the Third Edition

WHEN WE BEGAN WORK ON the first edition of this book shortly after the 2000 elections, the media environment was dramatically different, and this was true nowhere more than in campaign news. The so-called Big Three broadcast networks (and particularly their flagship nightly newscasts) defined the daily news agenda for presidential candidates and voters alike, as they had for decades.

The memorable moments of the past half century of presidential elections were all linked to televised images—the youthful-looking John Kennedy besting a haggard Richard Nixon in the first televised presidential debate in 1960; the 1968 Democratic convention held in the shadow of violent demonstrations and a police riot in Chicago; the "selling of the President" in 1972, when Nixon brought Madison Avenue techniques to bear on his choreographed campaign; Jimmy Carter's demonstration that a political unknown could generate a burst of media momentum by winning the previously overlooked Iowa caucuses in 1976; Ronald Reagan taking televised communication skills to a whole new level; George H. W. Bush's telegenic flag-factory visit and attack ads featuring the furloughed murderer Willy Horton in 1988; Ross Perot's televised infomercials in 1992; the "free airtime" the networks granted to Bill Clinton and Bob Dole in 1996 in a gesture of noblesse oblige; the list could go on indefinitely.

But the traditional campaign news system dominated by network television had already started to crack in 1992, when Bill Clinton discovered that he could take his case to the syndicated talk shows, Perot announced his candidacy on CNN's *Larry King Live*, and Rush Limbaugh brought talk radio into the campaign discourse. And this was only a warm-up for the really profound changes that were just around the corner. In 2000 cable news first surpassed the broadcast networks as a source of election news. In 2002 Fox News Channel, with its groundbreaking blend of populism and conservative opinion, became the most-watched cable network. By 2004 not only talk shows but late-night television comedians had become popular sources of campaign information.

For the first time since the 1960s, however, the most lasting and far-reaching changes were taking place in a new medium of communication. During the 1990s email and the World Wide Web had begun to revolutionize the ways in which ordinary people obtained information and communicated with each other. But use of the Internet as a political tool was still in its infancy. At the turn of the new millennium, as George W. Bush and Al Gore fought out one of the most hotly contested elections in history, only five million Americans had broadband connections. By 2004 the number had risen to thirty-three million, and by 2008 to sixty-eight million. In less than a decade, the latest "new media" had gone mainstream.

But most politicians were slow to use these new tools. In retrospect the 2000 candidate websites look primitive and rudimentary, and they played little role in that year's presidential campaign. It wasn't until the 2004 election cycle that Democratic primary candidate Howard Dean demonstrated the power of the Internet as a fundraising tool. In the 2004 general election online bloggers demonstrated their growing clout when they helped force CBS to retract a story claiming that George W. Bush had received preferential treatment in his National Guard duty during the Vietnam War.

Still, it was not until 2008 that Barack Obama became the first presidential candidate to succeed in integrating online with traditional campaign tools, especially in his use of social media. His success insured that no future GOP candidate will emulate John McCain in failing to appreciate the importance of Facebook, YouTube, and Twitter, not to mention any other online tool that shows promise in influencing voters in 2012.

For all the recent and coming changes in the media environment, however, television news has shown remarkable resilience in remaining the premier instrument of campaign communication. Over twenty million people still tune in to the three broadcast network evening news shows, several times the combined audience of their cable news counterparts at any point in prime time. And while growing numbers of citizens get their campaign news on the Internet each election cycle, that's not the same as getting their news *from* the Internet. In 2010 the Pew Research Center's Internet & American Life Project reported that the most popular online news destinations were portal sites like Google News and AOL (which mainly pass users along to traditional news media sites), followed by broadcast and cable news network sites. These options easily outdistanced blogs, social-networking sites, and news and commentary sites like the Drudge Report and the Huffington Post (Pew 2010). In addition, regular users of such sites know the considerable extent to which the commentary that appears online is derived from mainstream news content, much of it originally airing on television.

So it's still far too early to write off television news or even those alleged dinosaurs, the network evening news shows, as key agenda setters and information sources in presidential campaigns. They're still very much in the game, although the days are long gone since they could claim to be the whole ball game. Nonetheless, any serious study of campaign news these days must venture far beyond the nightly news to encompass the multidimensional media landscape that surrounds today's voters.

For the third edition of this book, we were able to meet this challenge with the help of remarkable research carried out by the Project for Excellence in Journalism (PEJ), which is itself a project of the Pew Research Center in Washington, D.C. During key periods of the 2008 primary and general elections, PEJ conducted a content analysis of campaign news that encompassed every major segment of the contemporary news media, including broadcast and cable television, talk radio, national and local newspapers, and online news sites.

We are extremely grateful to PEJ director Tom Rosenstiel for sharing the findings from that study with us, including material that had not previously been published. These data give our analysis of the 2008 campaign cycle a breadth and depth beyond the studies we had conducted for the elections from 1988 through 2004, which were incorporated into previous editions of this book. At the same time, our own study of the network evening newscasts in 2008 provides continuity with our previous studies and permits direct comparisons of our findings across the past six presidential elections.

Acknowledgments

O UR GREATEST DEBT FOR THE current edition of this work is owed to the Project for Excellence in Journalism, whose generous data sharing both broadened and deepened our analysis. It is in recognition of their crucial contribution, not only to our own work but also to that of the entire field of political communication, that we have dedicated this book to Tom Rosenstiel and his colleagues at PEJ. (Of course, we bear full responsibility for the interpretations of their data that appear in this volume.)

But a project of this scope would not have been possible without the efforts of many individuals over the years. The support, encouragement, and advice of Diana Owen and Jim Lengle of Georgetown University and Jack Kramer and Lew Fickett of the University of Mary Washington proved invaluable in helping us develop the ideas and arguments that appear in this volume. At the Center for Media and Public Affairs, we are especially indebted to Richard Noyes, Mary Carroll Willi, and Daniel Amundson, who directed the CMPA Election News studies on which this book is based.

When Rich directed the first CMPA study in 1988, no one had imagined that a real-time content analysis of election news was possible. By the time he directed his final study in 1996, he was a nationally recognized authority on media and campaigns whose insights are summarized in *Good Intentions Make Bad News* (coauthored with Robert Lichter 1995).

Rich Noyes was ably assisted in 1992 and 1996 by Mary Carroll Willi, whose skills and dedication were once again demonstrated when she took over as director of Election Watch 2000. While making a smooth transition in a chaotic environment, Mary Carroll also somehow found the time to provide the updated data and tables used in the first two editions of this book.

In 2004, CMPA formed a partnership with the international media research organization Media Tenor to analyze the presidential election coverage. Mary Carroll Willi and CMPA research director Dan Amundson worked with several Media Tenor staffers to ensure that the data were comparable to previous CMPA election studies. Our thanks go to Cynthia Ozick, Ray Mock, Markus Rettich, Senja Post, Günther Töpel, and Rob Jekielek; special thanks to Media Tenor founder and CEO Roland Schatz for making this project possible.

In addition, Dan Amundson helped develop the initial coding system and provided invaluable counsel and assistance before taking over sole direction of the study in 2008. As CMPA's vice president, the late Dr. Linda Lichter contributed her expertise to developing the coding system at the outset and her patience and moral support thereafter. Finally, we thank the many students who have worked on these projects as coders and research assistants at CMPA over the years, as well as the George Mason University graduate students whose research contributed to the 2008 study—Kelly Schoeninger, Kim Michael, Kate Yates, and Melissa Masone.

Tanya DeKona offered not only her support but also her patient, careful reading of this manuscript. Without her continuing encouragement, this project would not have been possible. And from inception to publication of the first edition of this book, the patience and dedication of our editor Jennifer Knerr served as a reminder of how great a contribution a good editor can make to a manuscript. We also thank Niels Aaboe, the editor of the second and third editions, Lea Gift, April Leo, Renée Legatt, and Elaine McGarraugh of Rowman & Littlefield for their help with various editions of this project.

Over the years, too many journalists for us to single out have given us the benefit of their insights into how the process works from the inside. They include the reporters and editors of the Washington bureau of the *Los Angeles Times*, the *Kansas City* (Missouri) *Star* and *Times*, the *Burlington* (Vermont) *Free Press*, the *Rutland* (Vermont) *Daily Herald*, States News Service, and Fairchild News Service. But special thanks go to four who contributed lengthy formal interviews for this book, and to Luke Britt, who conducted the interviews: Michael Barone of *U.S. News & World Report*, Larry Barrett of *Time*, Peter Brown of *Scripps Howard*, and Joe Klein of *Newsweek*. Similarly, our research depended on the efforts of many other CMPA staff members, student coders, and research assistants, whom we also thank collectively.

Among the scholars upon whose personal support and expertise we relied over the years, special thanks go to Stephen Hess and Tom Mann of the Brookings Institution, Norman Ornstein of the American Enterprise Institute, Diana Owen of Georgetown University, Bruce Buchanan at the University of Texas at Austin, Larry Sabato at the University of Virginia, Tom Rosenstiel of the Project for Excellence in Journalism, and, primus inter pares, Marvin Kalb and Tom Patterson of the Shorenstein Center on Press, Politics, and Public Policy at Harvard University. We benefited as well from the writings of other scholars who have done pioneering work on the media's role in elections, including Michael Robinson, Doris Graber, Chris Arterton, and Kathleen Hall Jamieson.

Finally, this project was made possible by the generous support of several private foundations and universities. Funding for various phases of this research came from the American Enterprise Institute, Brookings Institution, Earhart Foundation, George Mason University, Harvard University, J. M. Foundation, John and Mary Markle Foundation, the University of Mary Washington, Pew Charitable Trusts, Robert Stuart Foundation, Smith College, Smith Richardson Foundation, and Wellesley College.

Even as we express our appreciation for the assistance of the foundations that supported this work over the years, the scholars and journalists on whose insights we relied, and the coworkers who contributed their efforts to this project, we recognize that many may disagree with some of the arguments and conclusions that we drew from our research. For all our debts to others, we take full responsibility for the opinions expressed in this book and for any errors or omissions it may contain.

1

The Media and Presidential Elections: Studying News Content

THE NEWS MEDIA ARE OFTEN viewed as equivalent to a fourth branch of government, with authority and importance comparable to the Supreme Court, the presidency, and the Congress (cf., Cook 2005; Sparrow 1999). This vision of the "fourth estate" is not misplaced, since the news media influence the presentation and interpretation of campaigns as well as the performance and evaluation of those who are ultimately elected. For generations, journalists have been vital sources of information regarding American government, policies, and politicians. In recent decades, reporters have become even more important sources of information for citizens. Smoke-filled rooms where party bosses once selected presidential nominees have been replaced by nationally televised primary debates.

Candidates have adapted by increasingly taking their messages to the voters directly through campaign websites, YouTube videos, and online social-networking sites (Frantzich 2009; Owen 2009). Reaching citizens through innovative uses of media is a long-term trend in American politics: in a less-wired era John McCain's Straight Talk Express campaign bus dominated the cable news networks in 2000, and Ross Perot's televised infomercials were key parts of his 1992 independent presidential campaign (Owen 2002; Patterson 1994; Polsby and Wildavsky 2000; Vavreck 2001).

Journalists continue to play an important role in keeping political candidates and government officials accountable. But the mainstream media increasingly shares this role, sometimes uncomfortably, with a variety of additional voices. The growing list includes ever-more aggressive cable news channels, online news sources and aggregators, television comedians and talk-show hosts, and even peer-to-peer communicators (Owen 2009; Pew 2008b, 2009). Even as these newer information sources are changing candidate marketing and voter learning, however, traditional journalists remain key voices in defining the public agenda (Farnsworth 2009; Frantzich 2009; Owen 2009; Pew 2008b).

Everyone seems to have an opinion about the quality of campaign news. Sometimes reporters are seen as pro-establishment tools of big corporations, sometimes as leftist attack dogs, and still other times as scandal-obsessed character cops (cf. Alterman 2003; B. Goldberg 2002; McChesney 1999, 2004; Sabato et al. 2000). What we offer here is empirical evidence, and lots of it, regarding the quantity and quality of news coverage in a series of presidential-election campaigns. Using objective content analysis—the careful dissection of each news story into fragments that can be classified along several different dimensions—we analyze the news media's coverage of presidential elections over the course of the past two decades.

This study, conducted by the Center for Media and Public Affairs (CMPA) at George Mason University, represents the most comprehensive and systematic examination of campaign news ever assembled. The data set includes *every* campaign news story on the broadcast network evening news shows across the past six election cycles from 1988 through 2008, as well as stories from Fox News Channel, PBS, television talk shows, and daily newspapers in selected elections. Moreover, the content analysis of news coverage is supplemented by analysis of communications from the campaigns themselves in speeches, TV ads, and website postings.

In addition, our analysis of the 2008 election makes extensive use of an extraordinary content analysis conducted during key periods of the 2008 primary and general election campaigns by the Project for Excellence in Journalism (PEJ), a division of the Pew Research Center. The PEJ study covers an extremely broad and detailed compilation of news sources. It includes morning and evening broadcast network news shows; cable news network shows from daytime, early evening, and prime time; liberal and conservative talk-radio programs, as well as National Public Radio; national and local newspapers; and online news sites, including both providers of original reporting and aggregators of existing material. Finally, PEJ examined the content of candidates' websites at various points during the campaign.

In the wake of every presidential campaign, reporters promise to improve next time, and sometimes they even apologize for their past performances (cf. Downie and Kaiser 2002; Russert 1990; Rutenberg 2004a, 2004b; Rutenberg and Zernike 2004; Sabato 2002; Shogan 2001). Despite the frequent promises and occasional regrets, however, the content analysis evidence demonstrates that the media's coverage of presidential elections has not improved over the years; on many measures it has even declined. Like Tolstoy's unhappy families, each campaign news cycle disappoints in its own way. For sheer erroneous reporting, nothing (so far) can compare with election night 2000. On that excruciating night, the television networks declared that Al Gore had won Florida, then that the race was too close to call, then that George Bush had won Florida, and then that the race was too close to call once again (Jamieson and Waldman 2002). Given widespread recognition that Florida's twenty-five electoral votes would likely be decisive in the contest, the networks' mistakes effectively declared one candidate the winner of the White House, then the other, in a contest that was not settled until more than a month later when the Supreme Court stopped the recounting of Florida ballots and handed the presidency to Bush in a contentious five-to-four decision (Bugliosi 2001; Nelson 2001; Sunstein and Epstein 2001).

These devastating miscalls, as bad as they were, are only part of a broad pattern of coverage that has declined in both quantity and quality over the past six presidential elections. In particular, television's portrayal of presidential contests has been marked by a host of shortcomings: a tendency to emphasize the campaign's horse race over matters of substance, a frequently controversial performance with respect to the core values of accuracy and fairness, a declining amount of attention paid to candidates (as opposed to that lavished on the journalists covering them), and declining volume of coverage of the election overall. Different shortcomings are more prominent in different election cycles, but at least some of these criticisms apply to every recent presidential election.

The study of campaign news coverage is a very controversial area, as people tend to have strong opinions about the media's performance. These emotional reactions can make it difficult to evaluate the news media objectively. For example, readers and viewers often remember particular stories that resonate for them personally, including those that make them angry or irritated or provide information that is consistent with their existing opinions (Paletz 2002). These isolated impressions (and sometimes misimpressions) may produce unrepresentative opinions about a particular news outlet or the news media as a whole (Graber 1988). For these reasons, it is very important to study the media as scientifically as possible.

This is why we rely on content analysis, in which each segment of a news story is carefully coded into categories that describe whether the segment was positive, negative, or neutral toward each candidate, as well as who the source of that commentary was (e.g., candidates, citizens, outside experts, and reporters themselves). Each story is also coded into categories that describe which topics were addressed (e.g., policy issues, candidate traits, campaign strategy, etc.). Each news story is analyzed along several different dimensions that allow for studies of media content from many different perspectives. The central core of the study is a database on every campaign news segment that aired on the evening news programs of ABC, NBC, and CBS during every presidential election campaign from 1988 to 2008, including the general election, the primaries, and the campaign preseason.

This content analysis, conducted by the Center for Media and Public Affairs (CMPA), a nonpartisan research institute affiliated with George Mason University, permits an unusually wide-ranging and thorough examination of campaign discourse. The 9,260 network news campaign stories analyzed here from two decades of presidential campaigns are part of a larger CMPA content analysis of more than 25,000 campaign communication items examined from the past six presidential elections. All are employed to make the arguments in this book (though we obviously do not discuss each of them individually).

The data allow for a quantitative study of how television news coverage has changed from election to election along key dimensions including the focus on the horse race rather than on matters of substance, the problems of accuracy and fairness, the focus on reporters rather than on candidates, and the amount of campaign coverage overall. The evidence offered here illustrates the ways that the mediated presentation of reality on network television, generally speaking, has worsened over time.

The collected data also permit comparisons between network news and other media outlets, as well as comparisons between network news coverage and unmediated candidate discourse. These analyses find that network news falls short when compared to other media outlets and to what the candidates and the campaigns actually said. The more than 31,000 items analyzed by CMPA and the Project for Excellence in Journalism that are *not* from the broadcast networks' evening news programs include segments aired or printed by a wide variety of media outlets, including the Public Broadcasting Service (PBS), Fox News, CNN, MSNBC, the *New York Times*, the *Wall Street Journal*, and the *Washington Post*. The PEJ content analysis project also includes talk-radio content, reports from online news sites, and various forms of campaign discourse, including speeches, interviews, advertisements, and campaign websites. Through these additional data, we compare the content of the network evening newscasts with other media outlets and with what the campaigns and the candidates themselves actually said in their speeches, debates, advertising, and websites.

The comparison of television news and its competitors allows us to determine the ways in which the "mediated" perspectives on the campaigns on network television differ from those of public television, cable television, talk radio, and newspapers. Both network news and other media outlets are also compared in chapter 5 to the "unmediated" messages put forward by the campaigns and the candidates themselves. (The appendixes more extensively discuss the campaign news items contained in this analysis.)

Mediated versus Unmediated Campaign Information

Many critics have found fault with television news campaign coverage in the past, but rarely have these criticisms had the support of such extensive and detailed evidence. Our comparative data allow us to say that many other news outlets—including other television news outlets and several of the nation's leading newspapers—often do a far better job of providing citizens with the information needed to understand and evaluate the campaign, the candidates, and the issues. We also compare what candidates and campaigns actually said versus what the reporters *said* the campaigns and the candidates said. The differences between the campaigns' messages and the media's messages are immense. We demonstrate that candidates and campaigns do a far better job of responding to citizen desires for substance, fairness, and comprehensiveness than the television networks do. In other words, the mediated coverage of much campaign news has become so negative and so inaccurate that the unmediated speeches, advertisements, and Internet websites of the highly self-interested campaigns produce more-substantive, more-useful, and more-accurate forms of campaign discourse.

Examining network news coverage of the most recent presidential elections is central to our understanding of how these contests operate. Candidates and their teams design campaigns to maximize positive television exposure because television news remains a major source of public learning about candidates and political issues (Hollihan 2001; Paletz 2002; Pew 2008b). Since the vast majority of information about presidential elections received by ordinary citizens is mediated information, television news reports play an important linkage role in our electoral process—arguably more important than even the political parties themselves (cf. Patterson 1994; Wayne 2001, 2003). While the audience for network television news is far smaller than it was a generation ago, large numbers of voters continue to tune in to these evening newscasts or examine their cable and online offshoots.

For good or for ill, television news programs remain central players in the operation of elections as well as in the process of governing in this country (Cook 2005; Graber 2006; Patterson 1994; Sparrow 1999). Reporters tell us much of what we learn about the issues, the candidates, and how they are faring on the campaign trail. Even online bloggers often address campaign developments by writing about what they read in the morning paper or saw on the television news.

For most of us, the mediated reality portrayed directly on television or indirectly via online commentary is the reality we perceive (Iyengar and Kinder 1987; Patterson 1994). The poor quality of television's performance in covering presidential campaigns, therefore, is an important warning sign regarding the health of our electoral process. TV networks that reduce the quality and quantity of election coverage shortchange not only the candidates but also the voters who choose each successive president.

What Voters Want from Campaign News

Above all, what the voters say they want from journalists is better coverage, reporting that is more informative, more issue-based, and less biased. Arguably the most powerful evidence that the media are not giving citizens the desired campaign news content is found in the evaluations citizens give journalists at the end of the campaign season. Numerous polls in recent years have demonstrated the low regard with which the American public views the news media in general and election news in particular. The most useful long-term consideration of this public frustration with the press is found in surveys conducted by the Pew Research Center for the People and the Press, which every four years asks respondents to assign letter grades to the performance of various participants in the election process.

Over the six presidential election cycles considered here, the public has consistently given the media poorer grades than the parties, candidates, pollsters, and even the much-criticized campaign consultants (Pew Research Center for the People and the Press [hereafter Pew] 2000c, 2004c, 2008c). In 2008, only 35 percent of those surveyed gave the media an A or a B grade. In previous elections, the combined A and B ratings have ranged from a high of 37 percent in 1992 to a low of 29 percent in 1996 and 2000. Even the relatively favorable 2008 ratings reflect troubling partisan differences: "Fully 62 percent of Democratic voters give the press positive grades, up from 46 percent in 2004. By contrast, just 13 percent of Republicans now give the press an A or B, and more than four-in-ten Republicans (44 percent) give the press an F grade (up from 28 percent in 2004)" (Pew 2008c). In contrast, 67 percent of those surveyed said that the voters deserved an A or a B grade, and 49 percent would give even the campaign consultants high marks (Pew 2008c). Given these scores, it comes as no surprise that the public wants journalists to have less influence over presidential elections. A November 2008 postelection survey by the Pew Center (2008c) found that 46 percent felt the news media had too much influence on the political process.

Media coverage of the horse race in recent elections is not simply a response to what viewers want from media coverage of campaigns and elections. Considerable evidence suggests that we the people want more substantive coverage than we get from the television networks. For example, an examination of the questions asked by citizens calling in to *Larry King Live* on CNN during the 1992 campaign also found a gap between what the media focused on— mainly campaign strategy—and the issues that mattered to those ordinary citizens who asked then-president George H. W. Bush questions about trade with Mexico, aid to Russia, and how to make the economy work better (Patterson 1994, 55–56). Reporters clearly have a different perspective about what citizens need to know than citizens themselves do: "The voters possess a different schematic outlook [than do reporters]. They view politics primarily as a means of choosing leaders and solving their problems. As the voters see it, policy problems, leadership traits, policy debates, and the like are the key dimensions of presidential politics" (59).

However, some scholars think there is a great difference between what people say they want from the news and what they actually desire. Despite all the public protestations calling for serious, issue-based news, scholars have found that citizens are drawn to strategic ("horse-race") campaign coverage in practice (Iyengar et al. 2004).

Citizens frequently express concerns about potential media bias, with Republicans far more likely to think their party suffers from media unfairness. A November 1996 Harris survey found that 63 percent of the public believed the news media favor one side when presenting news on social and political issues, and 77 percent saw a "great deal" or a "fair amount" of political bias in news coverage (T. Smith et al. 1997, 119). Conservatives were particularly troubled by media bias: 45 percent of Republicans viewed journalists as more biased than most people, as compared to 27 percent of Independents and 28 percent of Democrats (101).

In a December 2000 Gallup poll, 65 percent believed reporters' news stories were "often inaccurate," up from 45 percent in a 1998 survey, 44 percent in 1989, and 34 percent in 1985 (Wayne 2003, 131).

The November 2008 Pew postelection survey showed public frustration over the tone of media coverage, particularly among conservatives. Two-thirds of those surveyed (67 percent) felt that coverage of the Obama campaign was fair, compared to 53 percent who regarded news coverage of McCain as fair (Pew 2008c). As one would expect, there were distinct partisan cleavages: 83 percent of Democrats thought that coverage of Obama was fair, while only 22 percent of Republicans thought McCain was treated fairly by reporters.

In a study of perceptions of bias regarding various media outlets, C-SPAN programming, the *NewsHour* on PBS, the Sunday morning news magazines (like *Meet the Press*), and CNN were seen to be particularly evenhanded, while local call-in talk radio and Rush Limbaugh's talk-radio program were seen as the most biased (Dautrich and Hartley 1999, 100). Network news finished in the middle of the pack, just below local newscasts and just above the *New York Times*.

But public opinion regarding journalists is not entirely negative, particularly when reporters are compared to politicians. Three-quarters of those surveyed expressed support for the news media's role as a watchdog on government (Smith et al. 1997), and 63 percent on balance thought that reporters help democracy more than hurt it through their reporting. Three-quarters of those surveyed said that reporters should hold public officials accountable for what they do, and two-thirds said it was "very important" for the media to protect the public from abuses of power (T. Smith et al. 1997, 50). In fact, more than 40 percent of those surveyed called for a more aggressive media, saying reporters could do more to scrutinize public officials and to guard against government abuses of power.

Ellen Hume, at that time the director of the Democracy Project on PBS, said at a news conference releasing the Harris survey's results that it is important for reporters to make more of an effort to tailor their reporting to such public concerns: "We should try to design news programming that actually helps citizens figure out what their role is in this great landscape in America. So often the news is encrypted in Washington. It is about what the insiders are saying around the dinner table. That might be interesting to some people, but I do think that citizens deserve better" (Hume, quoted in T. Smith et al. 1997, 5).

What Voters Get from Campaign News: Past Content Analysis Research

Horse Race versus Substance

Three decades ago, political scientist Thomas Patterson (1980) observed that television focused heavily on the question of which candidate was ahead and who was behind, a far cry from the much more issue-oriented coverage of the 1940s. Although Patterson focused on the 1976 presidential election, the same trends were found in subsequent contests. Throughout the 1980s and 1990s, we were told more and more about who was ahead in the polls and who was behind, rather than where candidates stood on the issues (Lichter and Noyes 1995; Patterson 1980, 1994).

In their comprehensive study of campaign coverage by CBS News and by United Press International (UPI) wire service during the 1980 presidential contest, Michael Robinson and Margaret Sheehan (1983) found that 59 percent of CBS election news stories failed to contain a single sentence about policy issues, even though the scholars identified more than ninety issues on the 1980 campaign agenda. For UPI, 55 percent of the stories failed to reference a single issue: "'Horse race' permeates almost everything the press does in covering elections and candidates. We found that in our wire copy and videotape about five of every six campaign stories made some meaningful reference to the competition, but, by comparison, well over half of the same stories made no mention of issues" (148).

In recent presidential campaigns, new polls are conducted every day to give us constant updates regarding the fortunes of each candidate. In the New Hampshire primary, for example, ever since 1992 daily tracking polls have measured the horse race every twenty-four hours during the month before the election (Farnsworth and Lichter 1999, 2002, 2003, 2006b). Reporters may have little understanding of the uncertainties of polling, including such things as margins of error, but that does not stop them from talking about polls frequently during the half-hour nightly news programs (Larson 2001; Owen 2002).

But voters do more than learn regularly of each candidate's standing when watching the nightly news; they actually begin to support in greater numbers the candidate who reporters said was winning. Patterson (1980) called this a *bandwagon* effect. Bandwagon effects make it harder for a candidate who is believed by reporters to be behind—or who really is lagging in the media-reported polls—to catch up with the front-runner. If news consumers are told over and over again that poll numbers are the most important thing in the campaign, it should come as no surprise that the voters also consider poll standings when comparing candidates: "The press-game schema is more pervasive now than it was even a few decades ago. The change coincides with the shift to an electoral process that depends on the press as its chief intermediary. In the same period that the press has taken on the mediating role once performed by the political party, a number of trends within journalism have combined to make election news a less-suitable basis for voter choice" (Patterson 1994, 60).

Our data in the chapters that follow show that conditions have deteriorated even further since Patterson wrote those words. Questions of the heavy horse-race emphasis of network television news are taken up in chapter 2.

Scandal Coverage

The campaign news agenda also tilts heavily toward personal scandals and gaffes, which crowd out coverage of policy matters. Larry Sabato (2000) found a growing emphasis on scandal among reporters in the wake of Vietnam and Watergate, when public lies by government officials had become commonplace.

The rise in recent years of new media, including cyber-journalism and talk radio, has increased the opportunity for scandals and gaffes to balloon into major controversies (cf. Davis and Owen 1998; Drudge 2000; Hall 2001; Seib 2001). For example, a 2008 remark by Barack Obama at an "off-the-record" fundraiser about how small-town working-class voters "get bitter" and "cling to guns or religion" was picked up by a citizen journalist and generated a media "feeding frenzy" during the nomination campaign (Owen 2009, 21).

Even reporters and editors who may want to restrain themselves from scandal coverage find it hard to do so in an increasingly competitive media environment. Being left behind is not an appealing prospect for any reporter or editor, given the intense public and media interest in personal scandals like (to name a few) Bill Clinton's efforts to avoid service in Vietnam and allegations surrounding his relationship with Gennifer Flowers (R. K. Baker 1993), the 2000 reports concerning George W. Bush's quarter-century-old drunk-driving arrest (Burger 2002), questions of what George W. Bush and John Kerry did—or did not do—during the Vietnam years, and, most recently, the theological and racial musings of the Obama family's pastor, Reverend Jeremiah Wright (Denton 2009; Egan 2004; Milbank and Allen 2004; Nagourney 2004; Rasmussen 2004; Roig-Franzia and Romano 2004; Seelye and Blumenthal 2004; Wilgoren 2004).

Just being a responsible journalist may mean being left behind in scandal coverage. During the 1992 presidential primaries, all three broadcast networks at first refused to run a story on Gennifer Flowers's statement that she and Bill Clinton had had an extramarital affair when Clinton was governor of Arkansas, because they could not document the allegations. Nevertheless, one NBC news executive was shocked to find the story leading the 11 P.M. local news on his network's New York affiliate that same night (Rosenstiel 1994, 63).

A few years later, *Newsweek* lost out on its scoop of the Clinton-Lewinsky matter to Internet journalist Matt Drudge in January 1998, largely because *Newsweek* executives wanted more time to evaluate the reporting on such an explosive scandal (Drudge 2000; Sabato et al. 2000; Seib 2001). By 2004, the rush to publish was so great that few media outlets scrutinized claims against the candidates effectively before airing them (Eggerton 2004; Kurtz 2005; Orkent 2004; Trippi 2004).

Our analysis of the news media's focus on scandals is found in chapter 3.

Fairness, Accuracy, and Allegations of Media Bias

The news media's power to set the agenda is particularly troubling if reporters fail to meet standards of objectivity and fairness. Conservatives are more likely to charge that reporters are biased toward the Democrats, though in the 2004 election many liberals alleged that reporters went too easy on George W. Bush over the failure to find weapons of mass destruction in Iraq (Fallows 2004; Greenberg 2003; Massing 2004; Pew 2004b; Risen 2006). In the 1992 campaign, when allegations of media bias were particularly high, many Republicans put bumper stickers on their cars that read "Annoy the Media: Re-elect Bush."

Scholars have a range of opinions on the question of whether reporters are biased. Some say that reporters are biased only by the norms of the news business: things such as deadline pressures and the need to make stories interesting enough to attract interest (Robinson 1976). Others say that reporters try to be fair, but when inadvertent bias finds its way into news stories it is more likely to reflect the liberal perspectives held by most journalists (Lichter et al. 1990). Still other media researchers focus on the corporate structures of the news business and argue that the conservative orientations of corporate executives and owners are the true sources of bias (Ginsberg 1986; Gitlin 1980; Herman and Chomsky 1988). As the diversity of opinion suggests, researchers have not yet reached a consensus on the nature of any alleged media bias (cf., D'Alessio and Allen 2000). Further, the findings for one election may differ greatly from those for others. In this project, we use the CMPA and PEJ content analysis to search for evidence of bias in television news over the past twenty years to see whether any such network bias is reflected in other media coverage. Our analysis of bias is found in chapter 4.

While scholars and politicians argue over the existence of ideological bias, there is much stronger evidence that the television networks' coverage has been largely negative in tone over the past several elections. This negativity, directed against nearly all viable candidates in most election cycles, can powerfully impact public orientations regarding government. Citizens exposed to negative media portrayals of political candidates and of government are thought to become increasingly cynical about government (Cappella and Jamieson 1997; Hetherington 2001). Voter turnout in the United States remains below that of other Western democracies, and many scholars think media negativity is one of the reasons why nearly half of the nation's eligible adults have chosen not to vote in recent presidential elections (Putnam 2000). An examination of media negativity and its effects on voter turnout and on a president's ability to govern can be found in chapter 4.

Debate over the media's ability to get the facts right often begins with the television networks' miscues on election night 2000 (Owen 2002; Sabato 2002). The bungled *60 Minutes II* coverage during the 2004 campaign of George W. Bush's National Guard years suggested CBS had not learned much from 2000. But the debate shouldn't end there. As in every presidential election at least since the 1960s, the news media—especially television—established the information environment within which the general election was contested. Public debate over media coverage began long before the double miscalls of 2000 that left the network anchors with not just egg but an entire omelet on their faces, in Tom Brokaw's wry image. At various points during that campaign, commentators complained that news reports were distorting the images and trivializing the messages of both major party candidates (Kurtz 2000a). During the party conventions, other critics charged that the broadcast networks, traditionally the industry leaders in covering presidential elections, were ignoring their public-service responsibilities by basing their diminished coverage on ratings rather than the intrinsic importance of events (AuCoin 2000; Kloer 2000). And throughout the fall campaign, media critics and journalists alike debated the scope, focus, and tenor of campaign coverage (Buckley 2000; Hess 2000a, 2000b; Papai and Robinson 2000; Taylor 2000). This study devotes considerable attention in chapter 4 not only to the Swift Boat Veterans for Truth and the *60 Minutes II* reports of 2004 and to the events of election night 2000 but to earlier—and subsequent—news media errors in the coverage of American political campaigns.

The Shrinking Sound Bite and Journalistic Self-Obsession

Of all the declines in the quality of network television news in recent decades, perhaps none has been as dramatic as the reduction in a presidential candidate's ability to address the issues in his or her own voice on network television news during the presidential campaign. A study by Kiku Adatto (1990) found that the average length of time presidential candidates spoke in their own words on network television news during the 1968 campaign was forty-two seconds. The average sound-bite length in 1988 fell to ten seconds, a decline of more than three-quarters over that twenty-year period. The results triggered a good deal of soul-searching among reporters when they were first released, and the networks promised longer candidate sound bites in 1992 (Patterson 1994, 160). Nevertheless, the CMPA data, presented here in chapter 3, demonstrate that these snippets of candidate discourse continued to shrink before finally rebounding in 2008.

If the candidates aren't doing the talking, who is? Thomas Patterson described media coverage of a presidential election as a struggle among reporters and candidates to be heard and to set the tone. The reporters, of course, have a great advantage in this struggle as they have access to the news programs in a way that candidates do not. As a result, we hear a lot more in campaign coverage from the reporters than from the candidates. In the 1960s, candidates and other partisan sources were much more able to set the tone of an article, and to be heard at greater length, than in more recent decades

(Patterson 1994). Matthew Kerbel (1998) later found that the trend has become overwhelmingly biased toward reporters and away from presidential candidates. We apply the CMPA data to this issue in chapter 3.

The question of content cannot be addressed without considering how much impact the news media have over voter perceptions of the candidates, the campaigns, and the issues. Although our focus is on the content of media messages rather than their effects, review of past research on media effects can help place the content analysis research in perspective.

Content's Consequences: Three Models of Possible Media Effects

The Hypodermic Effects Perspective: Heavy Media Influence

In addition to the content of news, scholars have focused their attention on its impact on public opinion. This area of research properly begins with the Martians on the radio. When Orson Welles broadcast a fictionalized radio account of an alien invasion of New Jersey as a Halloween prank in 1938, millions of Americans were fooled (Cantril et al. 1940). The effects of this "War of the Worlds" broadcast suggested that citizens may be highly susceptible to media images. Seeing (or hearing, at that time) was believing. Scholars dubbed this perspective on media influences the *hypodermic effects* model, as the effect was seen as immediate, direct, and powerful—much like getting an injection at the doctor's office.

The rise of Adolf Hitler in Germany and Benito Mussolini in Italy shortly before World War II also seemed to support this theory of very powerful media effects on public opinion. Both came to power in part through their news appearances in the then–relatively new media of radio and filmed newsreels, which allowed for rapid and easy transmission of messages to large numbers of people. *The Triumph of the Will*, a pro-Hitler pseudodocumentary made during this era by Leni Riefenstahl, was seen as one of the most-effective exercises of propaganda ever: the film starts with Hitler descending through the clouds as if he were an Aryan god (he is returning to earth by airplane) and shows Hitler receiving the fervent adoration of cheering multitudes throughout (Mast 1971). Scholars who looked at the Nazis' effective use of the media became convinced that ordinary citizens were very susceptible to media messages, particularly messages put before our eyes and ears over and over again. Ever since, dictatorships have tried to create cults of worship of the national leader through this sort of propaganda—China was once filled with portraits of Mao, and Iraq was only recently filled with portraits of Saddam Hussein.

Radio and film were not the first media formats, of course. But they were the first *national* media sources, particularly in the United States. They were the first to provide identical messages from coast to coast through broadcast networks and through national distribution in motion-picture theaters. Newspapers, even when part of a national company, tended to be much more localized in their coverage and did not provide a pervasive national message comparable to that offered by radio networks, newsreels, and later the television networks (Postman 1985; Schudson 1978; C. Smith 1977).

Although the hypodermic effects model may seem appealing at first glance, it didn't seem to work all that well, at least in the United States, once social scientists developed techniques sophisticated enough to allow for data-based studies of media effects on public opinion. Researchers looked for opinion change among voters exposed to media content about candidates for office, but they did not find much evidence that would support the hypodermic-effects approach (Lazarsfeld et al. 1948). The hypodermic effects theory may have explained media influence on citizens in the 1920s and early 1930s when radio and film were novelties, but the model was not supported by quantitative evidence that examined media use and candidate preferences of U.S. voters in the 1940s.

Why didn't this first theory work better in practice? There are several possible explanations: Perhaps U.S. citizens became more sophisticated with respect to media messages as we became more accustomed to these new media sources, more wary of propaganda as a result of World War II, and less susceptible due to steadily increasing education levels. Perhaps this model of heavy media influence does a better job of explaining cultural trends than partisan political behavior. Or perhaps the model never was all that effective. We just don't have enough public-opinion research from before World War II to know for sure whether the model ever truly worked well. Some researchers believe that, upon further reflection, the early studies that laid the foundation for this perspective were not that solidly constructed to begin with (McQuail 2000).

The Minimal Effects Perspective

If the news media could not change minds, as scholars started to observe in the late 1940s and 1950s, perhaps mass media sources were not so influential after all. Social scientists then reversed course and settled on the idea of *minimal effects* to explain the relationship between the media and the people. They proposed a "two-step flow," in which media messages particularly influenced political elites—opinion leaders like executives, union officials, and heads of families (Klapper 1960). These elites then used what they learned to organize their own discussion of issues, thereby transferring the substance of the media message to those who might have missed it or were not paying attention.

But this theory of modest-media effects also became unpopular as scholars began to look for empirical evidence to support it. Unfortunately for the theory's supporters, the evidence against this approach seemed consistent and powerful, almost from the time it was first offered. Civil rights became a front-burner issue in the 1960s, once television started broadcasting pictures of African American children being attacked by police dogs and adults being clubbed by Southern sheriffs (Graber 2006). Public support for U.S. involvement in Vietnam declined drastically once the television networks began suggesting the war was a stalemate in the wake of the 1968 Tet Offensive (Braestrup 1983; Mueller 1973). More recently, a variety of issues—homelessness, health care, nuclear-weapons proliferation—became highly important when television focused on them, only to lose their importance to citizens once the networks moved on to other topics (Adams et al. 1994; Iyengar and Kinder 1987; Paletz 2002).

The Media Effects Perspective: Setting the Public Agenda

For the past quarter-century, many media researchers have favored a third theory, known as *media effects* or *more-than-minimal effects*. This perspective, pioneered by Michael Robinson (1976) and Maxwell McCombs and Donald Shaw (1977), is located between the high-impact and low-impact extremes contained in the earlier hypodermic and minimal effects theories. They argued that the media's most powerful influence on American society relates to agenda setting—not telling us what to think so much as telling us what to think about. A great deal of survey research supports the media-effects position. People seem to evaluate candidates and government officials, for example, along the lines of the issues that are the focus of televised news reports. Studies show that citizens are primed to focus on what reporters have told the country were the most important matters, such as whether Vice President Hubert Humphrey should be blamed for the war in Vietnam, whether President George H. W. Bush should be fired for alleged economic bungling, whether Bill Clinton should be impeached and then removed from office over the Monica Lewinsky scandal, and whether George W. Bush should be reelected because of how he handled the "War on Terror" (Dimock 2004; Edwards 2004; Gregg 2004; Iyengar and Kinder 1987; McGinniss 1969; Owen 2000; Robinson 1976).

The media effects theory does not presume the overwhelming media impact suggested by the hypodermic model, but the agenda-setting function is still seen as an important source of media influence (Iyengar and Kinder 1987;

Iyengar 1991). Scandal coverage demonstrates how media messages do not always translate into public opinion. President Clinton was treated extremely negatively on television for his handling of the Clinton/Lewinsky scandal, yet public opinion consistently opposed his removal from office (Sabato et al. 2000). At most, this highly negative media treatment of Clinton triggered modest declines in public ratings of his personal character, though public evaluations in that area were not that high before the scandal became public. Media treatment of Clinton scandals involving Gennifer Flowers and allegations of draft-dodging during the Vietnam years were likewise extensive and quite negative in tone before the 1992 New Hampshire primary, and many pundits thought the Clinton campaign had been fatally wounded by them (Kurtz 1992a). But then the former front-runner finished second, declared himself the Comeback Kid, and got back on track to win the Democratic nomination (Ceaser and Busch 1993; Palmer 1997).

Another limitation on media effects research is the huge body of evidence that citizens remember only some of the news they hear, see, and read. A news item is most likely to register and be remembered if it is consistent with one's core values about people and politics (Graber 1988).

The agenda-setting idea suggests that the topics that reporters emphasize will also play an important role in evaluations of candidates. The changing role of economic evaluations in presidential elections provides a useful example of how this process works: Economic conditions are usually one of the most important measures by which incumbent presidents (and subsequent nominees of the president's party) can be rewarded or punished (Campbell 1992; Fair 1978; Lewis-Beck and Rice 1992). In a year when negative news abounds, like 2008, there is little a nominee of the incumbent president's party can do to reverse the tide, as Senator John McCain (R-Ariz.) found to his regret (Ceaser et al. 2009). In 2008, 90 percent of those surveyed said the nation's economy was worse off than the year before, and McCain won only 44 percent of those voters (Abramson et al. 2010, 180). Sixteen years earlier, President George H. W. Bush's 1992 reelection campaign likewise ran aground on poor economic conditions (Farnsworth and Lichter 2006a; Fitzwater 1995; Gold 1994).

In fact, media agenda-setting effects sometimes are strong enough to outweigh personal experiences. One study of the effects of economic news coverage, for example, found that people who were exposed to a large amount of macroeconomic news tended to emphasize societal economic conditions and deemphasize their own personal economic situations (Mutz 1992).

Conversely, if the media focus is not on the economy, the public focus is also likely to be directed elsewhere. In 2000, when reporters said little about the condition of the national economy—which had been growing at a healthy pace for the eight years of the Clinton presidency—one would not expect the national economy to be that significant a factor for voters. Indeed, exit polls in 2000 showed that only 18 percent of those casting a ballot in the Gore-Bush contest considered the economy to be the most important issue that year, as compared to 43 percent who thought so eight years earlier, when Clinton defeated President Bush and Texas billionaire Ross Perot (Frankovic and McDermott 2001). In 2004, only 21 percent of those surveyed said that "the economy/jobs" was the most important issue (Pew 2004c). In contrast, 63 percent of voters said the economy was the most important issue in the 2008 election (Pew 2008c). Not surprisingly—given the focus in 2004 on "moral values" during the Bush reelection campaign and on the Iraq occupation—both "moral values" and "Iraq" were more important to voters that year than the economy (Pew 2004c). With examples like this to draw on, it is no wonder that the media effects perspective became popular among media and elections scholars relatively quickly.

Broadcast news, with its national reach, long offered the opportunity for a shared national schema, or shared orientation toward a particular subject (Graber 1988)—before parts of its audience moved away toward the much wider range of information and perspectives provided by talk radio, cable-news channels, and the Internet (Davis and Owen 1998; Owen 1996). The fact that the networks have faced more competition in recent years is an important issue to consider as we examine coverage of recent elections in the variety of media outlets analyzed in this edition.

At the same time, the media effects perspective is far removed from the minimal effects model. Citizens are consuming much of the news themselves, rather than having others digest it and translate it for them. Indeed, the fact that an increasing number of citizens are seeking out sources beyond the television networks is hardly consistent with the two-step flow of information at the center of the minimal effects model. The media effects approach, which seemed to make sense to many media scholars before the Internet, appears even more relevant in a time when individual news consumers are increasingly searching for their own news content.

The Changing News Media Environment

The six presidential elections covered in our study have taken place during a time of rapid transformation of the news media environment. When Michael Dukakis and George H. W. Bush battled in 1988 over the opportunity to succeed Ronald Reagan as president, there was no Internet, there was hardly any talk radio, and the only cable news network was a lightly watched upstart operation that posed no competition to the broadcast networks (Davis and Owen 1998; Graber 2006; Kovach and Rosenstiel 1999). At the start of this period, network television stood astride the media world as an eight-hundred-pound gorilla. America stopped to listen every evening when the nation's network anchors described the most important events of the twenty-four hours since they had last visited our living rooms. The share of the network news audience had fallen some, from 75 percent of the audience in the 1970–1971 season to just under 70 percent in the 1980s, but when Dan Rather, Peter Jennings, and Tom Brokaw spoke, America listened (Kurtz 2002b).

What a difference twenty years makes (Halperin and Harris 2007). With its unprecedented twenty-four-hour-a-day news coverage, CNN came into its own during the 1991 Persian Gulf War, becoming the place to turn to for up-to-the-minute news during times of international crisis (R. Goldberg and Goldberg 1995). In 1992, it was on CNN's *Larry King Live* that Ross Perot announced he was running for president. Indeed Perot ran for president in 1992 largely through CNN appearances and through his own self-financed and highly rated infomercials on network television (R. K. Baker 1993; McWilliams 1993). Rush Limbaugh became a talk-radio icon at about the same time. Limbaugh, an in-your-face conservative who drew considerable public attention during the 1990s, peppered President Clinton with a never-ending series of attacks and helped promote the rise of a more combative Republican Party that achieved majority status in the U.S. Congress following the 1994 elections (Owen 1996, 1997). Fox News provided considerable positive coverage of George W. Bush's first term (Farnsworth and Lichter 2006a) and by 2004 was at least as important to cable news viewers as the more established CNN (Pew 2004c). The Internet became an obsession for millions of Americans and the source of constantly available news and information—sometimes of dubious quality—about virtually any topic (Davis and Owen 1998; Drudge 2000; Hall 2001; Seib 2001). And what about the once-dominant Big Three television networks? Their audience share plummeted to 43 percent of the audience by George W. Bush's first term, a drop so dramatic that media experts wondered if the half-hour nightly news programs were long for this world (Kurtz 2002a, 2002b).

Howard Kurtz, who covers the news business for the *Washington Post*, blames demographic and technological changes for the decline of the network evening newscasts:

> The audience is shrinking—and graying—because of changing lifestyles and more media choices. Older folks who came of age in the precable era are accustomed to tuning in for news at 6:30. Most younger people never acquired the habit, are still working at that hour, or are just plain less-interested in news, surveys show. A growing number get their information online, essentially becoming their own editors. (Kurtz 2002b, A20)

Attention paid to network news coverage of presidential elections has shown the same dramatic decline in viewers, and in influence, as has network news overall. Table 1.1 contains the results of a series of election-year surveys

Table 1.1
Media Use Trends, 1992–2008

Question: "How did you get most of your news about the presidential election campaign—from television, from newspapers, from radio, from magazines, or from the Internet?" [Accept two answers. If only one response is given, probe for one additional response.]
[If the respondent answered *television*, ask:]

(2008) "Did you get most of your news about the presidential election campaign from: (randomized list) local news programming, ABC network news, CBS network news, NBC network news, CNN cable news, MSNBC cable news, the Fox News cable channel?" [Accept up to two answers.]

(2004) "Did you get most of your news about the presidential election campaign from: (randomized list) local news programming, ABC network news, CBS network news, NBC network news, CNN cable news, MSNBC cable news, the Fox News cable channel, CNBC cable news?" [Accept up to two answers.]

(1992–2000): "Did you get most of your news about the presidential campaign from network TV news, from local TV news, or from cable news networks such as CNN or MSNBC?" [Accept up to two answers.]

(Results in percentages)

	2008	*2004*	*2000*	*1996*	*1992*
Television (overall)	68	76	70	72	82
Network	18	29	22	36	55
Local	10	12	21	23	29
Cable	44	40	36	21	29
Newspapers	33	46	39	60	57
Radio	16	22	15	19	12
Magazines	3	6	4	11	9
Internet	36	21	11	3	n/a
Other	2	2	1	4	6
Don't know/refused	*	1	*	1	1

(1996–2008) "Did you happen to get any news or information about the [2008] elections from the Internet, or not?"

Yes	56	41	30	10
No/don't know	44	59	70	90

* Less than 0.5 percent.
n/a = not asked.
Because two answers were accepted, columns do not add up to 100 percent.
Source: Pew Research Center for the People and the Press (Pew 2000b, 2004c, 2008c).

that show what news sources citizens say they are using as they collect information about that year's presidential contest.

News consumers are voting with their eyeballs with respect to electronic news coverage, and as more alternative sources have become available people have begun looking elsewhere. They are choosing sources that our content analysis demonstrates sometimes are more thorough, less negative, and more informative than network news. The expansion of cable news in particular has cut greatly into network television's share of the news audience. In 2000, for the first time, more people turned to cable news than to the networks for information about a presidential election. Cable news increased its advantage in 2004 and 2008. In 1992, 55 percent of the public said that the network news programs were one of their top-two media sources for information about presidential elections. By 2008, only 18 percent made the same claim.

Other media sources have also seen declines, though they tend to be less dramatic. The audience share of local TV news fell from 29 percent to 10 percent over the sixteen-year period, and, like network television, newspapers suffered a hard fall in recent years. By 2008, only 33 percent listed newspapers as a top news source, a significant decline from the 57 percent of those surveyed in 1992 who said they relied on newspapers for political news.

Despite these declines, network television news continues to attract huge audiences, and some of the cable and online alternatives are network-owned offshoots that sometimes use the same reporters and even the same stories. A case could be made, to paraphrase Mark Twain, that reports of the death of network evening news have been greatly exaggerated. During an average week in January 2010, for example, the three evening newscasts drew a nightly average of twenty-five million viewers (Moore 2010). Although these audience figures are smaller than they used to be, the audiences are larger than those who tune in to leading cable news outlets or public television (Kurtz 2002b; de Moraes 2002). Sean Hannity, who hosts one of the leading cable news programs on the Fox News Channel, was bringing in just under seven million viewers a night, and Bill O'Reilly was drawing just over five million viewers (Nielsen 2010).

Nonetheless, news coverage of presidential elections has been marked by a steep decline in public attention to the Big Three evening news programs as some viewers have moved in the direction of higher quality news. In 1992, network news was about as commonly used a source of election information as newspapers. But a steady decline since then in network news performance—a decline amply demonstrated through our content analysis—has led to a dramatically increased gap between these two formats. A two-percentage-point gap favoring print in 1992 opened up into a fifteen-percentage-point gap favoring newspapers over network television news sixteen years later.

There has also been a move toward other media that are available on demand, as shown in table 1.1. Network television news had a twenty-six-percentage-point advantage over cable news in 1992; by 2008 this had become a twenty-six-point deficit. There weren't enough people online in 1992 to even ask about the Internet as a major place to obtain news, but by 2008 the online world trumped network television as a leading source of news by a two-to-one margin.

But where do people go for news online? Table 1.2 shows that online campaign news consumers consulted a wide range of sources during the 2008

Table 1.2
Top Websites for Campaign News, 2008

Question: [Asked of those who said they obtained any campaign information online, N = 817] "What websites did you use to get information about the election? Just name a few of the websites you went to most often." [Accept up to three answers.]

(Results in percentages)

	All Voters	Obama Voters	McCain Voters
CNN	27	35	18
Yahoo!	17	20	14
MSNBC/NBC	13	14	13
Candidate websites	13	15	10
Fox	11	5	18
MSN/Microsoft	9	9	10
Google	7	8	6
New York Times	6	9	2
Local newspaper/TV/radio	5	4	6
AOL	5	5	5
Other conservative blogs/sites	5	*	10
Political parties/organizations	4	3	5
Drudge Report	4	1	9
Polling sites and aggregators	3	3	4
Washington Post	3	3	2
YouTube	2	4	1
Huffington Post	2	4	*
Other liberal blogs/sites	2	3	1
BBC	2	3	1
ABC	2	2	2
Other blogs	2	2	1
Politico	2	2	1
ISP/cable provider	2	1	2

* Less than 0.5 percent.
Because up to three answers were accepted, columns do not add up to 100 percent.
Source: Pew Research Center for the People and the Press (Pew 2008c).

election: some that generate their own news, others that primarily present news reported by others, and still others that offer an ideological coloring to their comments. In this survey, researchers found that only one news source—CNN—was consulted online by one out of every four voters (27 percent). This speaks volumes about how widely the online news audience is disbursed, particularly when one considers that everyone surveyed could give up to three answers.

The second-most popular site was Yahoo!, a news aggregator, which was mentioned by 17 percent of those who obtained campaign information online. Only three other websites were listed by more than 10 percent of online news consumers: MSNBC/NBC (13 percent), candidate websites (13 percent), and Fox's online operation (11 percent). Table 1.2 lists the top twenty-three websites identified in the survey, along with every website that was listed as a major source by at least one out of fifty online news consumers. The fact that so few people view these major sites as that important demonstrates how likely today's citizens are to have very different information from each other as they evaluate candidates and policies.

One other important observation to draw from table 1.2 is how much one's partisan loyalty continues to affect where one goes for news online (cf. Iyengar and Hahn 2009; Mutz 2006). CNN and Fox were each listed as a major source for 18 percent of McCain voters obtaining news online. Among Obama voters, Fox was a major source for only one out of every twenty online news consumers, a tiny fraction of those who frequently use CNN (35 percent of online news users). Nine percent of Obama voters relied on the *New York Times* webpage, as compared to 2 percent of the McCain voters. The Drudge Report, famous for breaking the Clinton-Lewinsky scandal a decade ago, had an audience skewed in the opposite direction. Nine percent of McCain voters regularly checked in with Drudge for political news, as compared to 1 percent of Obama voters.

Some online Web outlets drew roughly equal shares of their frequent users from supporters of both Obama and McCain. Online, MSNBC/NBC and the *Washington Post* had roughly equal levels of interest among supporters of the two candidates, as did the MSN/Microsoft, Google, and AOL Web operations.

The declining audience for mainstream media outlets offline and the considerable competition they face online illustrate the great challenges faced by today's largest media operations. Citizens have grown more negative toward the mainstream media, criticizing it as too negative, not focused enough on the issues, and too biased (or at least not biased in the direction they prefer). And media researchers—ourselves included—find that television has become even more worthy of criticism in its coverage of recent presidential elections. It is to an outline of this content analysis methodology that this chapter now turns.

An Overview of the Content Analysis Evidence

For the last six presidential elections—from 1988 to 2008—CMPA's content analysis focused largely on the Big Three (ABC, CBS, and NBC) broadcast-network evening news shows. As we have noted, despite their recent decline in viewers—and with new anchors on all three evening newscasts—these flagship broadcasts continue to draw large audiences. They also control many of the alternative news outlets on cable and influence greatly online political news content, where material from the evening newscasts can be recycled for cable news programming (this is particularly common for NBC and MSNBC) or simply used to generate copy elsewhere. In addition, this core network news sample provides a basis for comparison with television news coverage of earlier presidential contests. The 2008 content analysis applied most of the same coding categories that were used in previous years, which allows for direct comparisons over time. The CMPA comparisons are further enhanced by a content analysis of campaign stories on Fox News in 2004 and in 2008 and on the *NewsHour* on PBS during the 2000 campaign, as well as an expanded version of the study for 1996, which included additional variables and a larger and more diverse sample, including print as well as broadcast outlets. The 1996 study also measured candidate discourse in several different formats, including campaign-trail speeches and paid television ads. CMPA also analyzed nonnetwork news outlets for the 1988 and 1992 elections, allowing for content comparisons overall for all six presidential elections considered here.

The networks' evening news coverage was examined to determine its thoroughness, substantive focus, valence (i.e., positive or negative tone with respect to the candidates), and level of mediation (i.e., the degree to which the story of the campaign was communicated through the candidates' own utterances, as opposed to the comments of journalists and other on-camera sources). The amount of coverage, the topics and issues that were addressed, the context in which public-policy issues were framed, the speaking time given to the candidates (both cumulatively and in terms of average duration, as measured by individual sound-bite length), and the evaluative tone of comments about the candidates were among the dimensions measured for each news story.

Table 1.3 demonstrates how news content can be very clear-cut, as confusing or complicated statements are often stricken from newscasts. Reporters know that readers and viewers are sometimes distracted. They may be listening to music when reading the paper or fixing dinner when watching the evening news. As a result, journalists often try to present simple, clear news content with a minimum of both complexity and guile. While such reports may not reflect the messy reality of the world beyond the television screen

Table 1.3
Content Analysis: Coding News Content during the 2008 Campaign

Read the sentences below, and try to determine which candidate is the subject of each statement and whether each statement is positive or negative in tone. (Answers are below.)

1. "Neither one of them comes even remotely close to representing my values."
   - Evangelical Voter, quoted on CBS, 08/02/2008
2. "Obama worked to open a jobs center. He also helped residents fight to rid their housing projects of asbestos. People in this [Chicago] community say Barack Obama's work inspires them to this day."
   - Kevin Tibbles, NBC, 10/2/2008
3. "Obama's dollar deluge is possible because he broke a promise to accept public funding."
   - John Berman, ABC, 10/19/2008
4. "McCain has shown that he can work on both sides of the table to help this country."
   - Voter, quoted on ABC, 10/10/2008
5. "Palin's carefully cultivated 'Joe Six Pack' image is now bumping up against a six-figure wardrobe."
   - Nancy Cordes, CBS, 10/22/2008

Answers:
1. Negative toward Obama and McCain
2. Positive toward Obama
3. Negative toward Obama
4. Positive toward McCain
5. Negative toward Palin

or the printed page, the lack of nuance does allow researchers to undertake content analysis with little disagreement among coders looking at the same news story.

Coders worked from videotaped newscasts. For all variables reported here, intercoder reliability—the extent to which one coder agreed with a second coder looking at the same taped news segment—exceeded 90 percent. Reliability tests were conducted on stories taken from previous applications of the system, and spot checks were conducted on current stories during the 2008 campaign to provide additional confidence in the content coding. The overall news story was treated as the unit of analysis only for measures of topical focus. Other variables were measured by coding individual statements (message units) within stories. This procedure permits far-more precise differentiation of campaign discourse than story-level coding affords.

For five of the six presidential election cycles, the general election study period began on Labor Day, the traditional kickoff date for the general election campaign, and concluded with the broadcasts aired the night before election day. We had to change the length of our study period for 2008, because Republicans decided to hold their nominating convention after Labor Day, immediately after the Democratic National Convention. We could have started our analysis in mid-September after both conventions had concluded, but that didn't seem to reflect the campaign season's dynamics. In particular, John McCain's selection of Sarah Palin as his running mate set off an ongoing media frenzy that dominated the entire campaign for several weeks. So we defined the 2008 campaign season as starting on August 23, right before the start of the Democratic National Convention. Where appropriate, we reported both lengthened campaign season and regular-season campaign statistics to maximize the comparability of 2008 with earlier years.

The ever-shifting political calendar caused problems with the primary season calendar for 2008 as well. From 1988 through 2004, the primary election news period began on January 1 and lasted until a nominee was selected, usually by mid-March. When the 2008 Iowa caucuses were moved up to January 3 and the New Hampshire primary to January 8, however, starting the primary season coverage on January 1 made little sense. So for the 2008 election cycle, the primary season is measured as starting on December 16, 2007. The nominating process not only started early, it also ended late, at least for the Democrats. We define the primary season as ending on March 22, 2008, by which time all but eight of the fifty states had held primaries and caucuses, and both nominees were virtually assured.

Finally, the election "preseason," which previously covered the calendar year before the presidential contest, ended on December 15, 2007, because of the early nominating events of 2008. Although few voters may be paying much attention a year before a presidential election, jockeying to win a party's presidential nomination starts even earlier than that, particularly in the states that vote early.

This study also includes findings drawn from a content analysis of 18,836 campaign news stories during 2008 by the Project for Excellence in Journalism. The broadcast news portion of this study includes 3,977 stories from the first thirty minutes of the morning shows and the entire thirty-minute evening news shows on ABC, CBS, and NBC, as well as the PBS *NewsHour*. The PBS analysis rotated daily between the first thirty minutes and the last thirty minutes of the hour-long newscast.

The 9,202 cable news stories analyzed by PEJ were drawn from CNN, MSNBC, and Fox News Channel. Some material was drawn from daytime offerings and some from the early-evening and prime-time reports. The cable sample includes both news-oriented programs, like CNN's *Situation Room*, and more opinion-oriented programming, like Fox's *O'Reilly Factor* and MSNBC's *Countdown with Keith Olbermann*.

The 2,919 stories on radio programs include news reports on National Public Radio and a sampling of talk radio from both conservatives, such as Rush Limbaugh and Sean Hannity, and liberals, such as Ed Schultz and Randi Rhodes. The 1,264 online stories PEJ examined came from sites that created their own material for their websites (like CNN.com and MSNBC.com) and sites that provided material either entirely or largely generated by others (like Yahoo! News, AOL News, and Google News).

Finally, the newspaper portion of the PEJ study includes 1,474 front-page stories from both major papers and smaller news outlets. The *New York Times* was coded every day, and four other major papers—the *Wall Street Journal, Washington Post, Los Angeles Times,* and *USA Today*—were coded roughly every other day. A sample drawn from sixteen regional and local newspapers was also coded, with the papers selected for the analysis changing from day to day.

What Comes Next?

This first chapter has introduced the research project and outlined existing academic theory and research on news media content and effects with respect to election campaigns. Chapter 2 begins by comparing the content of network television newscasts from past presidential elections. Here we will demonstrate how the amount of coverage overall has declined and how the coverage that remains has often focused on the horse race rather than on more substantive matters, like discussion of policies and character—areas that would be very useful for voters trying to decide which candidate to support. For the 2008 election, the PEJ data allow us to compare findings for network news with those of other news outlets looking at the same campaign events.

Chapter 3 deals with another damaging change in the way journalists have covered presidential campaigns over this period: the amount of attention they devote to themselves. Not only has the amount of campaign coverage overall declined, so has the amount of coverage in which candidates speak for themselves. The content analysis reveals that only a small share of television airtime is devoted to their comments and that the fragments of candidate remarks (sound bites) have become smaller and smaller. In this chapter, we demonstrate how this degradation of coverage forces candidates to reduce their ideas to the simplest and most "media-friendly" descriptions if they expect to receive media attention. The trend even encourages candidates to pepper each other with "sound barks," rather than reason with each other on the campaign trail. Simplistic attacks are also a tempting campaign strategy in this media environment. Finally, we also consider the ways television reports frame candidates, reducing some of them to little more than stereotypes. Of course the network newscasts are not the only places that candidates are framed by media. The PEJ data for cable, print, and online news content allow us to compare the traditional networks with other media outlets during 2008.

Chapter 4 turns to questions of negativity, accuracy, and bias in a consideration of network coverage. The astonishing series of media blunders that marked the 2000 Bush-Gore contest comprises only the greatest errors of judgment in a process that frequently has been marked by inaccurate and more negative coverage over time. The decision by the television networks to pool their resources to create the Voter News Service has led to similar (if less-egregious) errors in the past. The race to be first, which has intensified as media technologies have improved and as use of the Internet has become more widespread, has led to increasing recklessness in the calling of elections, and not just in the notorious 2000 Florida race that decided the entire election (Nelson 2001; Owen 2002; Sabato 2002). Our PEJ data allow us to compare network news with major media rivals on this dimension for 2008 as well.

Errors are only part of the problems relating to accuracy and bias. Recent elections have been marked by little civility in the news coverage, with reporters increasingly focusing on the negative aspects of each candidate. The media cynicism created decades ago by the lies of Vietnam and Watergate continues to deepen, as a decreasing fraction of what is said about a candidate qualifies as positive. Indeed one of the major issues of the 2004 election was what Bush and Kerry did—or did not do—during the Vietnam era more than three decades earlier. Major issues of 2008 included the thoughts of Barack Obama's minister and the validity of Obama's birth certificate. Another major issue focused on the wardrobe choices of Sarah Palin and who paid those bills. By focusing on relatively petty matters, media triviality and negativity may encourage potential voters to tune out the candidates (and the media) and not even go to the polls on election day. Or dispirited voters may refuse to accept the eventual winner and resist every White House initiative for the following four years.

In chapter 5, we argue that the disparities seen in media content in 2008 are not unique but rather are part of a pattern going back several elections. The evidence against the television networks is particularly compelling when compared to other media sources over the years, including public television and leading daily newspapers that help set the national media agenda—papers such as the *Washington Post*, the *Wall Street Journal*, and the *New York Times*. Fox News and the *NewsHour* on PBS offer important contrasts. Despite having a slightly smaller amount of airtime, PBS devoted far more air time to election 2000 news than all of the Big Three evening news shows combined, was far more focused on substantive issues than on the horse race, and was less prone to bias. Four years later, Fox News was even more biased in its coverage of the candidates than were ABC, CBS, and NBC. But by 2008, the tables had turned, with Fox more even-handed in tone than any of the Big Three networks.

Chapter 5 also discusses the large gap between the way presidential campaigns are presented by the news media and the way that these campaigns actually unfold. There is a great deal of difference, the CMPA content analysis demonstrates, between what the candidates said and what the networks said they said. This discrepancy is found across types of campaign discourse, including candidate speeches, campaign websites, and even the much-maligned campaign advertisements.

Chapter 6 presents potential reforms to improve the performance of network television or in the alternative to make the networks even less significant in citizen assessments of presidential candidates. While network television does not appear likely to follow the lead of the *NewsHour*, which has far lower ratings than any of the three network evening news broadcasts, there are possible ways to improve the broadcast networks' performance in covering presidential elections. Potential reforms debated here include hour-long network newscasts, free broadcast airtime for candidates to present unmediated messages, and the growing opportunities for interested citizens to go beyond the nightly news through consultation of Internet sources.

2

A Need-to-Know Basis? Covering
Issues of Substance and the Horse Race

E VERY FOURTH NOVEMBER, more than 120 million Americans cast a vote
for a presidential candidate. The campaigns for president, and before
that the preliminary battles for the Democratic and Republican presidential
nominations, are extended seminars on the state of the nation: how well (or
how poorly) the incumbent president has handled the always-pivotal issues of
war and peace and the state of the economy. Candidates debate other issues
that could affect presidential performance as well, which—depending on the
year—could include energy, the environment, health care, tax cuts, and even
the country's moral climate. But more than just a look back, presidential campaigns are also about looking forward. Candidates discuss where the country
should go in the years ahead and how the nation can deal with some of its
most vexing problems: terrorism, crime, poverty, the massive federal debt,
the tens of millions of Americans who lack health insurance, and the potential insolvency of Social Security and Medicare in the coming decades. Even
for a country as wealthy as the United States, there are many challenging and
highly contested policy areas considered at length by people who campaign
to be president.

In the media, though, a different picture emerges. The debate is not primarily over whether Social Security needs fixing and, if so, how to fix it. The
mediated discussion is often not over whether the American economy needs
a boost and, if so, how to provide a little macroeconomic help. Rather, reporters talk mostly about who is ahead and who is behind in the presidential
polls. The discussion of public policy matters that does occur in the media is
often framed in the context of this very same horse race. Campaign programs

proposed to fix Social Security or cut taxes or revamp welfare are seen as ways to woo the farmers, soccer moms, senior citizens, or other interest groups. As data presented in this chapter show, reporters often spend more time judging the political wisdom of the appeal than the policy and its substantive merits. The horse-race-focused election presented by the news media is the one that most of us see. Few Americans attend presidential campaign rallies in person, and less than half of the nation's voters use the daily newspapers as our major source of campaign news. If we attend campaign rallies and carefully scour online news sources and some of the country's better newspapers, we might see or read more discussion of policy options, more discussion of matters of substance. But searching for hard-to-find substance-based coverage is a lot of work to ask of voters, who turn to the media for accessible discussions about where the candidates would take the country. As we discuss in this chapter and in chapter 5, other news outlets suffer from many of the same problems that afflict network news.

The CMPA content analysis (described in chapter 1) demonstrates how television coverage often focuses on the horse-race aspects of the presidential campaign rather than more substantive matters, like issues and candidate character. Even in years with reduced amounts of horse-race coverage, the "sports" of politics still remains at least as significant a part of campaign coverage as news dealing with policy proposals. In addition, the Project for Excellence in Journalism study finds that many other leading media outlets also focused on horse-race news at the expense of matters of substance throughout the 2008 campaign.

Agenda Setting: The Power of News Content

In the first chapter, we discussed three leading theories of the news media's influence: the "hypodermic effects" model (where news content was thought to be more or less "injected" into citizens and of very powerful effect), the "minimal effects" model (where citizens were not seen to be affected very much by news content), and the "media effects" model ("more than minimal" effects), where the news media don't tell citizens what to think so much as what to think about). Few media scholars imagine citizens are "brainwashed" by what they see on television (the first perspective), and few believe citizens are only barely influenced by what is presented in the news media. Most academics who study the news media consider the third, the media effects, model, to be the most likely—believing that reporters and editors help set the agenda and frame the debate by the issues and perspectives they choose to emphasize (or to ignore).

Television has been a part of our lives for so long that it is easy to forget how much television news changed the political environment. Television, which became widespread in America during the 1950s, had the potential to be far more influential in politics than newspapers were for a variety of reasons: (1) it offered an expanded range of information—both moving pictures and words, (2) it offered the potential for being more credible (seeing is believing), and (3) it rapidly became the dominant source of information and entertainment in American households (cf. Grossman 1995; Ranney 1983; White 1961). The key events of American politics in the 1960s—the civil rights movement, the Vietnam War, the space race, the Cuban Missile Crisis, and the assassinations of John F. Kennedy, Robert F. Kennedy, and Martin Luther King, Jr.—all lent themselves to powerful (and emotion-invoking) visual images (cf. Gitlin 1980; Grossman 1995; Halberstam 1979; Lesher 1982; McGinniss 1969; Meyrowitz 1985; White 1978). It is no wonder that citizens turned to television in increasing numbers and for an increasing share of the news they consumed.

The rise of cable news programming in the 1980s and the Internet boom starting in the 1990s intensified many of these developments. The prominence of CNN, the first major cable news network, meant that news became available on television twenty-four hours a day, seven days a week, and the subsequent development of cable news and opinion programming on MSNBC and the Fox News Channel offered the options of more interpretative reporting and more ideological content. Finally, the World Wide Web exponentially increased the amount and range of material at the fingertips of news consumers (Graf 2008; Owen 2009).

Regardless of the media technology they encounter, candidates try to set the campaign agenda to maximize their chances of winning the election. Presidents in good economic times want to make the economy the issue, as Bill Clinton wished to do in 1996 (Ceaser and Busch 1997). Presidents in bad economic times want to make something—anything—else the issue, as George H. W. Bush did four years earlier (Gold 1994). Challengers also have their own preferred agenda: in 2008, Barack Obama wanted to run on hope in the face of economic hardship, while John McCain campaigned primarily on his national security credentials (Abramson et al. 2010; Ceaser and Busch 2001; Ceaser et al. 2009).

But candidates do not get the opportunity to set the campaign agenda unilaterally. The real power to set the agenda is in the hands of the news media, which control access to the columns of the nation's newspapers and the segments on the evening news programs (Ranney 1983). And in recent elections, bloggers and other Internet voices sometimes succeed in bringing new issues to the forefront (cf., Drudge 2000; Gronbeck 2009; Owen 2009). The process for candidates or their allies to engage with the media can be symbiotic, as candidates try to present information in media-friendly formats (Cook 2005; Edwards 2003, 2004; Entman 2005). Reporters sometimes use those "made for TV" efforts in their programming, as the media experts on the campaigns try to tailor what they offer reporters to correspond with what the reporters themselves desire to use in their stories (Cook 2005; Kellner 2002, 2003; Kumar 2003a, 2003b; Lewis and Rose 2002; Schechter 2003). But make no mistake about it—coverage decisions are made by journalists, not by candidates. Online activists may also try to convert an issue that is thriving online to one that is also a key part of the offline media conversation (cf., Farnsworth 2009; Gronbeck 2009). What the reporters choose to talk about is an important matter. When news consumers are exposed to what reporters and editors think are the important issues, they tend to consider these issues important themselves (Iyengar and Kinder 1987). This process of agenda setting can work in a number of different ways. When citizens are exposed primarily to horse-race news coverage, they do a better job of recalling that information than more substantive matters (Cappella and Jamieson 1997). If reporters talk and write about economic matters a great deal, as was the case in 1992, news consumers considered economic matters an important part of evaluating a president or a presidential candidate (Lewis-Beck and Rice 1992; Mutz 1992).

The reverse is also true. If the media do not say a great deal about economic matters, as was the case in 2000 and 2004, economic matters are not seen by citizens as an important issue to consider when selecting one's favorite presidential candidate (Campbell 2001; Lewis-Beck and Tien 2001; Pew 2004c; Wlezien 2001). When economic news tops the issue agenda, as it did in 2008, there is little that candidates can do to shift the media conversation and voter perceptions of salience elsewhere, even though John McCain greatly desired to talk about something—anything—else (Abramson et al. 2010; Campbell 2009).

Political scientists Shanto Iyengar and Donald R. Kinder (1987) offered one of the most extensive tests of the agenda-setting power of television news through a laboratory experiment in which subjects were assigned to watch newscasts with different content and emphases. The more extensively and prominently a topic was covered on television news, the more important it became to the viewer.

> Americans' views of their society and nation are powerfully shaped by the stories that appear on the evening news. We found that people who were shown network broadcasts edited to draw attention to a particular problem assigned greater importance to that problem—greater importance than they themselves did before the experiment began, and greater importance than did people assigned to control conditions that emphasized different problems. (Iyengar and Kinder 1987, 113)

As noted above, reporters do not have complete control over the campaign agenda. They cover candidates who are constantly trying to shape the agenda to their own advantage. And external events, such as wars and other crises, can alter the campaign agenda regardless of the issues that had been the focus of media attention (McLeod et al. 1994). Likewise, not all citizens accept the media assessments of the most important issues. Not every citizen is persuadable, in other words. Some voters are very strong supporters of one political party or the other, regardless of candidate, issues, or media content.

Another factor that can undermine the media's influence is that not everyone pays sufficient attention to understand political developments. Many citizens, even those who vote regularly, are not all that interested in political news. "For most Americans politics is still far from the most interesting and important thing in life," wrote Austin Ranney (1983, 11). "To them politics is usually confusing, boring, repetitious, and, above all, irrelevant to the things that really matter in life." Political scientist Doris Graber (2006) has argued that the disconnected facts received from television news make it hard for all but the most careful media observers to create meaningful wholes of the evidence they do receive, and this can discourage many citizens from even trying to make sense of the political world. In addition, the increasingly fragmented public audience for news content also works against the construction of a consistent campaign narrative in the mass public (cf., Pew 2008a, 2008b). Despite these challenges to public learning from the media, however, an extensive study of campaign discourse in 1992 found that citizens are far more capable of engaging in useful democratic discourse than many critics believe (Just et al. 1996).

The News Agenda: The Horse Race Matters Most

Applying the agenda-setting perspective to the study of presidential elections means turning to the horse race, which has long been a key area of media research (Bartels 1988; Patterson 1980, 1994; Ranney 1983). Thomas Patterson (1980, 1994) was an early critic of television's emphasis on horse-race coverage, saying that reporters talk too much about the electoral "game" rather than about governing. Citizens receive information about politics-as-sports, but not nearly enough about issues to enable them to choose effectively between the candidates. Why are reporters so obsessed with horse-race matters, and, as a result, with public opinion polls? Patterson laments the media's focus on polls, but he believes this pattern of modern reporting has more to do with news routines than with a deliberate choice on the part of reporters: "The news is not a mirror held up to society. It is a selective rendition of events told in story form. For this reason, the conventions of news reporting include an emphasis on the more dramatic and controversial aspects of politics. Above all else, reporters are taught to search for what is new and different in events of the past twenty-four hours" (Patterson 1994, 60).

Nearly every content analysis that examined television programming has objected to the heavy emphasis on the horse-race aspects of presidential campaign coverage (cf. Bartels 1988; Kerbel 1998; Lichter et al. 1988; Lichter and Noyes 1995, 1998; Patterson 1994; Robinson and Sheehan 1983). "In covering a presidential campaign," complained Larry Bartels, "the media tell us more about who is winning and who is losing than they do about who is fit to be president" (1988, 32), raising an objection widely shared by media researchers. Despite the objection from many critics, the media practice of describing politics as sports continues to train our collective focus on the horse race.

From the point of view of a well-functioning democratic polity, the horse-race focus during primary campaigns seems particularly troubling. Primary campaigns are intramural competitions where citizens no longer have partisan cues to guide them. In addition, these early struggles often involve several candidates who are not well-known, and if the primary race is fiercely contested, the eventual party nominee can be crippled going into the general election (Lengle 1981, 1987; Lengle et al. 1995).

The concerns here, therefore, go beyond the fact that network news is paying a great deal of attention to trivial matters. Television's frequent treatment of politics as sports is making this trivial matter influential—if not decisive—in the selection of presidential nominees, and that selection process itself may be an important factor in voter assessments in the general election. A key way that horse-race matters affect outcomes occurs through the process by which this coverage builds momentum for a candidate (Bartels 1988). In 1972, for example, Edmund Muskie won the New Hampshire primary by nine points, but the media's story was instead that he did worse than expected as the reporters focused on the "surprisingly strong showing by [George] McGovern" (Ranney 1983, 96). Bill Clinton proclaimed himself "the Comeback Kid" after finishing second in the New Hampshire primary twenty years later, and likewise the media's focus was on Clinton's stronger-than-expected showing and not on the candidate who actually won the primary (and won it by 8 percentage points), former senator Paul Tsongas of Massachusetts (Baker 1993). "Doing best in the early primaries is not simply a matter of getting more votes than the other candidates; it is getting substantially more votes 'than expected,'" wrote Austin Ranney (1983, 95). "Query: expected by whom? Answer: by the analysts of the press and the networks."

If you are underestimated and do quite well, like Bill Clinton in 1992, John McCain in 2000, John Kerry and John Edwards in 2004, and Barack Obama in 2008, you may bask in some of the most favorable coverage available. If you are overestimated and do not do as well as expected—even if you win several primaries or even the nomination itself —you may suffer from harsh media coverage, like President George H. W. Bush in 1992, former Vermont governor Howard Dean in 2004, and Hillary Clinton in 2008 (Farnsworth and Lichter 2006a, 2006b; Norrander 2009). Robert Shogan of the *Los Angeles Times*, one of the nation's most experienced political reporters, laments this focus on the expectations game in New Hampshire, arguing that it has "a profound and capricious impact" on presidential nominations and elections (2001, 31).

Fortunately for the candidates who "beat the spread"—including Obama, Kerry, Bill Clinton, McGovern, and Jimmy Carter—reporters continue to play the expectations game (Maisel 2002). Being badly mistaken in their predictions doesn't even cause the media to pause.

> Four weeks ago, just before the [1992] New Hampshire primary, the television wise men of *Inside Washington* were asked to assess the prospects for Bill Clinton's scandal-ridden candidacy. "I think he is a goner," said Carl Rowan. "I think Clinton is dead," said Charles Krauthammer. The governor of Arkansas, long since resurrected from the political graveyard, appeared well on his way to the Democratic nomination yesterday after convincing victories in Illinois and Michigan. And the press? Those folks who anointed Clinton the frontrunner long before the voters tuned in, then decided he had been de-Flowered in New Hampshire, then started chronicling his comeback? Well, it's a good thing they don't make their living playing the stock market. (Kurtz 1992a)

As political scientist Larry Bartels observes, "Analysts, observers, and pundits courageous enough to predict the outcomes of recent nominating campaigns have been routinely embarrassed" (1988, 6). But the predictions keep on coming. Indeed, if Democratic voters had listened to reporters about the "inevitability" of Hillary Clinton's huge fundraising and name-recognition advantages in the months before the 2008 Iowa caucuses, Barack Obama might never have become the Democratic nominee (Norrander 2009).

The erroneous predictions of Bill Clinton's fortunes by reporters during the 1992 New Hampshire primary, together with the mistaken assessment of former First Lady Hillary Clinton in the 2008 nomination contest, demonstrate the limits of media effects on the viewing and reading audience. Likewise, Bill Clinton's presidency was thought to be on life support in the days following the first public disclosure of that Clinton-Lewinsky scandal. Repeatedly during those early days, leading pundits said Clinton's presidency was over. Sam Donaldson, the longtime White House correspondent and host of ABC's *This Week*, opined: "If he's not telling the truth, I think his presidency is numbered in days. This isn't going to drag out. We're not going to be here three months from now talking about this. Mr. Clinton, if he's not telling the truth and the evidence shows that, will resign, perhaps this week" (Donaldson, quoted in Jones 2001, 199).

In fact, America was talking about that scandal a *year* later, and Clinton went on to finish out his eight-year term with relatively high approval ratings.

Howard Dean was the Democratic candidate with the same high expectations going into the 2004 nomination season that Bill Clinton had enjoyed back in 1992. As political scientist Barry Burden noted, "Howard Dean was on fire in the latter half of 2003. He signed up hundreds of thousands of 'Deaniacs' on the Internet, drew tremendous crowds, and raised enormous sums of money. . . . By the time Gore endorsed him in mid-December, Dean seemed unbeatable. If momentum exists in contemporary presidential nominating campaigns, Dean had it" (2005, 26).

Dean's rise during the 2003 election preseason was all the more surprising given the fact he had begun the year in the low single digits in the presidential preference polls. The former Vermont governor's support had risen from 19 percent in July 2003 to 45 percent in early December (Burden 2005, 27). Only John Kerry was competitive with Dean in fundraising during this period, and Kerry's support fell from 25 percent to 13 percent during the last half of 2003. For a while, it looked like Dean would surge to his party's nomination just like governors Jimmy Carter of Georgia, Ronald Reagan of California, and Bill Clinton of Arkansas had (cf., Ceaser and Busch 2005).

But Dean's fortunes soured once the caucuses and primaries began. After looking like the 2004 version of the odds-beating Jimmy Carter, Dean turned into the next Senator John Glenn (D-Ohio), the overhyped former astronaut whose 1984 presidential campaign never really got off the ground. Dean's support among New Hampshire voters fell rapidly in the final two weeks before that pivotal 2004 primary, where he finished second to Kerry by a margin of 38 to 26 percent (Farnsworth and Lichter 2006b). Kerry's victory in New Hampshire, coupled with a similar come-from-behind victory over Dean in Iowa earlier in January 2004, effectively finished off the Dean campaign and secured Kerry's nomination (Burden 2005).

The horse-race-based media expectations game can have real consequences. People can be elected president if they win the expectations game and face a weakened incumbent. Such was the case with George H. W. Bush, weakened politically by poor economic conditions (Patterson 1994). Jimmy Carter's 1976 victory was also helped considerably by the combination of these two factors (Bartels 1988; Ranney 1983). Although George W. Bush could not run for a third term in 2008, his party's nominee that year—John McCain—repeatedly suffered from the poor economic conditions that had developed during Bush's final year in office (Abramson et al. 2010).

What do journalists do when they are wrong? They write a new story—and when necessary add a 180-degree turn to their coverage. Reporters seeking to find explanations for their previous underestimations of a candidate can be quite generous, at least temporarily. Reporters describe candidates enjoying an unexpected rise in the polls as "suddenly more decisive, committed, inspiring, and in general a better candidate and person" (Patterson 1994, 118–19). Candidates falling in the polls receive more negative coverage, described by that particularly undesirable quality, "a likely loser."

Agenda-setting is not only the process of telling voters what to think about and what to ignore; it is also the process of telling voters whom to think about and whom to ignore. When third-party presidential candidates, like Ralph Nader and Pat Buchanan in 2000, get very little media coverage, voters are less likely to consider those candidates and their issues. In his report on his 2000 Green Party presidential campaign, Nader faulted the networks for not taking his campaign seriously, even though the third-party candidate generated large crowds and raised issues other candidates failed to address.

> There is a major problem for anyone who runs for president, especially a third-party candidate. No matter how long or extensively you campaign in every state of the union, no matter how large your audiences become, you cannot reach in direct personal communication even 1 percent of the eligible voters. In essence, you don't run for president directly; you ask the media to run you for president, or, if you have the money, you can pay the media for exposure. Reaching the voters relies almost entirely on how the media chooses to perceive you and your campaign. In short, this "virtual reality" *is* the reality. (2002, 155; emphasis in original)

The focus on horse-race news is damaging for the polity, according to some researchers. If the news focuses largely on polling, some otherwise uncommitted citizens will pay a great deal of attention to which candidate is ahead and which is behind when they decide which candidate to support (Patterson 1980).

Shanto Iyengar (1991) argues that the news media's unwillingness to take issues seriously undermines the ability of politicians to send issue-based appeals and of voters to receive them.

> Instead of forcing the candidates to address the issues of clear social or economic significance, television news coverage of the 1988 campaign focused on the Pledge of Allegiance, patriotism, prison-furlough programs, flag desecration, membership in the American Civil Liberties Union, and other issues more symbolic than substantive. (142)

This trend is particularly problematic for a democratic society, because it does not give citizens the information necessary to "connect the dots" and appreciate the complexities of modern public policy debates (cf. Just et al. 1996; Wayne 2003). The fault for the public's inability to appreciate such political contradictions lies largely with the media, Iyengar (1991) concludes:

> Because of its reliance on episodic reporting, television news provides a distorted depiction of public affairs. The portrayal of recurring issues as unrelated events prevents the public from cumulating the evidence toward any logical consequence. By diverting attention from societal and governmental responsibility, episodic framing glosses over national problems and allows public officials to ignore problems whose remedies entail burdens to their constituents. Television news may well prove to be the opiate of American society. (143)

Amount of Network News Coverage

General Elections

Even before the general election begins, the networks routinely face criticism for cutting back on their live coverage of the party conventions. Critics saw these reductions in coverage as evidence of how the network news departments pay less attention to "hard" political news and more to "soft" news of lifestyle trends and human-interest stories (Patterson 2000). Broadcast executives claimed that the conventions had grown too dull and too stage-managed to justify covering extensively and argued that interested viewers could find more coverage on cable television.

Even so, network television executives may be listening to their critics. During the 2008 presidential election, network television provided more news on the campaign than in all but one of the six presidential elections examined here. The culmination of five hundred stories on the presidential election on ABC, CBS, and NBC during the fall campaign season was comparable to the 2004 presidential election, when the networks aired 504 stories. When measured by number of minutes devoted to the election, the results are even more striking: the 1,187 minutes (nineteen hours and forty-seven minutes) devoted to the 2008 election was almost 11 percent more than the 1,070 minutes (seventeen hours and fifty minutes) of campaign news in 2004 and well above the comparable figures for 2000 and 1996. Still, the 2008 coverage remained well below the total for 1992.

Reporting campaign news from Labor Day to election day, as we have done in previous years, creates a problem when we attempt to compare the 2008 campaign with previous years. In past years, both conventions took place before Labor Day, but in 2008 the GOP convention took place after the traditional start of the campaign season. For purposes of comparing the amount of coverage over time, we report results from this conventional campaign kick-off day for earlier years in table 2.1.

But the different calendar for 2008 leaves researchers with a dilemma. To start our analysis at Labor Day would include one party's national convention and exclude the other's. To start our analysis early enough to include both conventions creates a campaign season roughly two weeks longer than the other years analyzed. With this caveat, we use the extended study period (which includes both conventions) for CMPA data except where otherwise indicated. For measures of news volume in table 2.1 we include both the extended period (designated in the tables with the initials *EP*) and a more conventional campaign period starting on September 5. This allows readers to select their preferred timeframe. For other measures elsewhere in this book, we generally rely on the extended period, which in our opinion more accurately reflects the complete general election campaign dynamics of 2008. It is also a fairer measure of substance and tone than the shorter conventional campaign period.

The amounts of network coverage for the last four general elections pale before the massive news coverage CMPA recorded for the campaign in 1992 (twenty-three hours, twenty-two minutes).

The light coverage of the 1996 general election, representing barely half the 1992 level, was initially attributed to a dull and uncompetitive contest between two well-known candidates. With the media coverage of the 2008 election now precisely quantified, the comparably smaller amount of coverage previously recorded in 1996, 2000, and 2004 now appear to be part of a longer-term trend of reduced network television coverage of presidential elections. A campaign that pitted the first African American major-party nominee

Table 2.1
General Election News, 1988–2008

Amount of Coverage	2008EP*	2008	2004	2000	1996	1992	1988
Number of stories	683	500	504	462	483	728	589
Stories per day (ave.)	9.4	8.8	9.0	7.3	7.7	11.5	10.5
Minutes per day (ave.)	22.0	20.8	19.1	12.6	12.3	24.6	17.0
Total time (minutes)	1,606	1,187	1,070	805	788	1,402	1,116

*The general election campaign period starts with Labor Day evening newscasts on ABC, CBS, and NBC and continues through the day before election day for 1988–2004. The 2008 period covers from the end of the Republican National Convention through the day before election day (September 5 through November 3). The 2008EP (extended period) included here adds the party conventions, which occurred on either side of Labor Day. To include both conventions, the 2008EP covers the evening newscasts starting on August 23 through the day before election day. As a result, the 2008 total figures are not directly comparable with those for previous years.

for president with one of the most visible senators seems highly compelling. Presidential elections don't get much more interesting than they were during the economic crisis year of 2008, but the amount of coverage in that election was far less than the general election phase of the 1992 presidential election. But the general election trend, at least as of 2008, remains better than some other recent election years.

Nomination Contests

As one would expect from the first presidential election cycle since 1952 in which neither a sitting president nor vice president was competing for a presidential nomination, the amount of news coverage of the 2008 nomination contests was extraordinary. Add the first viable African American and female presidential candidates to the mix, and you have the makings of a record-breaking primary season.

And so it was. From December 16, 2007, through March 22, 2008 (when the competitive phase of the Democratic primary was over), the evening newscasts of ABC, CBS, and NBC broadcast 932 stories on the Democratic and Republican presidential nomination contests, for a total of 1,710 minutes (28.5 hours) of campaign news (see table 2.2).

As shown in table 2.2, news reports of the 2008 nominations burst past the amounts of nomination news coverage from the previous five cycles. The amount of campaign news analyzed for 2008 was roughly a month longer than in past years for two reasons: (1) the nomination contests started earlier than ever before, and (2) Obama and Clinton kept up a long-running contest for the Democratic nomination that lasted well beyond Super Tuesday, by which point both parties' nominees are usually determined.

Table 2.2
Primary Election News, 1988–2008

Amount of Coverage Parties with Viable* Contests	2008 D, R	2004 D	2000 D, R	1996 R	1992 D, R	1988 D, R
Number of stories	932	356	550	699	370	597
Minutes per day (average)	17.6	11.2	13.4	16.9	10.7	13.3
Total time (minutes)	1,710	684	882	1,202	738	1,126

* Defined as at least two nationally known figures competing for a given party nomination.
Note: 2008 data covers ABC, CBS, and NBC newscasts from December 16, 2007, through March 22, 2008 (when the competitive phase of the primaries was effectively over); 2004 data covers from January 1 through March 1 (Super Tuesday); 2000 data covers from January 1 through March 7 (Super Tuesday); 1996 data covers from January 1 through March 12 (Super Tuesday); 1992 data covers from January 1 through March 10 (Super Tuesday); and the 1988 data covers from January 1 through the Illinois primary on March 15.

Because of the differing lengths of the nomination campaign in different years, the number of stories per day may be the best comparison over time. The average of 17.6 network news stories a day in the 2008 cycle was markedly more than the 16.9 stories per day for 1996, when then-senator Bob Dole and television commentator Pat Buchanan fought for the chance to be the Republican to challenge Bill Clinton's re-election operation. The amount of coverage for the 1996 nomination campaign still represents a record for years when only one party had a viable nomination struggle.

The amount of coverage in 2008 is particularly notable when compared to the 2004 primaries, which generated the fewest number of stories and the least coverage of the past six primary election cycles. The 2008 performance is also striking when compared to the results of other years when both parties had nomination contests: 2000, 1992, and 1988. Even though 1992 was the best year for the amount of campaign coverage during the general election, that year fell far short of the amount of primary campaign news in the historic year of 2008.

Within the primary season, a key period of media coverage is the month or so before the New Hampshire primary, traditionally the first presidential primary. The New Hampshire primary enjoys a wildly disproportionate influence in American presidential nomination politics, as the voters of that small and unrepresentative state have long been able to narrow considerably the field of candidates for the primaries and caucuses that follow (Adams 1987; Baker 1993; Duncan 1991; Mayer 1987, 1996, 1997, 2001; Palmer 1997; Rosenstiel 1994; Stanley 1997, 2001).

From December 16, 2007, through the eve of the New Hampshire primary on January 8, 2008, network television devoted eighty-two stories to Hillary Clinton and eighty-two stories to Barack Obama. The evenhandedness in volume of coverage reflected the status of the campaign at that point—Obama had upset Clinton in the Iowa caucuses on January 3, 2008, and had caught up with her in fundraising and in the national preference polls during this period (Norrander 2009). But the "proportionate representation" of coverage did not extend to John Edwards. The former senator from North Carolina, who had kept up with his two chief rivals in pre-caucus polls in Iowa, was the subject of only fifty-two network news stories in the weeks leading up to the primary. Edwards finished a distant third in the Granite State, dealing a near-fatal wound to his campaign (Norrander 2009). [Of course, given Edwards's extramarital affair and the eventual scandal created (Bosman 2010), Democrats might consider themselves lucky Edwards did not get more media attention or more votes.] Other Democratic candidates, further back in the polls than Edwards, received even less media attention.

The 2008 nomination news story was much the same on the Republican side, with the leading candidates getting far more attention in the run-up to the New Hampshire primary than other rivals. Former Arkansas governor Mike Huckabee, the winner of the 2008 Iowa caucuses (and now a news commentator on Fox), was the subject of seventy news stories in the three weeks leading up to the New Hampshire primary on January 8. He edged out former Massachusetts governor Mitt Romney, who was the subject of sixty-eight stories. John McCain, the eventual nominee—and the winner of the 2000 New Hampshire primary—was third in the amount of Republican coverage, the subject of sixty-one stories. The coverage pattern matched their standings in Iowa, where Huckabee had won, Romney had finished second, and McCain had finished third. But the coverage did not reflect the subsequent outcome in New Hampshire, where McCain finished first, Romney second, and Huckabee a distant third. Once again, candidates farther back in the polls—like Congressman Ron Paul (R-Tex.), a darling of libertarians—received little attention.

Previous nomination cycles showed similar patterns, as the news media frequently focus on the top two—or at most three—candidates, leaving others in the dust. In 2004, Edwards also received a relatively small amount of coverage when compared to Howard Dean, the former Vermont governor, and John Kerry, the party's 2004 nominee. Former senator Bill Bradley (D-N.J.), who ran against then vice president Al Gore in 2000, had a similar problem, albeit a bit later in the nomination contest. After Gore won the New Hampshire primary, the media basically stopped covering the Democratic contest, focusing instead on the competition between McCain and George W. Bush on the Republican side (Farnsworth and Lichter 2008; Stanley 2001). In 2004, the volume of media coverage suggested that Kerry and Dean were the most viable candidates for the nomination, a perspective also reflected in their fundraising advantages over their rivals (Burden 2005). But these coverage patterns shortchanged the less well-known candidates from outside the region, including Edwards and former U.S. Army general Wesley Clark, an Arkansas native. Both Dean and Kerry had been elected repeatedly in states bordering New Hampshire, and their own states' television signals carried into the Granite State, furthering their advantages over rivals hailing from more distant states. Media decisions to devote less coverage to Edwards and Clark helped doom their 2004 candidacies. A candidate who fails to finish first or second in New Hampshire has never won the party's presidential nomination in the modern era (Farnsworth and Lichter 2006b). However effective a wartime president former general Wesley Clark might have been, the expectations game made him a fourth-place finisher in media coverage, as well as a fourth-place finisher in the New Hampshire vote (Farnsworth and Lichter

2006b). With his talk of economic hard times in small-town America, Edwards might have made an appealing presidential nominee for the Democrats interested in spreading the party's appeal beyond the states that went for Gore in 2000. But Edwards's third-place finish in both volume of media coverage and the New Hampshire vote totals made it nearly impossible for him to catch Kerry in the contests that followed.

With the historic dimensions of the 2008 nomination campaign, and the fact that there were two vigorously contested party nominations, the amount of preseason coverage also set a new record. As shown in table 2.3, there were twenty-two hours and sixteen minutes of preseason election news on the Big Three networks during 2007, nearly 59 percent more preseason coverage than the second-place year of 1995. The total number of stories increased dramatically, from 187 in 2003 to 651 four years later. News coverage of the preseason in 2003 involved the smallest amount of time and smallest number of stories during any of the six presidential election preseason years examined here, probably because that year also marked the invasion of Iraq and the problem-filled occupation in the months that followed the defeat of Saddam Hussein (Burden 2005; Harris and Martin 2009). (The recordbreaking 2007 preseason coverage reported here does not include the final two weeks of 2007, which were transferred to the nomination–campaign news category because of the caucuses and primaries started in early January 2008. So a fully comparable time period would have increased the gap between 2007 and earlier years.)

As we saw in chapter 1, the increased amount of coverage has not restored the fortunes or the audiences of the once-dominant network news operations. By 2008, wired political junkies were able to find all the information they desired on the cable news programs and the web sites that are maintained by all major news organizations and others seeking to shape the nation's political discourse. (In fact, the network news websites contain far more information on the election, the candidates, and their issue positions than do the nightly evening newscasts evaluated here.)

Two decades into the e-mail age, though, some people continue to find it harder than others to go online. Not everyone has easy access to a computer, and not everyone possesses the skills needed to scan the Web for relevant

Table 2.3 Preseason Election News, 1987–2007

Amount of Coverage	2007	2003	1999	1995	1991	1987
Number of stories	651	187	294	485	211	379
Minutes per day (average)	3.8	1.1	1.2	2.3	1.1	2.1
Total time (minutes)	1336	320	420	842	383	683

2007 data from January 1 through December 15; 1991–2003 data for full year; 1987 data from February 1 through December 31.

information. The losers in this new information environment will be the television viewers who catch up on campaign news by watching the evening news shows, but who do not or cannot seek out more information on websites. While the volume of news did increase on several dimensions during the last presidential election cycle, the online world contains information to fill all of anyone's available time.

As a result, the information gap between political elites and the mass public may intensify and increase the difficulties faced by lawmakers trying to divine and respond to public opinion on policy matters (Hetherington and Globetti 2006). Further, these information gaps may make it easier for frustrated citizens to feel negatively about government. This negativity can lead to a corrosive cynicism that can make citizens very negatively disposed toward the federal government and less likely to support government policies and programs designed to address important national problems (Balz and Cohen 2009; Cappella and Jamieson 1997; Craig 1993, 1996; Easton and Dennis 1969; Farnsworth 1999a, 1999b, 2000, 2001; Hetherington 2001; Hibbing and Theiss-Morse 1995).

Horse-Race Coverage

General Elections

The thoroughness of campaign news, along with its usefulness to voters, depends on the focus of the coverage as well as its sheer volume. This issue has long been raised by critics of the media's concentration on the horse race and the strategies and tactics adopted by the campaigns (Broh 1980; Ranney 1983; Sigelman and Bullock 1991). But it also involves the more specific topical agenda that the news features—the major foci of discussion.

This has become more central to the debate over campaign news since the 1992 election. Many journalists regarded the 1988 general election battle between Bush and Dukakis as a campaign marred by negativity, superficiality, and factual distortions. The network news divisions responded by vowing to pay greater attention to the topics that journalists considered most relevant to the public interest, regardless of the candidates' spin on issues and events. In other words, more than a dozen years ago broadcast journalism adopted a more active role in setting the campaign agenda, in order to better serve the voting public (Alter 1988, 1992; Bode 1992; Boot 1989; Russert 1990). This commitment toward a more-heavily mediated approach has been a goal of network television since 1988, though as this study shows—and as others have shown—the effects of this effort have been mixed at best (Kerbel 1998; Lichter and Noyes 1995, 1998; Owen 2002; Patterson 1980, 1994).

Table 2.4
Horse-Race Coverage: General Election News, 1988–2008

Focus of Coverage (percent of stories)*

	*2008EP***	*2004*	*2000*	*1996*	*1992*	*1988*
Horse race	41	48	71	48	58	58
Policy issues	35	49	40	37	32	39

* Stories can include a horse-race and a policy focus (or neither focus); numbers therefore do not sum to 100 percent.
** The general election campaign period starts with Labor Day evening newscasts on ABC, CBS, and NBC and continues through the day before election day for 1988–2004. The 2008EP (extended period) included here adds the party conventions, which occurred on either side of Labor Day. To include both conventions, the 2008EP covers the evening newscasts starting on August 23 through the day before election day.

With a more active role comes increased responsibility for the tone and substance of campaign news. How did the networks respond to this challenge in the past five presidential elections? As table 2.4 illustrates, the 2008 general election marked the best performance in this troubling category among the six election cycles we examined. During the extended period of the 2008 general election campaign (which started on August 23 rather than Labor Day), 41 percent of all stories contained a discussion of the candidates' standings and prospects (we defined *discussions* as lasting a minimum of thirty seconds of air time or one-third of very brief stories). This figure was lower than the previous record, the 48 percent figure from the 2004 and 1996 campaigns, and far less than the 71 percent of the discussions devoted to horse-race matters in the razor-thin 2000 election.

But the news wasn't all good on this front. As table 2.4 also shows, the amount of news devoted to policy matters during the 2008 campaign remains relatively low. The 35 percent of coverage devoted to policy issues was the second lowest of the six elections. Four years earlier, 49 percent of the discussions focused on policy issues. Taken together, the horse race has attracted more network news attention than policy debates during five of the past six presidential elections. The exception was 2004, when stories containing policy discussions edged out those reports containing horse-race coverage by a single percentage point. (The percentages do not add to 100 because some discussions address other topics, such as candidates' "character" issues.) Such personality-oriented discussions were particularly prominent in 2008 because of the character-oriented campaigns waged by both parties (cf., Abramson et al. 2010).

News coverage of issues in 2008 focused on economic policy matters to a far greater degree than four years earlier, a natural result of the near-collapse of the banking and auto industries, rising unemployment, a steep decline in the stock market, and heightened consumer economic anxieties (Ceaser et al. 2009). Economic news was covered more frequently than foreign policy by a more than six-to-one margin, and discussion of economic matters trumped health care by a margin of more than ten-to-one. All three issues would play a key role in Obama's first year as president, which was marked by an economic stimulus package, a significant increase in the number of U.S. troops in Afghanistan, and efforts to reform the nation's health care system (Murray et al. 2010). During the fall campaign, there were 174 stories on economic matters, with seventy-two of them focusing on economic conditions and another forty-four on the bailout of the banking industry. Of the twenty-eight foreign policy discussions on network news, ten dealt with Iraq.

What a difference four years makes: Foreign policy had dominated campaign news during 2004, which featured 936 evaluations of foreign policy issues, more than three-quarters of them focusing on Iraq (504) or terrorism (223). Four years earlier, in 2000, there had been only a handful of foreign-policy evaluations during a general election campaign that focused on domestic matters and the personal characters of George W. Bush, Al Gore, and Bill Clinton (who was leaving the Oval Office after that election). In fact, the combined 2000 total of ten stories on all foreign policy crises was exceeded by the sixteen stories that aired about the discovery that a youthful Bush had been arrested for drunken driving in the 1970s. (That story, which broke only days before the general election, may have cost Bush hundreds of thousands of votes in the narrowly decided election [Burger 2002].)

Network television's lack of attention to foreign stories in 2000 failed to allow voters to evaluate the candidates on what was to become the single most important matter of the new presidency: the September 11, 2001, terrorist attack on the World Trade Center in New York City and the Pentagon just outside Washington, D.C., and America's subsequent military response. Foreign policy, where presidents often have a much freer hand than in domestic policy (Cronin and Genovese 1998; Neustadt 1990; Nincic 1997), is always important to consider when evaluating a president, and the events of 2001 made this policy area even more important than usual. Indeed, Bush's presidency was marked largely by foreign and military policy matters, including wars in Afghanistan and Iraq, as well as disagreements with Iran, Russia, China, and several European nations (Harris and Martin 2009; Woodward 2006).

As rare as policy coverage is, a large portion of the "issue-oriented" coverage that does occur is actually framed in terms of horse-race news (Patterson 1994). That is, the candidates' records and positions are discussed not in terms of their relevance for public policy but as indicators of their strategies and their standings in the polls. Patterson's point was reinforced by CMPA's expanded content analysis of the 1996 election, which found that nearly half

(43 percent) of all policy-oriented discussions on network news focused on the insight they provided into campaign tactics or their implications for the horse race. (For example, a story on Clinton's family leave policy focused on whether it helped him gain votes among married women, rather than the specifics of his proposal or its likely impact on American society).

The CMPA study also found that even fewer issue stories met any of three criteria that we established to gauge the depth of policy-oriented discussions: Only 35 percent specified any detail of a candidate's position (such as the dollar amount of a proposed tax reduction), 31 percent contained any background information about an issue (such as the demographics of welfare recipients in a story on welfare reform), and 37 percent considered the consequences of any proposal for the country (e.g., whether a tax cut would create new jobs or hamper deficit reduction).

A mere nine percent of all network news stories met all three criteria. Thus, measures of both the quantity and quality of issue coverage suggest that viewers are more likely to learn more about the political consequences of policies than their substantive details. This lack of information puts viewers who depend on TV news at a disadvantage when it comes to evaluating those policies. Without specific information about a given policy voters are hardly in a position to consider whether a candidate's proposal on any issue is in the country's interest, or their own.

Of course, the question of who is likely to win the election is a perfectly legitimate one for the voters to hear about. This question is particularly likely to be a focus of media coverage when the answer is highly uncertain, as it was leading up to—and even for several weeks after—election day in 2000. The 2004 election was also close, though an undisputed victory in Florida that year prevented a replay of the 2000 debacle. In 2008, when Obama took a slight lead in the polls conducted after the financial crisis erupted in mid-September and retained a narrow advantage throughout the rest of the campaign, there was less uncertainty and correspondingly less discussion of the horse race than in more closely contested elections.

Citizens do not seem as focused on the horse-race dimension of the campaigns as are reporters, but there is substantial evidence that citizens learn more about the race than about candidate policies. Polls have repeatedly shown that voters have a very good idea of which candidate is likely to win the presidency, but voters are less able to demonstrate their knowledge of issue stands, policies, and other examples of political knowledge more removed from the horse-race component of campaigns and elections (Hibbing and Theiss-Morse 1995; Lichter and Noyes 1998).

Voters frequently criticize television's heavy horse-race news coverage, though some research suggests they are more interested in horse-race news coverage than they admit (Iyengar et al. 2004). The low grades that the reporters receive in citizen evaluations of the media lately have been a matter of "how low can they go?" As television news has become more and more focused upon campaign standings and strategy, the public has become increasingly critical. Citizens surveyed by the Pew Research Center gave reporters a grade of 1.8 (where 4.0 is an "A" and 2.0 is a "C") for their coverage of the 2008 campaign (Pew 2008c). Previous surveys showed citizens had given reporters average grades between 1.7 and 2.0 during all the contests dating back to 1988 (Pew 2000c; 2004c; 2008c).

There is further evidence that the television networks are on the wrong track when reporters focus on horse-race concerns rather than on a discussion of issues. Whenever voters are given a chance to question candidates—and in recent presidential elections they often have been given opportunities to do so—the citizens' questions focus far more on issues than do the questions asked by reporters (Just et al. 1996; Patterson 1994). The town meeting–style debates that have become a staple of presidential debates focused in 2008 on more substantive matters raised by audience questions, like the economy and the war in Afghanistan. That year, questions for presidential candidates even arrived via YouTube!

The discrepancy between what the voters want (more discussion of issues) and what the networks provide (coverage dominated by the horse race) frequently has been observed by scholars. Looking at the 1992 presidential election, Patterson (1994, 55–56) observed a sharp contrast between the questions asked by voters who called in to query Governor Clinton on *Larry King Live* and the campaign questions asked of President George H. W. Bush by the White House press corps. On that talk show, citizens asked about U.S.–Mexican trade relations, Clinton's views on African American and African issues, whether he would increase aid to Russia and free up loans to Israel, and what policies he would adopt to help promote an economic recovery. In contrast, reporters asked Bush whether he would debate Clinton and Ross Perot, whether Bush felt Perot was trying to buy the presidency, whether the polls indicated the public has rejected the Bush message, and whether Pat Buchanan's support in the primaries suggested Republican voters wanted an alternative to Bush. According to Patterson, such differences reflect the fact that reporters often are too focused on perceiving politics as sport to provide voters with a more comprehensive perspective.

In the game schema, a change in a candidate's position, however slight, is a calculated attempt to manipulate the electorate. In a different schema, that of governing, flexibility and compromise, are a vital part of the political process. Campaigns have historically served an educative function for candidates. As they travel the country, their ideas are tested against public opinion and regional problems. They learn which of their ideas are sound and which need adjustment if they are to garner the support necessary to make their programs work if and when the voters put them in office. The campaign would be a failure if the public's reactions did not feed back into the candidate's programs. (Patterson 1994, 87–88)

The comments and questions reporters put to then-president Bush in 1992 offered a distinct contrast to what citizens will ask candidates when they are given the chance, as has been the case in recent elections and primaries. Particularly since 1992, voters have stopped being little more than passive repositories of opinions for pollsters and reporters to survey. Citizens have also become direct questioners of candidates in talk shows and in presidential debates.

For each of the past five presidential contests, one of the three general election presidential debates has been reserved for questions offered by an audience of ordinary citizens. The significance of this new campaign format was apparent from the first question-and-answer general election debate, which was held in Richmond, Virginia, on October 15, 1992. At that town-hall debate, President Bush struggled with a question about how the nation's economic troubles had affected him personally. His uncertain, stumbling response gave the impression that he was aloof and out of touch on an issue central to many voters. In sharp contrast, Bill Clinton answered the question with a far more empathetic discussion about the severe economic hardships he knew many Americans were enduring at that time and how strongly he believed this suffering had to end (Germond and Witcover 1993; Owen 1995).

CMPA's study of the 1992 general election campaign found that economic matters were discussed more than any other issue in network news stories. But the coverage of these issues was almost always quite brief—"only 9 percent of the references to candidates' issues were reasonably extensive, detailed, and contextually meaningful presentations of their records and proposals" (Lichter and Noyes 1995, 95). The extensive back-and-forth questioning in the 1992 Richmond exchange went far beyond the often brief and routine treatment of economic matters in news stories. "Most [1992] media references (television and newspaper alike) to the candidates' programs resembled bumper-sticker slogans—brief, superficial, and without context" (95).

Nomination Contests

With two campaigns to cover in some years and usually more than two candidates to consider in years when only one party has a contested nomination, horse-race coverage often reigns supreme during the nomination campaigns. While the 2008 general election coverage provided a substantial amount of issue-oriented coverage, the horse race dominated coverage of the primary campaign. During the 2008 primaries, 71 percent of all discussions focused on the horse race, while only 14 percent focused on substantive matters. As shown in table 2.5, that 14 percent substantive coverage was the worst of the six primary seasons examined here.

But other years were also weak in this regard, with 18 percent substantive coverage during the 2004 nomination campaign and 15 percent substantive coverage during the 1988 primaries. For network news reporters and their viewers, the battle between Obama and Hillary Clinton or between McCain and Romney and Huckabee trumped important questions over the increasing troubles in Afghanistan and Pakistan, the economic recession, the rising federal deficit, and the collapse of home values.

Horse-race news dominated the 2000, 2004, and 2008 nomination campaigns far more than was the case in the three earlier election years examined here. While the horse-race percentage was roughly equivalent for the past three cycles (71 percent in 2008, 77 percent in 2004, and 78 percent in 2000), those three horse-race scores are at least 15 percentage points higher than any of the other primary years. But even with roughly the same amount of focus on horse-race matters, reporters in 2000 were able to provide viewers with slightly more discussion of policy issues than they did in 2008. Only about one in seven network news campaign stories during the 2008 nomination campaign focused on policy matters. The issues most frequently discussed on network television during the 2008 primaries were the economy (forty-five discussions), Iraq (thirty-six discussions), and race relations (thirty-six discussions). The latter stories focused on Obama's pathbreaking campaign, as well as the appearance of Obama's controversial pastor, Reverend Jeremiah Wright, in the campaign debate.

Table 2.5
Horse-Race Coverage: Primary Election News, 1988–2008*

Focus of Coverage (percent of stories)**

	2008	2004	2000	1996	1992	1988
Horse race	71	77	78	56	55	49
Policy issues	14	18	22	44	72	16

* 2008 data covers ABC, CBS, and NBC newscasts from December 16, 2007, through March 22, 2008 (when the competitive phase of the primaries was effectively over); 2004 data covers from January 1 through March 1 (Super Tuesday); 2000 data covers from January 1 through March 7 (Super Tuesday); 1996 data covers from January 1 through March 12 (Super Tuesday); 1992 data covers from January 1 through March 10 (Super Tuesday); and the 1988 data covers from January 1 through the Illinois primary on March 15.
** Stories can include a horse-race and a policy focus (or neither focus); numbers therefore do not sum to 100 percent.

Coverage of electoral reform was the fourth most frequent topic (twenty-three discussions), triggered by the debate among Democrats and Republicans over whether to seat convention delegates from Michigan and Florida, states that were accused of violating party rules in their nomination contests (Norrander 2009). Immigration ranked fifth (seventeen discussions), and the economy and jobs ranked sixth (thirteen discussions). As the year progressed, the economy worsened, making this topic a more significant part of the general election.

As has been the case in general elections for president, citizens have had an increasing ability to be involved in the questioning of candidates during recent primary contests. This again led to powerful contrasts between the questions the media believed needed to be asked of candidates and the questions ordinary citizens thought should be asked. These contrasts can be seen across the past several presidential nomination campaigns, as the venues for citizens' questions have expanded to include debates and call-in shows, and now even some news programs that offer candidate responses to questions posed via YouTube videos.

Thus, wherever one looks on the network television news—be it the coverage of general elections, primaries, or the preseason; the coverage directed to Democrats or Republicans; or the coverage of CBS, NBC, or ABC—the reporters favor a pattern of coverage tilted toward the horse race rather than more- substantial matters like the coverage of issues. Over time, this "politics as sports" focus—a concentration that does not appear to be shared by most voters—has become a key component of the political world as seen through the distorted prism of network television.

The Horse Race: Framing the 2008 Campaign Online, on Cable TV, and in Print

One frequently mentioned solution to the problems identified in studies of network television is to encourage citizens to look beyond ABC, CBS, and NBC for more-substantive information. But rarely have other media sources been subject to extensive analysis—and as long-term scrutiny—as has network television. Fortunately, we are able to compare the 2008 portion of our analysis of network television with that of a companion study conducted by the Project for Excellence in Journalism (PEJ), seen in table 2.6. The PEJ study examined campaign news content for network television (both morning and evening news programs), as well the campaign coverage for various cable television, online, print, and radio sources. (The full scope of the PEJ study is detailed in appendix A).

Table 2.6
Frame of Campaign Coverage by News Outlet, 2008

Focus of Coverage, September 8–October 16, 2008 (percent of stories)

	Total	Online	Print	Net-work**	MSNBC*	CNN*	FOX*
Political horse race	53	54	52	56	54	57	51
Policy	20	20	13	27	27	24	22
Advertising/fundraising***	10	6	12	6	9	8	15
Public record	6	7	7	2	7	4	1
Personal	5	4	9	4	2	2	5
Other	6	9	7	5	1	5	6

* Includes daytime and evening news reports and commentary.
** Includes morning and evening newscasts on ABC, CBS, and NBC.
*** Includes stories about the treatment of candidates by the press, the electoral calendar, and endorsements.
Note: Percentages may not add to 100 percent because of rounding.
Source: Project for Excellence in Journalism content analysis of 2,412 campaign news stories from broadcast and cable television, newspapers, radio, and online during a portion of the presidential campaign. Further details regarding the PEJ sample are found in appendix A. PEJ uses a larger number of categories than those used in the CMPA content analysis.

Although that study covered many more news outlets than CMPA's, it did so for a shorter period of time (September 8 through October 16). In order to have sufficiently large sample sizes for the subcategories of news, certain venues were combined (e.g., daytime and evening reports on Fox were combined into a single Fox category; all the online content analyzed was likewise grouped together). These data allow us to compare our findings for the entire 2008 campaign season on network television with the news content provided by a variety of outlets during more than a month of the peak campaign season analyzed by PEJ. We use the PEJ data to supplement our own analysis throughout this book.

Overall, the PEJ results show that horse-race coverage is a significant part of all the media outlets examined during this period. As table 2.6 shows, more than half of all stories are framed primarily as horse-race stories, with only one in five focused on a policy matter. There is little difference among outlet categories, with the percentage of horse-race coverage ranging from 51 percent to 56 percent of the news provided by the various outlets. This range of 5 percentage points seems quite narrow, considering the very different transmission systems used by these different media, as well as the different audiences these outlets seem likely to attract.[1]

The PEJ analysis demonstrates that a significant amount of time—10 percent of the coverage—looks at campaign advertising and fundraising, as well as coverage about the news coverage itself. The public record of candidates was the subject of 6 percent of the stories, and 5 percent of the stories dealt with personal matters, those of character and family. The remaining stories did not fit into any of the above categories.

Online news, sometimes portrayed as a salvation for those seeking more content than that found on television, turns out to be just as horse-race oriented as network television. While PEJ did not look at all online news content (who could?), the sample does include some of the top politically oriented web sites of the left, right, and center. (More details on how the online sample was created appear in appendix A.)

Nor does cable news look that much different from the broadcast networks. MSNBC, CNN, and Fox all focused on the horse race in more than half of their campaign coverage, though all three also had more policy coverage than the average for the outlets examined by PEJ. (Network television also has an above-average score on this measure of policy focus).

Surprisingly, less policy-oriented coverage was found in the newspaper sample, even though other studies have found evidence of higher-quality newspaper coverage in earlier years (cf., chapter 5 of this text, as well as Farnsworth and Lichter 2006a). Perhaps, as significant parts of the audience for news has migrated from newspapers to television, print outlets have sought to imitate the content of television more closely. But there were two notable differences in PEJ's findings: newspapers were more inclined to run process stories (e.g., fundraising, advertising, and coverage about the campaign coverage) and more likely to produce stories about personal and character matters than the other news outlets examined.

The heavy reliance on horse-race news for all outlets PEJ analyzed is particularly noteworthy considering the segment of the 2008 campaign covered by this study. The five-and-a-half-week period examined here contained as heavily a policy-oriented discourse as any part of the campaign. The PEJ study period includes all three presidential debates, the vice presidential debate, the discussions over and passage of the emergency bank-bailout legislation, as well as John McCain's abrupt decision to suspend his campaign to focus on the financial crisis legislation in Washington. If ever a time would seem likely to produce more policy-oriented news than average it would be the portion of the campaign analyzed by PEJ. Yet, even during this intense period, policy matters took a back seat to the horse race.

Consequences of a Horse-Race Focus

Many scholars of media effects in presidential elections have pointed to the media's role in shaping the agenda and framing the debate. The media's greatest influence, according to most media researchers, is in its ability to tell voters what to think about. The heavy concentration of horse-race matters on the flagship nightly television newscasts makes the candidates' campaign standings an important part of many citizens' evaluations of the election (Patterson

1980, 1994). This *bandwagon effect* makes it easier for candidates who hold a lead to keep that lead, as more and more undecided voters conclude that a majority of their fellow citizens are probably right. Many of these undecided voters ultimately do decide to vote for someone, and most decide to support the likely winner (Patterson 1980, 1994).

The bandwagon effect seems particularly prominent in nomination campaigns. Consider, for example, the list of early front-runners who eventually went on to win their party's nomination in recent years: Al Gore and George W. Bush in 2000, Bob Dole in 1996, Bill Clinton in 1992, George Bush and Michael Dukakis in 1988, Walter Mondale in 1984, and Ronald Reagan in 1980. While some challengers did well in an early primary or two (or three)— Mike Huckabee in 2008, John McCain in 2000, and Pat Buchanan in 1996, for example—very few dark horses ultimately end up being at the top of their party's ballot in November.

Though they rarely win, the tendency of television news to balance coverage through compensatory reporting can give underdogs a chance. Front-runners are subject to heightened media scrutiny as a result of their privileged status as likely winners, and therefore often to more negative substantive evaluations. Those negative evaluations may cause a candidate to stumble, as it did for both Clinton (over allegations of draft-dodging and womanizing) and Bush (over allegations of fiscal mismanagement) in 1992, the year with the greatest focus on issues and the least emphasis on the horse-race coverage during the primaries. In a few cases—including Howard Dean in 2004, Ed Muskie in 1972, and Gary Hart in 1984—a campaign may collapse under the weight of questions raised by the intense media scrutiny afforded temporary front-runners.

Most of the time, though, horse-race reports are more prominent and more numerous than issue coverage on network television. Even in the unusually issue-oriented primary season of 1992, after all, the CMPA content analysis found that more stories focused on the horse race than on candidate issues. Given the "media effects" perspective on agenda-setting, greater coverage of the horse race means that horse-race matters will likely trump matters of substance in the minds of many network television viewers. Compensatory coverage, in other words, can only go so far. In most contests, matters of substance are likely to be drowned out by the heavy network television emphasis on the horse-race aspects of the campaign.

To test this theory that horse-race-dominated television coverage helps convince voters to also view the campaign primarily through this same "politics-as-sports" perspective, we have created the most difficult test we could imagine. Our test of media effects and horse-race coverage brings us back to New Hampshire, the state that enjoys special status as home to the first and most important presidential primary.

Many would-be presidents have met their downfall in New Hampshire (such as Muskie in 1972, Bush in 1980, and Dole in 1988), and others (including Carter in 1976, Reagan in 1980, Bush in 1988, Kerry in 2004, and McCain in 2008) owed their eventual nominations in large measure to the huge boosts their campaigns received from this tiny and unrepresentative jurisdiction. A third group of presidential candidates (most notably Bill Clinton in 1992, Dole in 1996, George W. Bush in 2000, and Barack Obama in 2008) finished second in New Hampshire, doing well enough to survive to fight another day and to become their party's nominee in the subsequent weeks.

Supporters of the New Hampshire's first-in-the-nation primary argue that the state is small enough for many voters to meet individuals face to face, at community coffees, town meetings, and church suppers (Palmer 1997; Rueter 1988; Sprague 1984; Vavreck 2001). Other scholars argue that while the state has become more reliant on mass media, mass campaign mailings, and other things common to elections elsewhere, there is still a more direct connection between candidates and voters than is the case in any other part of the presidential nomination and election process (Buhr 2001). In the main, these arguments add up to the conclusion that network television is likely to be less effective in the Granite State than in other primaries, much less in a November nationwide presidential election. In other words, mediated images are thought by a number of scholars to be more dominant sources of information used to assess candidates outside the New Hampshire primary.

Thus, television may face its toughest agenda-setting test in New Hampshire. In the weeks before the 1996 Republican primary, about 20 percent of those polled in a WMUR–Dartmouth College survey said they had met a candidate running for president or had at least seen one in person, a figure far higher than would be found in most other primary states, where candidates spend less time and there are many more voters to reach (Buhr 2001). The personal encounters involving presidential candidates and New Hampshire voters before the state's primaries—which along with meetings with Iowa caucus-goers are the closest things to unmediated personal contacts in American presidential politics—give those voters more of a chance than voters elsewhere to reach their own conclusions about candidates and issues (Vavreck 2001). Above all, the New Hampshire contests offer an opportunity for citizens to evaluate potential presidents more removed from the video screen than is the case elsewhere in television-hungry America.

We obtained tracking-poll statistics provided by the American Research Group, Inc., a Manchester, New Hampshire, polling firm, for four separate New Hampshire primaries—the 1992, 2000, and 2004 Democratic contests and the 1996 Republican contest—and compared them to network news coverage as measured by the content analysis used throughout this project

(Farnsworth and Lichter 1999, 2002, 2003, 2006b). Tracking polls chart the daily course of the campaign, indicating—on a day-by-day basis—which candidates are gaining ground and which are losing. Although tracking polls have the potential for a significant amount of error, they are the best tools available to help identify the sudden changes in a particular candidate's fortunes during the course of a campaign. Used widely by academics and by political practitioners, tracking polls are the most effective measures of day-to-day changes in voter sentiments in the days leading up to an election or primary.

Conceptually, the test we applied to check for the significance of horse-race agenda setting in New Hampshire is simple. We looked at what evening news programs on the Big Three networks said about each candidate on each of the days in the month before that year's New Hampshire primary. We divided the comments into positive and negative statements about each candidate as those statements related to the horse race and to more substantive matters like character and issue positions. We then compared the content of the daily newscasts to the daily tracking polls that started surveying state residents that evening.

Our research considered two basic questions: (1) Did what was said about the candidates on network television appear to affect their popularity with New Hampshire voters in subsequent surveys? And, (2) if so, did network television's focus on the horse-race aspects of the campaign mean that voters took horse-race matters more seriously than matters of substance in their evaluations of candidates?

In all four primary contests we studied, the answers to these two questions were yes and yes. We could predict effectively in all four elections whether a candidate's fortunes would rise or fall based on what was said about that candidate on the three network newscasts aired shortly before the polls were taken. Also, in a state other scholars have seen as particularly resistant to the messages offered by network television, matters of the horse race trumped matters of substance in all four New Hampshire primaries we studied. These findings do not indicate that New Hampshire is any more media-dominated than other parts of America, only that the facts do not support the claim that New Hampshire is a special place where network television has little influence.

Voters in the Granite State are moved by network television's drumbeat of horse-race coverage just like voters elsewhere in America (Farnsworth and Lichter 1999, 2002, 2003, 2006b; Patterson 1980, 1994; Robinson and Sheehan 1983). These findings speak volumes about television's influence, as one is hard pressed to imagine a political environment in the United States less hospitable to network news influences than the flinty, insular voters casting ballots in the New Hampshire primary.

Conclusion

Journalists love to talk about the horse-race aspects of presidential campaigns, and they do so at every stage of the process: the general election, the primary campaigns, and even the primary preseason. For the six presidential election cycles subject to the CMPA content analysis, horse-race news has been heavily emphasized on network television, usually at the expense of stories that focus on the policy proposals of the candidates. This trend has remained prominent despite the fact that the candidates have been a very diverse and often articulate bunch—ranging from Reverend Pat Robertson, Pat Buchanan, and Congressman Ron Paul (R-Tex.) on the ideological right, to Ralph Nader, Jerry Brown, and Congressman Dennis Kucinich (D-Ohio) on the ideological left. The "politics-as-sports" focus of network television news does not help raise the quality of candidate discourse, nor does it give citizens the information they need to evaluate which candidate would make a better president. And the data show that this trend has gotten much worse over the past twenty years.

Even in New Hampshire, where presidential candidates spend months trying to meet as many voters as possible in person before these crucial early primaries, network television is a powerful force for setting the campaign agenda. Even in that state, where the opportunities for face-to-face issue discussions with would-be presidents abound, the dominant network message—that the horse race is the most important thing to know—is being heard and is registering with voters.

Of course horse-race concerns are important. Campaigns, after all, are about winning elections, and presidential campaigns spend hundreds of millions of dollars every four years attempting to win control of the White House. While the network news audiences have been shrinking, tens of millions of Americans vote with their eyeballs and continue to tune in to hear anchors and reporters talk about the horse race. In other words, the "politics-as-sports" message is at least acceptable to many news consumers.

While horse-race matters are clearly part of the story, however, they are not all of it. Horse-race-dominated coverage shortchanges candidates who are trying to talk about issues, and voters who are trying to talk about issues, too. The questions citizens ask of candidates and—as we will discuss in subsequent chapters—the comments of the candidates themselves are about a lot more than who is gaining or losing ground in the latest poll or in the latest assessment of reporters and pundits. The movement in recent years toward increased use of cable television and the Internet suggests that increasing numbers of voters are hungry for the issue-oriented coverage that network television is becoming less and less able or willing to provide. Of course, not all people have equal access to, or equal ability to use, these alternative sources of information about candidates and campaigns.

Despite considerable ferment and reform efforts by mainstream journalists in recent years, public perceptions seem to echo scholarly studies that find little improvement in broadcast television election news. Meanwhile, the network news departments struggle to redefine their role in a rapidly expanding media landscape that already includes such new venues for election news as talk radio, cable news networks, Internet sites, and entertainment formats that range from *Oprah* to late-night comedy monologues.

Twenty years ago the broadcast network news departments had the field virtually to themselves among electronic media in setting the campaign news agenda. Today they struggle even to keep pace with nimbler rivals. Campaign 2000 marked the first time voters were more likely to rely on the wide-ranging offerings of cable than broadcast networks for election news, even as various talk-show formats were also becoming purveyors of information about the candidates (Pew 2000c, 2000d). The presidential contests of 2004 and 2008 extended this trend (Pew 2004c, 2008c).

Of course, the broadcast networks are staking their own claims in the new media landscape. For example, NBC reaches voters through the cable networks CNBC and MSNBC, along with their associated web sites, not to mention other news programs like *Dateline* and Jay Leno's jabs at politicians in his nightly monologues. The information at each network outlet is increasingly integrated with the others by cross-promotions that encourage viewers to learn more by visiting the appropriate web site. But the fact that a website URL appears at the bottom of the screen does not relieve network newscasters of their responsibility to do a better job of covering the campaign on air.

This chapter has demonstrated that the amount of campaign coverage overall has vacillated, even as the proportion of horse-race coverage has remained high over the past two decades. In chapter 3, we turn more directly to issues of mediation; the struggles among reporters, candidates, and voters to define the matters of greatest importance in a campaign; and the "framing" of the candidates themselves.

Note

1. The numbers in table 2.6 do not match up exactly to CMPA's network television findings for several reasons: PEJ looked at morning and evening network newscasts, PEJ examined news content for a different time period, and the coding system was similar, but not identical, to that used by CMPA. Despite these differences, the PEJ and CMPA findings are quite similar.

3

Who Elected You?
Candidates versus Reporters

R ECENT PRESIDENTIAL CANDIDATES have been hit with a double whammy in getting their messages out via television news. Not only is campaign-news airtime highly limited, the candidates' share of it remains quite small. As a result, today's candidates have little opportunity to speak for themselves in many parts of the mass media, particularly on television, where campaigns can reach the largest news audiences available at any one time.

This limited coverage forces candidates to reduce their ideas to the simplest and most media-friendly descriptions in order to receive media attention. Moreover, because reporters love conflict, candidates get more airtime when they provide some. These trends toward more conflict and ever-briefer televised snippets encourage candidates to pepper each other with harsh and pithy one-liners rather than engage in reasoned argument on the campaign trail. They have little alternative. Candidates who do not appear regularly on television—particularly during the primary election period—quickly become ex-candidates.

In recent years candidates have tried to gain more attention through their own efforts on YouTube and Facebook or with the assistance of bloggers and other online voices. These new media venues have helped some candidates but could not prevent them from becoming campaign footnotes. The viable candidacies that emerged in 2004 and 2008—including Howard Dean, John Edwards, and Barack Obama—did so in part because of their aggressive online efforts. But they only became viable candidates after the mass media took note of their appeal and began to cover them extensively. In effect a two-step flow developed where online attention and online fundraising led to mainstream media attention (cf., Farnsworth 2009; Trippi 2004).

Most media consumers look to cable news, network television, and newspapers (in both their online and offline formats) for a clear indication of what the most important issues are during a presidential campaign. As we saw in chapter 2, reporters traditionally present presidential election campaigns—whether in general elections, primaries, or even primary preseason periods—as being mostly about the horse race, the daily line on who is winning and losing. This dominant media frame of the campaign as a contest, together with the trend away from coverage of more substantial matters, has become pronounced in a variety of media outlets, as the PEJ found in its content analyses of the 2008 campaign. This does not mean that news consumers do not want to learn about substantive issues. It means that citizens are told over and over again by the networks that elections are at least as much about polls as policies.

Fortunately, many voters are resistant to television's trivializing paradigm. Campaigns are becoming increasingly open to ordinary citizens—the proverbial man and woman on the street now have opportunities to ask questions in at least one presidential debate as well as during the course of numerous talk shows, YouTube debates, and other citizen-centric formats—and important issues are still being discussed. With these new venues, voters do not have to rely on reporters to bring issues of substance to the forefront. In recent elections, ordinary voters have stepped up during debates and call-in shows to ask questions about policy matters, reminding everyone watching that issues matter more to many voters than many reporters seem to think they do.

Mediated Coverage and the Shrinking Sound Bite

To be sure, the horse-race frame frequently offered up by traditional news outlets, and many online outlets as well, has the potential to degrade our democratic debates. A less visible, but perhaps equally dangerous frame is one that is the result of news media narcissism. Perhaps as a result of the high salaries and pampered lives enjoyed by network television political reporters, these correspondents increasingly seem to believe that elections are largely about themselves as reporters and as interpreters of political events. In the eyes of reporters, their own difficulties on the campaign trail all too often trump the issues raised by the candidates who are actually running for office and who will end up shaping the country's future.

In his seminal work *Out of Order* (1994), political scientist Thomas Patterson presented election news as a zero-sum game in which candidates lose out as journalists increasingly set the tone of reportage. This proved increasingly true for print as well as for television reporters. In a study of front-page presidential election news stories from the *New York Times*, Patterson (1994, 114) found that candidates and other partisan sources set the tone of an article nearly two times out of three in 1960 and more than 70 percent of the time in 1964 and 1968. The trend reversed itself in 1972, when reporters set the tone about 60 percent of the time. Since 1972, candidates and other partisan sources never again set the tone even 40 percent of the time, and by 1992 reporters were setting the tone of a story about 80 percent of the time. Patterson attributes the reversal to the weakening of norms that once worked against such advocacy by reporters.

Patterson's critical findings have been both echoed and amplified by other students of recent presidential elections. In his analysis of the differences between news programs on ABC and CNN during the 1992 presidential election, Matthew Kerbel found few differences worth noting between the two outlets with respect to who tells the story. On both networks, Kerbel found that "better than three-quarters of all statements were attributed to news personnel—correspondents, anchors, or analysts solicited by the networks to make observations about the election" (1998, 22). The candidates, he found, were rarely heard in their own words. Kerbel found that the networks were also limited in their selections of independent voices, as few remarks came from nonpartisan individuals.

In her analysis of the 2000 presidential election, political scientist Diana Owen (2002) observed that network television reporters sometimes tried to focus attention on average citizens and their views, which was one of the key differences between broadcast news and cable news in some recent elections. But she found that they abandoned the practice as the campaign progressed, returning to the reporter-centered perspectives relatively quickly.

Reporters know better than to leave citizen perspectives behind entirely. They have seen how effective voter input can be elsewhere, such as on the call-in shows favored by CNN. Consider the remarks of two highly respected and influential journalists: the late Tim Russert, formerly host of NBC's Sunday political show *Meet the Press*, and David Broder, longtime political columnist for the *Washington Post*.

> There is not a program I've watched [during the 1992 campaign] where I've not learned something new about the candidates. It exposes people to politics who wouldn't normally be exposed to politics. It's healthy as hell for the media and the political process. (Russert, quoted in Kurtz 1992d)

> Politics has become—and has been treated by the press [as]—largely a sport for a relative handful of political insiders. . . . It is no longer meaningful to a great many of our fellow citizens . . . because there is no real connection between their

concerns in their daily lives and what they hear talked about and see reported by the press in most political campaigns. (Broder, quoted in Meyer 1993, 91)

Such comments by highly visible media practitioners notwithstanding, most reporters do not do nearly as much as they might to integrate the concerns and the views of ordinary citizens in their reporting. This is documented in previous research and is demonstrated through the new, expanded findings we present in this book.

Not surprisingly, a number of politicians have joined media scholars in concluding that reporters could do a better job of focusing on citizen interests and opinions. At one particularly frustrating moment during the 1992 primary campaign, for example, George H. W. Bush's White House spokesman Marlin Fitzwater tried to force reporters outside to see for themselves the enthusiasm that Bush was generating at a March 1992 campaign rally at Oklahoma Christian University. This rally occurred during a period of very negative media coverage of Bush, at a time when reporters were attacking the president over his management of the economy and when Bush was being challenged for reelection from within the Republican Party by Pat Buchanan, a conservative television commentator.

> When I opened the door to go out, the crush of the noise and excitement almost forced me back inside. It was like a grenade of excitement had gone off, with nearly twenty-thousand people straining at the barriers, covering the hillside under a bright and warm winter day. It was spectacular. I walked back into the press filing center, a lecture hall located not twenty feet from that magical crowd. There sat thirty to forty reporters, in an auditorium setting, listening to the president's speech on the public-address system. I appeared at the top of the seats, which formed a well in front of the professor's podium, with Ron Kaufman, the White House political director. My blood pressure was surging. . . . "It's a great day," I screamed. "C'mon. Off your asses and outta here." They thought I was laughing, but I was mad. . . . When I saw Rita [Beamish, of Associated Press] and Kathleen [DeLaski, of ABC News] in that Oklahoma Christian hallway, I blurted out, "I'm sick of you lazy bastards. Go out and cover the events." (Fitzwater 1995, 332–33)

Fitzwater was not able to convince reporters to focus on the enthusiastic crowd. Instead, his own complaint provided them with the story of the day, which was that of a troubled campaign's spokesman lashing out at the White House press corps. As Brit Hume, then of ABC News (and later anchor of Fox's signature evening newscast *Special Report*), reported on March 6, 1992, "Stung by news stories characterizing Mr. Bush's campaign events as lackluster, Press Secretary Fitzwater ordered the pressroom loudspeakers turned off, to force reporters—lazy bastards, he called them—to go outside and see the cheering crowds for themselves" (quoted in Kerbel 1998, 35).

The real significance of this event, like other reports about the struggles between campaigns and reporters, is that network television reporters and anchors found this recounting of their personal interactions with political figures to be sufficiently compelling to deserve precious network airtime. However much they retreated behind third-person pronouns, the story was often told by and about the reporters themselves. In fact, Kerbel (1998) found that one in five stories on ABC and CNN during the 1992 campaign referred explicitly to the media.

> One of the preeminent stories of the 1992 campaign was the reporters' own story: the interactions with candidates, the experiences on the road, the frustrations of covering a national campaign, and other similar items about the process of reporting a presidential election and the place of the press in that process. The experiences themselves were not new, but their appearance in a running miniseries deemed worthy of valuable news time represented a significant development in television's political role. (36)

A leading early cataloger of this important trend of the "story-about-the-story" coverage, Kerbel observed that the media reports about how tough life was for reporters or how close reporters were to the campaigns they covered frequently were reports that ordinary citizens could have lived without. Kerbel found the same self-referential coverage in the 2000 campaign as well, even in leading print outlets, like this T. Christian Miller story in the May 21, 2000, issue of the *Los Angeles Times*:

> Take the chaos of a circus, the conversation of C-SPAN, and the silliness of World Wide Wrestling. Throw in a ringmaster who enjoys discussing things like the Antiballistic Missile Treaty, a particularly unruly herd of reporters, and lots of lost luggage. This, pretty much, is the world of presidential-campaign travel. A typical day involves moving more than one hundred people, including the candidate, his staff, dozens of reporters, and security through stops in as many as six states per day. . . . But for all its complexity, the punishing demands of campaign travel are probably lost on voters. (quoted in Kerbel 2001, 112)

These media-centered trends in coverage are not trivial. Kerbel (2001), citing the Vanishing Voter Project at Harvard University, reported that large numbers of citizens exposed to such self-referential media fodder predictably described the fall campaign as "boring." This was an astonishing assessment, given the down-to-the-wire (and even past-the-wire) nature of the November 2000 general election. By any reasonable standard, the 2000 presidential general election clearly was livelier than those of 1996, 1992, or 1988. But if the reporters talk a lot about their troubles on the campaign trail rather than the candidates' future plans for the country, it is no wonder many citizens fail to find the campaigns interesting.

Even when candidates are given an opportunity to speak for themselves on network television, they had better be quick about it. The locus of the election narrative, and the heavy mediation it reflects, was first brought to public attention by Kiku Adatto (1990), who found that the average duration of network news sound bites by presidential candidates had decreased from forty-two seconds in 1968 to only ten seconds in 1988. Despite the widespread controversy that ensued (Kurtz 1992b), CMPA content analyses have since revealed a steady decline in the average length of on-air candidate statements from 9.8 seconds in 1988 to 8.4 in 1992, 8.2 in 1996, and 7.8 in 2000 and in 2004.

As seen in table 3.1, the length of the average presidential sound bite increased somewhat during the 2008 general election campaign, up to a level of 8.9 seconds. That figure, based on a sample of one-third of all presidential campaign news stories, is the second-highest recorded over the past six presidential elections, trailing only the 9.8-second average in 1988. (If we include the 2008 vice presidential nominees, however, the average candidate sound-bite length increases. Sarah Palin, the subject of several relatively lengthy interview segments on network television during the fall campaign, had an average sound bite length of 13.6 seconds in the sample we examined. Including both the presidential and vice presidential candidates in our calculation of sound-bite length for 2008 gives us an average sound bite of ten seconds in our sample).

Thus, the average amount of time that a candidate speaks on air without interruption seems to have stabilized during recent elections. It even appears to have improved in 2008. But the shrunken presidential candidate sound bite we now take for granted is about 10 percent below the figure that caused a furor when it was reported by Adatto six presidential elections ago. The

Table 3.1
General Election News: Presidential Candidate Sound Bites, 1988–2008*

	2008**	2004***	2000	1996	1992	1988
Candidate airtime (minutes)	N/A	N/A	98	102	168	N/A
Average sound bite (seconds)	8.9**	7.8***	7.8	8.2	8.4	9.8
Total time (minutes)	1,187	1,007	805	788	1,402	1,116

* The general election campaign period used here starts with Labor Day evening newscasts on ABC, CBS, and NBC and continues through the day before election day for 1988–2004. The 2008 period covers from the end of the Republican National Convention through the day before election day (September 5 through November 3). The 2008EP (extended period) is not used in this table.
** The 2008 average sound-bite figure is based on a random 33 percent sample of all election news stories.
*** The 2004 average sound-bite figure is based on a random 10 percent sample of all election news stories.

overall decline is massive, as the average candidate statement on network news during the 2008 campaign was nearly 80 percent below the 1968 level.

Expressing an idea, even a relatively simple one, in nine or ten seconds is a considerable challenge. The standard television commercial, which usually has a single, simple message along the lines of "buy these pants," uses twenty to thirty seconds to make its case—about three to four times as much time as a presidential candidate has to say "here is why you should vote for me" or "here is why you should support this policy" (these sentences can be said in about three or four seconds each, so each would be close to half an average sound bite by itself). Making the case as to why one should be president by speaking for nine seconds or less at a time is a massive—perhaps an impossible—challenge. After all, Old Navy wouldn't try to sell a pair of jeans that fast.

Of course, the reporters, not the candidates, control the airwaves, the print columns, and the many online websites. This heavy mediation can be seen clearly in table 3.1, which shows the amount of coverage received by candidates during recent presidential elections. In addition to documenting the shrinking sound bite, it shows that the combined candidate airtime was ninety-eight minutes during the 2000 election (this figure refers to the time the candidates' voices were heard during network television reports). The 2000 total fell below the 102 minutes the candidates' own words were heard on network news programs in 1996, the Clinton-Dole-Perot election.

Cumulative speaking time for the entire 2000 general election campaign was fifty-three minutes for Gore, forty-two for Bush, and three for Ralph Nader. By contrast, cumulative speaking time for journalists was nine hours, fifty-six minutes, during the roughly two-month general election campaign season. The total speaking time for presidential candidates dropped from 168 minutes in 1992 to 98 minutes in 2000, a 40 percent decline that represents a loss of more than an hour of direct communication with viewing audiences on the three networks.

Because our 2004 and 2008 data on candidates are based on random sample, we do not have comparable figures on cumulative speaking time for the most recent presidential election. We would expect from the sample, however, that the total 2004 and 2008 results on this measure would be quite similar to those of 2000.

Moreover, the numbers are even worse than they appear at first glance. To start with, those 2008 figures represent the cumulative candidate airtime on all three major networks. Since very few people (at least few people outside the Washington Beltway) watch more than one nightly newscast, the effective total amount of time even the most faithful one-news-show viewer would see these candidates would be one-third of the above figures. So, on average, a viewer watching his or her favorite network's evening news program every single night during the 2000 campaign period from Labor Day to election eve would have heard Gore make his case in his own words for a total of less than eighteen minutes and Bush make his case in his own words for exactly fourteen minutes. Since each newscast lasts thirty minutes minus commercials, if all the Gore quotes aired on any one network had been spliced together and broadcast one right after another they would not have been long enough to fill a single nightly newscast from which they were drawn. Had the same been done for the Bush, there would barely have been enough verbiage to make it just past the midpoint of that same newscast.

Now imagine a person who uses three VCRs to tape each network's nightly newscast and then spends ninety minutes a day between Labor Day and election eve watching each of those newscasts. If all the Gore comments this obsessive (and hopefully hypothetical) news consumer had seen were spliced together and aired one after another, they would take about as much time to air as a single night's episode of *CSI*. The weather segment on your local news station would have to be added to a similar tape of Bush's remarks in order to get an hour's worth of direct material from two months of nightly newscasts on these three broadcast networks.

Of course a third-party candidate without the vast personal fortune of a Ross Perot faces an impossible challenge when it comes to getting his or her message out on network television (Nader 2002). Ralph Nader's three minutes of sound bites during this period averages out to just sixty seconds per network—the length of two commercials over the course of a two-month general election campaign. If the Green Party candidate's sound bites during the 2000 campaign had been strung together just like those for Bush and Gore, you could have listened to everything Nader said on a single network three times in the length of time it would take to listen to a single song on the radio. The nearly total absence of Nader on network television evening news programs was particularly ironic, given his crucial influence in the final outcome of the 2000 presidential election.

Even in presidential primaries, when there are often a large number of lesser-known candidates clamoring for citizen attention, network television news retains its small-sound-bite rule. In fact, a CMPA study of the 1996 Republican primary season found an even shorter average sound bite than in the general election that year. The average sound bite in the 1996 primary campaign was 7.2 seconds, more than 10 percent shorter than the 8.2-second average sound bite in the general election that year. There was a total of 1,066 minutes of network campaign news between January 1, 1996, and the March 26 California primary and only 129 minutes of candidate airtime. Because primary elections generally involve less-well-known figures, and because partisanship does not work as a voting cue in Republican-only or Democrat-only contests, many voters would need even more information about a primary-election candidate than a general election one.

These snippets of unmediated commentary from Gore, Bush, and Nader in the 2000 election and from other candidates in other elections are hardly sufficient for a viewer to get a full sense of a nominee and his or her policies. Of course, interested viewers can go beyond the nightly newscasts for other information, including the more-thorough coverage found in most newspapers or on cable outlets like CNN and MSNBC. In fact, the declining overall coverage of the campaign, coupled with the tiny share of that coverage that allows the candidates to speak in their own words, practically invites citizens to look elsewhere.

And more and more citizens are accepting the invitation, as the downsizing of campaign coverage has been accompanied by a decline in the viewing audience (Norris 2001; Pew 1996, 2000a, 2000b). But the network news audience remains substantial, though it does tilt away from younger viewers (Kurtz 2002b; Mindich 2005). The problem is that by 2008 many of these alternative sources, like CNN, MSNBC, Fox, leading newspapers, and even leading online organizations, are offering very similar campaign news content. As the CMPA and PEJ studies have found, people cannot easily shift their allegiance to news outlets that are less focused on the horse race and more issue- and candidate-centered. Such information can be found, but experienced Web searching—and a substantial time commitment—is required.

In table 3.2, we report the results of a Project for Excellence in Journalism content analysis that looked at a variety of media outlets and the frequencies with which they focused on the candidates for president and vice president during 2008. Once again, one is struck by the similarities among old, newer,

Table 3.2
Amount of Candidate Coverage by News Outlet, 2008

Percentage of Campaign Stories Where Each Candidate Was a Significant Presence, September 8–October 16, 2008

	Total	Online	Print	Network**	MSNBC*	CNN*	Fox*
Obama	62	61	64	62	61	69	66
Biden	09	14	11	13	08	09	07
McCain	62	61	65	64	70	73	59
Palin	28	32	26	34	29	27	27

Note: A candidate is considered a significant presence if 25 percent or more of the story is about him or her. More than one candidate can be a significant presence per story, so the total percentage exceeds 100 percent.
* Includes daytime and evening news reports and commentary.
** Includes morning and evening newscasts on ABC, CBS, and NBC.
Source: Project for Excellence in Journalism content analysis of 2,412 campaign news stories from broadcast and cable television, newspapers, radio, and online during a portion of the presidential campaign. Further details regarding the PEJ sample are found in appendix A.

and newest media. Obama was a significant part of 62 percent of the campaign reports in these media during the content analysis period (September 8 through October 16). Individual media outlets focused on Obama within a narrow range, with only CNN at 69 percent more than five percentage points away from the mean. McCain was also the focus of 62 percent of the news stories overall, and only a few media outlets were outside a five-percentage-point range (70 percent on MSNBC and 73 percent on CNN). Palin was a significant part of 28 percent of the coverage and Biden a significant part of 9 percent, but each media outlet gave each vice presidential candidate about as much coverage as the other outlets did.

Lessons for Candidates

Some candidates learned too late about the consequences to their own campaigns of network television reporters' self-referential approaches and the shrinking candidate sound bite. Michael Dukakis, the Democratic presidential nominee defeated by Republican George Bush in November 1988, observed after the campaign's end,

> I said in my acceptance speech in Atlanta that the 1988 campaign was not about ideology but about competence. . . . I was wrong. It was about phraseology. It was about ten-second sound bites. And made-for-TV backdrops. And going negative. I made a lot of mistakes in the '88 campaign. But none was as damaging as my failure to understand this phenomenon and the need to respond immediately and effectively to distortions of one's record and one's positions. (quoted in Butterfield 1990)

Indeed, Dukakis had ample opportunity to learn during his ill-fated presidential campaign how not to run a presidential campaign. In an effort to make the rather soft-spoken Massachusetts governor appear tough on defense, the Dukakis campaign offered a "made-for-television moment" where the candidate peered out the top of a moving tank. Unfortunately this ridiculous image reminded many voters more of the "Peanuts" cartoon character Snoopy than U.S. Army general George S. Patton. "Reporters present at the scene laughed so hard they could be heard on the film soundtrack," observed political scientist Herbert Parmat (2002, 42–43).

Bush attacked Dukakis over and over again with television ads lamenting pollution in Boston Harbor and for not being sufficiently tough on defense, for not being adequately supportive of the Pledge of Allegiance, for not being protective enough of the U.S. flag, and for allegedly coddling criminals (Butterfield 1990; West 2005). To the end of his 1988 run for the White House,

Dukakis failed to mount an effective counterattack. "At his core, Dukakis was a cautious man, a reformer trained in the good-government tradition of Brookline, Massachusetts. He opposed negative campaigning, and he was committed to running on his own issues" (Hershey 1989, 87). He also lost forty states.

Other candidates learn much more quickly how little network television news time will spend on them and how mediated that presentation will be. In that same 1988 campaign, George H. W. Bush consolidated his campaign message into six famous—later to become infamous—words: "Read my lips: no new taxes." It took the president a little less than four seconds to say those words, so this brief snippet was clearly made for television with time to spare. In fact, he said this slogan at nearly every campaign stop (Hershey 1989, 79). Further, the tough-guy, confrontational approach conveyed by this motto helped the Bush campaign present the then–vice president as something other than the indecisive wimp that he had been labeled by the news media in the past (77). An editorial cartoonist of the time portrayed Abraham Lincoln in front of a television crew offering up the 1860s version of a sound bite: "Read my lips: no more slaves."

Governor Bill Clinton, the Democratic presidential nominee who faced Bush four years later, was a quick study. During the 1992 campaign, Clinton responded to attacks quickly, in a way that Dukakis did not. Clinton made Bush the issue, in a way that Dukakis did not. Clinton, who dubbed himself the Comeback Kid after his second-place finish in the 1992 New Hampshire primary, also knew the value of a sound bite in a way that Dukakis did not. Clinton attacked Bush for what the Arkansas governor described as a reckless promise not to raise taxes. This promise was broken by Bush, Clinton went on to observe, when the president signed the 1990 Budget Act. Perhaps most importantly, Clinton won the battle of the sound bites with a terse campaign motto: "It's the economy, stupid."

But the real master of the news media in 1992 may not have been Bill Clinton but rather Texas billionaire Ross Perot, who turned to the wide-open and relatively unmediated discussion format of *Larry King Live* as he tested the waters for an independent presidential run in 1992. As King subsequently observed, "Perot showed you could start a national campaign on a prime-time TV talk show" (quoted in Kerbel 1998, 213).

Of course Perot couldn't keep a campaign going solely through appearances on *Larry King Live*. After enduring negative network media coverage and criticism over his midyear decision to abandon his 1992 campaign, the Texan returned to the presidential election campaign later that year with an enhanced commitment to reach the voters through paid television specials (Lichter and Noyes 1995). Perot did little public campaigning during the

second phase of his 1992 campaign, and he undertook few media appearances after his early experiences that year. As CNN reporter Chuck Conder
observed of Perot in 1992, "If he wasn't available—and he never was—then
you couldn't ask him any questions about what was in the news on a given
day" (quoted in Kerbel 1998, 181).

Perot's infomercial campaign offered this independently wealthy candidate
a chance to reach the voters in an unmediated way. And reach them he did.
The down-home Texan's first infomercial—"Plain Talk about Jobs, Debt,
and the Washington Mess"—aired on CBS and drew sixteen million viewers.
Perot's infomercial finished first in its time slot, beating out *Quantum Leap* on
NBC and *Full House* on ABC (Lichter and Noyes 1995, 156).

Tom Shales, a television critic for the *Washington Post*, observed that the
success of Perot's dry charts-and-pointer seminars demonstrated the error of
network television's belief that citizens would not stay tuned to hear sophisticated discussions of policy alternatives (Lichter and Noyes 1995, 156–57). But
as we have seen, television news nevertheless continued to shrink candidate
sound bites and to cut its campaign coverage after 1992.

Perot's efforts to keep reporters away from his message earned their anger.
Reporters jealously guard their prerogatives as interpreters-in-chief of campaigns and elections, and when a candidate like Perot tries an end run, he
does so at his peril.

> What mattered after the TV revolution is what went on the evening news, not
> what happened on the campaign itself. Perot, who seemed not to care what went
> on the evening news, decided not to participate in the charade. He aimed his
> campaign at voters, using television to reach them in their living rooms. Such a
> strategy, however, cut out journalists' mediating roles, and they didn't appreci-
> ate it. As the Perot experience showed, the further candidates maneuvered away
> from the media's reach, the more determined the media effort to block them
> became. (Lichter and Noyes 1995, 160)

The reverse is also true. In 2000, Senator John McCain (R-Ariz.) was the
anti-Perot, at least as far as dealing with reporters was concerned (Maisel
2002). The senator waged a very media-oriented campaign aboard his
"Straight Talk Express" campaign bus and received very positive media coverage for his trouble—the most positive coverage of the four major candidates
seeking the Republican or Democratic nomination that year. CMPA content
analysis of the 2000 primary season showed that McCain received a total of
63 percent positive substantive evaluations during the primary season, edg-
ing out the 62 percent positive evaluations for Bill Bradley (whose campaign
was relatively receptive to the news media). The more cautious and media-
wary front-runners, George W. Bush for the Republicans and Al Gore for the

Democrats, received 53 percent and 40 percent positive substantive evaluations, respectively, during the primary season. The more a candidate sought to cozy up to reporters, the more he tended to receive positive evaluations.

Although he received very little news coverage himself, consumer advocate Ralph Nader, the 1996 and 2000 Green Party presidential nominee and an independent candidate in 2004 and 2008, was able to see close-up how this media and campaigning process works for major-party candidates who get the volume of airtime of which an independent candidate can only dream.

> The media is the message. When George W. Bush nuzzles up to two little schoolchildren, his handlers make sure that the AP [Associated Press] and other photographers on his campaign have good positioning. When Al Gore stands near some national park in his L. L. Bean attire, his handlers know they succeeded only if the image and a few choice words are played throughout the country. There are very few rallies anymore. Instead there are carefully orchestrated photo opportunities that often leave locals resentful, feeling they have been used. And, of course, they have been used, just as the candidates use journalists for their poses, or try to, and just as journalism uses them. (Nader 2002, 155)

In 2004, the short candidate sound bites, together with the highly divisive nature of the election environment, encouraged nasty attacks by both the campaigns and their surrogates, who were newly empowered by the unanticipated consequences of the McCain-Feingold campaign finance–reform law. As early as the spring, shortly after Kerry had secured the Democratic nomination, campaign advertisements and campaign sound bites from the incumbent President Bush were heavily negative (Milbank and VandeHei 2004). Kerry and his campaign allies responded in kind, with a prominent late-spring hit on the president coming from independent filmmaker Michael Moore in his production *Farenheit 9/11* (Finnegan 2004).

In some ways, the short-sound-bite format of network television news reports favored Bush. His direct, plainspoken demeanor dovetailed nicely with a campaign that offered a series of simple messages, mostly relating to his performance as commander in chief during and after the terrorist attacks of 9/11. Many controversial Bush policies were justified as necessary to prevent another terrorist attack (Allen 2003; Auletta 2004; Milbank and Pincus 2003). These issues could be raised simply and effectively in the brief sound-bite format. Likewise the Bush campaign could sow doubts about Kerry's fitness to be commander in chief with brief sound bites describing the Democrat as a "flip-flopper."

Kerry, who spent most of his political career in the long-winded U.S. Capitol, was clearly outmatched when it came to speaking plainly, particularly in the early stages of the campaign. His convoluted arguments and inconsistent positions on the Iraq War, including Kerry's famous claim that he voted for the $87 billion for the troops before he voted against it, gave rich fodder to the Bush attack operation (Ceaser and Busch 2005). So too did Kerry's admission late in the campaign that he would still have voted to send troops to Iraq, even had he known that the United States would not find weapons of mass destruction there (Easton et al. 2004). In late 2003, the plainspoken antiwar candidate Howard Dean surged as Kerry campaigned by speaking in "Senate-ese." After Kerry won the nomination, the Bush team simply ran Dean's play—let the Massachusetts Democrat speak himself into a corner on Iraq. Kerry eventually tried to respond to Bush's attacks by sounding more like Howard Dean on the war as election day drew closer, but that only helped convince wavering voters that Kerry really was a flip-flopper (Ceaser and Busch 2005).

In addition, Bush's rhetoric was more idealistic, Kerry's more rational. The more emotionally oriented claims of Bush clearly lent themselves to more effective one-sentence or two-sentence sound bites and were more likely to connect with voters. (The religious imagery contained in Bush's remarks also served to enhance his appeal to those voters familiar with the Biblical wanderings of Moses and the Israelites).

[Bush] We'll continue to spread freedom. I believe in the transformational power of liberty. . . . I believe that a free Afghanistan and a free Iraq will serve as a powerful example for millions who plead in silence for liberty in the broader Middle East. . . . We have been challenged, and we have risen to those challenges. We've climbed the mighty mountain. I see the valley below, and it is a valley of peace. (quoted in Pomper 2005, 60)

[Kerry] We have a different set of convictions about how to make our country stronger here at home and respected again in the world. . . . You want to know who could be a commander in chief who could get your kids home. . . . I have a plan for Iraq. I believe we can be successful. I'm not talking about leaving. I'm talking about winning. And we need a fresh start, a new credibility, a president who can bring allies to our side. (quoted in Pomper 2005, 61)

In the colloquial world of cynical journalists, this comparison demonstrates why reporters think that Bush and his administration "gave good quote." But to say the structure of sound-bite-oriented news coverage favors Bush rather than Kerry is not to say that the content of the news coverage actually favored Bush. This was clearly not the case, as we will discuss in the next chapter.

As the 2008 campaign dawned, the deep unpopularity of President George W. Bush made it a tough time to be a Republican. Economic troubles, rising deficits, and the continuing military difficulties in Iraq and Afghanistan created a very negative environment for the party. Democrats had recaptured majority status in both the House and Senate in 2006—the first time they controlled both chambers since 1994—and seemed poised for additional gains across the political landscape as Bush and his team prepared to take their leave (Balz and Cohen 2006, 2007; Crotty 2009).

Fortunately for the Democrats, they fielded a candidate who understood the mass media and could use the way news is produced to his advantage. U.S. Senator Barack Obama of Illinois first came to national attention during a prime-time address that electrified the delegates at the 2004 Democratic Convention. At that time, Obama was a state senator and a candidate for a U.S. Senate seat. Four years later, he stood before the party convention as their nominee. Obama understood that the media respond well to hopeful generalities and that the short sound-bite news format does not permit much in the way of detailed follow-up. The campaign's mantras of "change" and "hope" and the historic nature of the first viable African American presidential candidate were effective media storylines, and those broad themes—together with the intense horse-race coverage—combined to limit the amount of detailed discussions in the media about exactly what Obama would do about the many policy problems the nation faced (Ceaser et al. 2009; Farnsworth 2009).

While some of Obama's Democratic rivals were effective users of new media, their storylines were not as compelling, so much of the mainstream media paid little attention. John Edwards, the party's 2004 vice presidential nominee and Obama's major competitor for the anti–Hillary Clinton vote in 2008, announced the start of his 2008 campaign for president from the wrecked Lower Ninth Ward of New Orleans, looking like an earnest television correspondent reporting on the devastation that remained years after Hurricane Katrina (Homaday 2007). The moment was captured on YouTube and drew a huge audience. "'Our goal was to have people go and watch that video so they could hear directly from John what this campaign was about,' said Matthew Gross, chief internet strategist for the Edwards campaign. 'Within the first forty-eight hours or so, fifty-thousand people had watched that video'" (quoted in Cillizza and Balz 2007).

Hillary Clinton's Web strategy was less effective, in large part because it was quite conventional. She announced her campaign online via three evenings of online chats in January 2007. Clinton's Web statement portrayed the senator sitting in a gracious living room and was released around the time of Bush's 2007 State of the Union speech. The setting maximized Clinton's appearance as a confident establishment figure, looking rather presidential herself, a year before the Iowa caucuses (cf., Allen 2007; Balz 2007). What was uncertain at that time was whether Democratic primary voters were interested in an establishment figure or wanted something different.

Locus of Coverage

The viewing audience's experience of the campaign depends not only on the focus of coverage—which topics are highlighted and which are ignored—but also on the locus—the on-camera sources conveying the information. This is analogous to the voice of a literary work, in which an author's decision to tell a story in the first person or through an omniscient narrator will produce very different experiences for the reader. Television news can adopt a style of presentation that either transmits the behavior and ideas of the candidates as much as possible in their own words and those of their surrogates, or one that emphasizes the role of journalists who summarize, contextualize, and evaluate this material on camera. Most news stories fall somewhere along the spectrum anchored by these two poles, interspersing the statements of political actors with comments by anchors and reporters that frame the story and provide its narrative flow. The placement of the coverage along the spectrum itself represents the level of mediation.

The phenomenon of the "shrinking sound bite" is one example of the limitations presidential candidates face as they try to connect with viewers of network television. An even more important measure is the proportion of overall airtime that is allocated to various speakers.

During the 2008 campaign, two-thirds (68 percent) of all speaking time was allotted to journalists, with the remainder split between presidential and vice presidential candidates (23 percent) and other on-air sources (9 percent), such as voters, pundits, and policy experts. Thus, roughly three times as much campaign talk came from anchors and reporters as from the candidates themselves. The truncated appearances and utterances of presidential candidates on the evening news shows made it difficult for voters to take their measure as individuals, thereby abrogating a great advantage that television has over print as a transmitter of information. In short, little of what the voters heard *about* the candidates actually was *from* the candidates. Of course, if you examine only the presidential candidates only 15 percent of the speaking time was used by McCain (8 percent) and Obama (7 percent), creating a more than four-to-one gap favoring the anchors and correspondents at the expense of the major-party nominees.

The distribution of airtime between candidates and journalists during the campaign in 2008, shown in table 3.3, was comparable to that found in the 2004, 2000, 1996, and 1992 campaigns, despite the spark Ross Perot added to those races. (We do not have this information for 1988.) Moreover, since these percentages are based on declining amounts of overall campaign airtime since 1992, they understate the full decline of candidate visibility. This

Table 3.3
General Election News: Locus of Coverage, 1992–2008*

(Speaking-Time Percentage)	2008**	2004****	2000	1996	1992
Journalists	68%	67%	74%	73%	71%
Candidates	23%***	12%	12%	13%	12%
Other sources	9%	21%	14%	14%	17%

* The general election campaign period used here starts with Labor Day evening newscasts on ABC, CBS, and NBC and continues through the day before election day for 1988–2004. The 2008 period covers from the end of the Republican National Convention through the day before election day (September 5 through November 3). The 2008EP (extended period) is not used in this table.
** The 2008 results are based on a random 33 percent sample of all election news stories.
*** The 2008 figure for the candidates includes presidential and vice presidential candidates. (Previous years are limited to presidential candidates). For 2008, the percentage of speaking time for the two presidential nominees totaled 15 percent (8 percent for McCain and 7 percent for Obama). Palin had 6 percent of the speaking time, and Biden had 1 percent. (Percentages do not add to 100 percent because of rounding.)
**** The 2004 results are based on a random 10 percent sample of all election news stories.

trend also helps to explain the increasing tendency of candidates to bypass traditional news venues in favor of talk shows from *The Daily Show* to *Late Night with David Letterman.* Along with the presidential debates, they represent rare televised opportunities for candidates to address audiences for more than a few seconds at a time. We talk more about the explosion of late-night political-campaign communication during 2008 in chapter 5.

This pattern of mediated discourse in mainstream media is not limited to general elections. A detailed content analysis of the locus of coverage of network news reports conducted by CMPA on the 1996 presidential primary season found a very similar pattern to that found in the four general elections presented in table 3.3.

Journalists also dominated network news coverage of the 1996 Republican primaries—which we analyzed from January 1, 1996, to the California primary on March 26, 1996. Reporters took 74 percent of the 1,066 minutes of network airtime for themselves, leaving only 12 percent of the airtime for the candidates. Other voices, including voters and independent analysts, took the remaining 14 percent of campaign airtime.

In sum, viewers of the 2008 campaign's news continued to learn about presidential campaigns mainly through the words of journalists, rather than hearing either the candidates or voters speak for themselves. The trend has been clear in the past four presidential elections, as well as through our analysis of the 1996 Republican presidential primaries. Relatively speaking, sad to say, this is the good news. Many other measures used in this book to assess network television news find the quality of coverage has declined. Here we see yet again that the network news coverage is unsatisfactory—an overwhelming coverage bias in favor of reporters rather than candidates hardly seems desirable—but here we can say that the network news coverage of presidential elections does not seem to be getting worse.

Media Framing: Past Research

In 1944, as World War II raged, a desperately ill Franklin Delano Roosevelt ran for an unprecedented fourth term as president. Thomas Dewey, the Republican presidential nominee that year, charged that Roosevelt was not doing enough to guard against Communist infiltration into the U.S. government, particularly through New Deal programs (Burns and Dunn 2001, 481). During that 1944 campaign, a Republican congressman from Michigan complained that the president's dog, Fala, had been retrieved at taxpayer expense by a destroyer sent to collect the wayward pet, which had mistakenly been left behind during a presidential trip.

This line of partisan attack contained a number of things FDR did not want to talk about in mid-1944. The last thing the White House needed as Allied forces made their way across France was domestic pressure on the alliance with the Soviet Union against Nazi Germany or a "Red Scare" in a U.S. government struggling to oversee a global war effort. Doubts about the New Deal programs were not an optimal subject for discussion, either, as the administration clearly had been devoting more energy to the war than anything else throughout Roosevelt's third term (Goodwin 1994). The GOP attack also subtly planted doubts regarding the president's vigor—perhaps even raising indirectly questions of the long-serving president's obviously failing health (Burns and Dunn 2001; Goodwin 1994). And questions regarding the judicious use of taxpayer funds during wartime also were explicit in the reference to the Fala incident.

What's a president to do? When facing trouble in American politics, talk about the family dog.

> Then came his rebuttal of the Fala story, his dagger lovingly fashioned and honed, delivered with a mock-serious face and in the quiet, sad tone of a man much abused. "These Republican leaders have not been content with attacks on me, or my wife, or on my sons. No, not content with that, they now include my little dog, Fala. Well of course I don't resent attacks, and my family doesn't resent attacks, but Fala—being Scottish—*does* resent them!" Some reporters saw this as the turning point of the campaign. (Burns and Dunn 2001, 482, emphasis in original)

In mid-1952, with his Republican vice presidential nomination in jeopardy over charges of political corruption, then-senator Richard Nixon gave a nationally televised statement, known as the Checkers speech, to defend himself and salvage his place as Dwight Eisenhower's running mate. Like Roosevelt eight years earlier, Nixon had sense enough to reframe the controversy around the family dog.

> One thing I should probably tell you, because if I don't "they'll" probably be saying this about me too: we did get something—a gift—after the election. A man down in Texas heard Pat mention on the radio the fact that our two youngsters would like to have a dog. And believe it or not, the day before we left on this campaign trip we got a message from Union Station in Baltimore saying they had a package for us. We went down to get it. You know what it was? It was a little cocker spaniel dog that he sent all the way from Texas. Black-and-white spotted. And our little girl—Tricia, the six year old—named it Checkers. And you know, the kids love that dog, and I just want to say right now that, regardless of what they say about it, we're going to keep it. (Nixon, quoted in Aitken 1993, 216–17)

In agenda setting, reporters—sometimes with the intervention of politicians—tell citizens what to think about. In framing, the subject of this next section, reporters—sometimes with the intervention of politicians—tell citizens *how* to think about a subject (McCombs and Shaw 1993). In the two examples above, savvy politicians deftly changed the focus of discussion in ways that suited them. In both instances, reporters knew a good story when they heard one and went along for the ride (Aitken 1993; Burns and Dunn 2001). By trying to frame allegations of Communist infiltration into government, an ailing president's health, and careless war spending into a joking tale of a dog defending the family honor, FDR was able to dissipate with a laugh potentially troubling issues. By converting charges of political corruption into a story of how Nixon's enemies will not be satisfied until they take away a young girl's dog, efforts to have the nominee stricken from the second spot on the GOP ticket evaporated. In a battle where partisan politicians stand on one side and a dog stands on the other, a man's (or his daughter's) best friend is going to win every time.

Normally, though, politicians don't have that much influence over how an issue or controversy or even their own character will be framed by the media and ultimately in the public consciousness. Roosevelt and Nixon (at least until Nixon's Watergate cover-up) demonstrated considerable abilities as media "spinmeisters" (Aitken 1993; Gellman 1999; Goodwin 1994; McGinniss 1969), and both men operated in a time of a far-less-assertive press than that covering today's politicians (Sabato 2000). Today's journalists have a great deal more control over the content of campaign news stories than do the subjects of those stories, the politicians. If presidents (or their advisers) have a good sense of how to package their messages, they can sometimes influence the framing process (Farnsworth and Lichter 2006a; Hertsgaard 1989; Jamieson 1996), but clearly the majority of the control over news content is in the hands of reporters and editors.

Framing—that is, the process of putting the information into a broad context—is not a trivial source of media influence. Reporters can choose not to cover a political actor's assertions, they can reduce the influence of these assertions by increasing the attention given to alternative voices, and they can even investigate and find them to be false or misleading (Bennett 2005). All these responses can contribute to the way the story is told, which may be as important to political conceptualizations of the issue as the fact that the subject is being talked about in the first place.

Context can be decisive for a politician's fortunes, as it was for President Clinton during the controversies over his scandal involving former White House intern Monica Lewinsky. If Republicans had succeeded in their efforts to frame Clinton's cover-up as a criminal matter of perjury—that is, the felony of lying under oath—they might have had greater success in their efforts to drive him from office. Instead, the media frame of the Clinton scandal was largely that the president's alleged lies were of a less-sinister nature, that of covering up an extramarital affair. This latter perspective generated far less public pressure for the president to resign or be forcibly removed than the "criminal Clinton" frame offered by the Republicans on the House Judiciary Committee (Bennett 2005; Farnsworth and Lichter 2006a; Klein 2002; Owen 2000; Sabato et al. 2000).

> Framing is often used to analyze how news stories emphasize or deemphasize different aspects of reality, which both shape and reflect the cognitive categories politicians, journalists, and citizens use to make sense of the political world. . . . The fundamental premise of framing is that people generally cannot process information without (consciously or unconsciously) using conceptual lenses that bring certain aspects of reality into sharper focus while relegating others to the background. Frames are the basic building blocks with which public problems are socially constructed. (Lawrence 2001, 93)

If information is presented absent a context, as news often is presented through the fragmentary, brief stories that are the norm on America's evening newscasts, the contents of those stories are not likely to be recalled or to play a significant role in citizen evaluations of political figures and issues (Graber 1988; Iyengar and Kinder 1987; Postman 1985).

> Media frames, largely unspoken and unacknowledged, organize the world both for journalists who report it and, in some important degree, for us who rely

on their reports. Media frames are persistent patterns of cognition, interpretation, and presentation, of selection, emphasis, and exclusion, by which symbol handlers routinely organize discourse, whether verbal or visual. (Gitlin 1980, 7)

Journalists' disjointed, horse-race-oriented campaign coverage is particularly likely to be presented in a decontextualized manner (A. Simon 2001). Addressing this issue more systematically, Shanto Iyengar (1991) divides media framing of political issues into two categories: episodic and thematic. Episodic framing undermines citizen evaluation of issues, while thematic framing helps place matters into context. Iyengar says,

> the episodic news frame takes the form of a case study or event-oriented report and depicts public issues in terms of concrete instances (for example, the plight of a homeless person or a teenage drug user, the bombing of an airliner or an attempted murder). The thematic frame, by contrast, places public issues in a more general or abstract context and takes the form of a "takeout" or "backgrounder" report directed at general outcomes or conditions. Examples of thematic coverage include reports on changes on government welfare expenditures, congressional debates over the funding of employment training programs, the social or political grievances of groups undertaking terrorist activity, and the backlog in the criminal-justice process. (14)

Because episodic stories tend to have better pictures, can be told more briefly, are easier to prepare, and are less susceptible to charges of bias—four items that dramatically improve a story's chances of being aired on a television newscast—far more stories are episodic than thematic, according to Iyengar (1991). Society may be worse off if citizens receive episodic-dominated media coverage, because voters will not be as inclined to recognize the importance of key policy issues including such topics as education, gradual environmental degradation, and the consequences of budget deficits. Such controversies, though clearly important matters for public discourse, do not lend themselves to brief discussions and good visuals. "The premium placed on episodic framing means many issues of significance have not received and will not receive the news coverage necessary to permit the public to become critical observers of national affairs. Many social problems tend to be invisible because they lack immediate or readily traceable symptoms" (Iyengar 1991, 141).

This episodic framing, in the context of president elections, is yet another reason why reporters may give short shrift to issues and instead focus on more-simply told stories, like horse-race matters, character traits of the candidates, and other topics that can be discussed in less than two minutes and offer the potential for good visuals. This approach likewise reduces political pressure on candidates to try to respond to social problems.

The frame of politics as sports also has serious consequences for citizen perspectives on politics, above and beyond the fact that issues are given short shrift. Public knowledge is also affected, according to past research on the consequences of framing. In his study of the 1984 Democratic presidential-nomination struggle, Larry Bartels (1988, 42) observed that 581 of 583 Democrats in a 1984 poll who recognized Gary Hart's name could give an estimate on his chances of securing the nomination, while 149 of the 583 refused even to guess on a basic policy question, such as whether he favored cutting government services. This horse-race frame so quickly picked up by citizens is not likely to go anywhere soon, because, according to Bartels, it is particularly easy for reporters to use because poll numbers change over time and those standings provide a shorthand estimate of the success of the overall campaign.

How can candidates fight back? Traditionally, they have done so through aggressive media management efforts, trying to spin the story in a more favorable direction. They could hope that the reporters would follow their lead and change the topic or at least allow the conversation to be redirected. Sometimes the strategy worked, as it did for Bill Clinton in his White House extramarital scandal. Other times media management efforts failed, as when George Bush tried to talk about something—anything—other than the Iraq war during the 2006 midterm elections (cf., Abramson et al. 2010; Ceaser et al. 2009; Crotty 2009; Farnsworth 2009).

Candidates view the new media environment, particularly the posting of videos on YouTube, as an ideal place to define their character and their policies themselves. Such venues are a way to get over, around, and under the mainstream media's focus on the horse race. Unfortunately, new media can also be used to undermine a campaign's representations.

Defining Candidate Character through Media Frames

Perhaps the best general example of media framing can be seen through the news media's focus on the horse race. But equally important to individual candidates are the ways they are defined through media frames regarding character. Every now and then a candidate seems to attract an extra measure of ridicule from the campaign press pack. Ideology does not seem to matter much, as both liberals and conservatives can be made out to be the campaign's comic relief. Although dark horses are often the butt of reporters' campaign humor, they are sometimes lionized. On the other hand, even viable candidates can get this dismissive treatment. Although there is no consistency over who gets the extra helping of ridicule in a given campaign, it is a serving that no candidate desires.

Former California governor Jerry Brown, a candidate for the Democratic presidential nomination during the 1980s and 1990s, is a liberal who was portrayed in an unflattering light. One could certainly have envisioned Brown as a credible national candidate in a nomination contest that in previous years was won by less-well-known governors of much smaller states. But the media consensus was formed early: Brown's presidential campaign efforts were frequently reported as humorous asides rather than as sources of serious policy alternatives. Although Brown suffered from little coverage as a presidential candidate, the sporadic coverage he did receive could be dismissive: "His rhetoric was unconventional. Whatever the specific content of his proposals, the language and the concepts he used—his talk of colonizing space, of holistic health—were alien to most reporters, who responded with barely concealed derision. His scant coverage consisted largely of snide swipes at his asserted typical California weirdness" (Paletz and Entman 1981, 42).

The alternative approach, of course, would be for reporters simply to report Brown's issues without the sarcasm and leave it to the voters to evaluate the candidate through his own words. The general unwillingness to do so represents a pattern of media bias that is applied to candidates of all ideological stripes.

Conservatives, liberals, and centrists are all framed in one fashion or another by network news. As reporters move into analyzing presidential candidates and their psyches rather than just reporting on the campaign, they rely on shorthand to describe candidates. For example, in 2000 Al Gore was seen as a "serial exaggerator" who would say just about anything to be elected, while George W. Bush was presented as an amiable dunce (Abramson et al. 2002). Anytime something happened consistent with these perspectives, a claim about inventing the Internet here or creating the word *subliminable* there, reporters jumped on the story (Ceaser and Busch 2001). This was a chance to replay the candidate's theme song—a song the reporters themselves had penned. The more evidence there was in support of a given candidate's media-created frame, the more savvy reporters seemed to have been for having developed the perspective for that candidate in the first place. Most candidates have little choice but to endure such media-created frames, particularly given the fact that reporters get to say a sentence for every word uttered on air by a candidate.

The character frames of candidates—even of the same candidate—can vary from year to year. In 1988, for example, Democratic nominee Michael Dukakis was seen as a cold technocrat while George H. W. Bush struggled to get beyond his wimp image. In 1992, Bush was portrayed as a clueless blue blood, while Clinton was seen as "Slick Willie," the sleaziest politician ever to ooze out of Arkansas. In 2004 George W. Bush was seen as either tough or stubborn, depending on recent developments in Iraq. Kerry tended to be seen as either a flip-flopper or a competent technocrat, again depending on recent developments in Iraq. We will have more to say about this general network news negativity, an important form of media bias, in chapter 4. Here our discussion of framing is designed to provide another instance of the many ways in which reporters take it upon themselves to expand their role beyond simply reporting on campaigns.

The frame that reporters developed for Jerry Brown was that the former governor of the nation's most populous state was a flake who was little more than a sideshow attraction in the primaries. Consequently he rarely was taken seriously by reporters and received virtually no coverage, particularly during the critical early phase of the 1992 primary season (Farnsworth and Lichter 1999). Brown, who eventually emerged in 1992 as the strongest challenger to the well-financed Clinton primary operation, was featured or mentioned in only seventeen network news stories during the month before the New Hampshire primary, as compared to sixty-eight features and mentions for Clinton; thirty-nine for Senator Tom Harkin of Iowa; thirty-five for Paul Tsongas, the former senator from Massachusetts who won the primary; and thirty-one for Senator Bob Kerrey of Nebraska (Farnsworth and Lichter 1999). The lack of an image during the early part of the 1992 campaign was every bit as damaging to the former governor's ability to convince voters to support him as the media's rough handling of Dan Quayle, Michael Dukakis, and President George H. W. Bush was to theirs.

When Brown did become a focus of media coverage in the 1992 primaries, it had nothing to do with his policy positions on taxes or international trade. Although Brown's overall coverage in 1992 was more positive than it had been in his previous nomination campaigns, an important area of media coverage of the former governor that year had to do with a personal scandal that tended to reinforce his media-defined reputation as offbeat. The most commonly reported personal matter on ABC and CNN regarding Brown in 1992 was the allegation that he had been smoking marijuana while California's governor. Kerbel (1998, 64–67) found that issue, the subject of 103 references during a one-week period in April 1992, ranked third among the scandals on network news during the primary season that year, behind only Clinton's top two scandals: questions over his relationship with Gennifer Flowers and over whether he tried to evade the military draft during the Vietnam War. ABC was the network that broke the story of the drug allegations against Brown and pursued it aggressively for several days. The charges eventually fell away as Brown's angry denials were soon followed by doubts regarding the source of the network's original report of gubernatorial "pot parties" in Sacramento (68).

For Brown, at least, the story does not have an entirely unhappy ending. Although he lost the 1992 Democratic nomination to Clinton and subsequently fell even farther below the national media's radar screen, in 1998 Brown was elected mayor of Oakland, one of California's largest (and most troubled) cities. After two largely successful terms as mayor, Brown was elected California's attorney general in 2006. Clearly many California voters viewed this politician with greater seriousness than did the national media. As of this writing, he is the Democratic Party's candidate for governor of California in 2010 (McKinley 2010).

On the other side of the political aisle, a leading Republican source of media merriment has been former vice president Dan Quayle, often portrayed as a half-wit who could not win a spelling bee even if he competed against elementary school students. Consider as well the media frame of President George H. W. Bush as so out of touch that he didn't understand the economic troubles of ordinary citizens. In fact, he was presented by the *New York Times* and other media outlets as someone who had been stunned in 1992 to see a department store's price scanner in action.

The objective truth of the matter used to construct these media frames is sometimes beside the point, at least to the reporter involved. The *New York Times* report of Bush's alleged amazement at seeing a price scanner in operation failed to mention that the president was actually being shown new features about the price scanner's technological advancements. Bush's amazement was over the scanner's ability to reassemble a universal product code ripped and jumbled into five pieces, not over the existence of price scanners themselves (Fitzwater 1995, 329).

> The [*New York Times*] story indicated that the president didn't know how a scanner worked and was out of touch with American life. Other newspapers and TV stations picked up the story, all suggesting that the president was out of touch. It was one of those stories where the truth never catches up with the lie. No other reporter at the event wrote the story that way. Reporters started arguing about what actually happened. I urged all reporters to go view the pool videotapes of the episode. Then we contacted NCR [the manufacturer of the device] and asked them to give interviews about what really happened. NCR also sent a letter to the president, confirming that it was brand-new technology involved. (Fitzwater 1995, 329)

Marlin Fitzwater, Bush's press secretary, said that Bush eventually received his due, not from the *New York Times*, where the story originally appeared, but from the Associated Press and Charles Osgood of CBS Radio (331).

In a 1994 interview, President Bush also pointed to that checkout-scanner story as one of the most frustrating news reports of his presidency:

Even though [the *Times* reporter] wasn't there, he wrote a piece that said I was startled to find out there was a checkout counter that recorded prices when a package was swept across it. The fact was, I had been shown something else, some mind-boggling new technology, and that was what I referred to, not a routine checkout scanner. The company that displayed the technology pointed that out, and a CBS reporter looked into the facts and reported that what I'd said was true. But the myth had been created by the *New York Times.* I wrote the publisher, Mr. Sulzberger—one of the few instances when I complained to a publisher—and I pointed out the facts and said their coverage was inaccurate and grossly unfair. And other reporters who were there pointed that out. But the *Times* refused to correct it, and it was picked up by my opposition. So it became not a report but an attack story. (quoted in Gold 1994)

The image that this story conveys of Bush, framed by reporters as an out-of-touch president, was hard to shake and was seen by the former president as one of the reasons he lost his 1992 bid for reelection (Gold 1994).

Gary Bauer, a candidate at the opposite end of the ideological spectrum from Brown and at a substantial ideological distance from President (and GOP moderate) George H. W. Bush, nevertheless got this same abusive treatment. Bauer, a long-shot Republican candidate for the 2000 presidential nomination, was another candidate who, like Brown, received little media coverage except when a scandal was alleged. Bauer first drew substantial media attention in September 1999 when he denied allegations of an alleged affair with a member of his campaign team. The story was not even so much about Bauer as about the culture of scandal that the story represented, as demonstrated by the September 30, 1999, *Los Angeles Times* article by Geraldine Baum and Mark Z. Barabak quoted below. Bauer's troubles were another self-referential story about news created and reported by the media.

The real news was the wall-to-wall press throng that showed up to listen [to Bauer's denials]. Most Americans probably had never heard of Gary Bauer, a Republican White House wannabe, let alone the allegations he vociferously denied. Still, it was standing room only for forty-five minutes of question-and-denial, as fifty journalists—including eight TV crews—chronicled the latest turn in Washington's Wheel of Scandal. Just last week, when Bauer delivered a fifteen-page address about his views on U.S.–China policy, a measly five print reporters and three local TV crews showed up, and the event garnered scarcely a line in most newspapers. (quoted in Kerbel 2001, 117–18)

Bauer disappeared from the 2000 campaign about as quickly as did the allegations of an extramarital affair, which were never substantiated. Had journalists reported on Bauer's issue concerns, however, they would have provided coverage that proved quite prescient. One of Bauer's signature issues was his deep concern over U.S. relations with China. One of the first international crises the new Bush administration faced involved a U.S. surveillance plane that was attacked by a Chinese jet fighter and forced to land in China, with its crew taken hostage. Of course the often-prickly relations between the two nuclear-armed nations, like the impending crisis the United States would soon face in Afghanistan, barely registered on the media's radar screen during the nomination and general election phases of the 2000 election.

Framing candidates, then, has great appeal for reporters. Media-manufactured frames allow reporters to tell a story about a candidate in simple terms: this guy is dumb, that guy is out of touch, this guy has a zipper problem, and that other guy is just plain from another planet. Reporting and recycling such simplistic characterizations does not require a great deal of homework or initiative from the reporter.

Revisiting the campaign frame is particularly appealing for television news, when the amount of time spent on politics during a newscast is in decline and a newer theme would take longer to introduce. These media frames of candidates tend to be self-reinforcing, as the reporters use examples of these individual themes to tell a continuing story. Reporters also return to these themes to justify the images (or stereotypes) they have bestowed on candidates in the first place. Framing also allows reporters to practice the sort of "gotcha" journalism that they can substitute for the more time-consuming, less-glamorous, and more-expensive investigative reporting. Framing represents a chance to go negative without having to work too hard or say too much. Returning to established frames also offers reporters ample opportunity to talk about themselves, since they created the frames in the first place. In these ways, candidate framing is the news media's gift to itself, and it is a gift that keeps on giving.

Given the convergence of media opinion regarding how much time reporters should spend talking about themselves and to each other in news reports, it is impressive how many voters rebel and try to redirect campaign discourse in the direction of more substantive matters. This trend, of course, is consistent with the media effects model discussed in chapter 1. During a 1992 Clinton campaign appearance on his show, for example, Phil Donahue became the target of criticism from Melissa Roth, a twenty-five-year-old member of the show's studio audience—who later said she was a Republican. "I think, really, given the pathetic state of most of the United States at this point—Medicare, education, everything else—I can't believe you spent half an hour of air time attacking this man's character. I'm not even a Bill Clinton supporter, but I think this is ridiculous" (Roth, quoted in Rosen 1992, 35).

Even though Donahue ran a talk show rather than a network newscast, the woman's comments produced cheers and applause from the audience. This offers yet another example of the gap between media coverage of a candidate and how voters would like to see a campaign covered (Rosen 1992). Donahue was, after all, pressing Clinton for answers about the same character issues the network reporters had been stressing throughout the primary season.

Polls verify that the electorate agrees with many reporters that campaigns are largely about the journalists, though perhaps not in a manner that reporters would find encouraging. In the wake of the 1988 campaign, for example, only 17 percent of the voters blamed the candidates for the deplorable nature of the campaign. Instead, the *Newsweek* poll found that 40 percent of those surveyed believed that the "news organizations covering the campaign" were the real problem (Lichter and Noyes 1995, 136).

Events seen as pivotal by reporters do not have to be rooted in an established frame to generate intense, self-referential media coverage. One of the major dustups reported in the media's portrayal of the 2000 elections was George W. Bush's ill-advised assessment of a newspaper reporter at a campaign rally. In front of a live microphone, the Republican nominee observed *New York Times* political writer Adam Clymer in the audience and described him as a "major-league asshole" (Sabato 2002). Dick Cheney, the Republican vice presidential nominee who was sharing the stage with Bush, readily agreed: "Yeah, big time," he replied. Both comments clearly were not intended for the audience. Nevertheless, they were carried by that live microphone and were heard by reporters and viewers around the country as the tape of the incident was broadcast and rebroadcast (sometimes with the offensive word excised) on the evening news. This "major-league" story was hardly that, particularly when compared to the scandals that plagued Clinton from 1992 onward (Klein 2002; Sabato et al. 2000).

What Bush said was hardly novel. Many political figures have an abiding distrust of if not outright contempt for the press, so Bush probably expressed what many political figures say privately about reporters in even stronger terms. President Clinton's unguarded moments likewise showed a profound contempt for—and frequent rage against—reporters. But he did not make accidental remarks in front of live microphones. Instead, insight into Clinton's personal views of the media came indirectly, through leaks from and books by administration insiders (Morris 1997; Reich 1998; Stephanopoulos 1999; Woodward 1994).

One damaging facet of the media's self-referential reporting is a journalist's inclination to determine the newsworthiness of an event by the extent to which it conforms to previous media consensus regarding the candidate. Marjorie Hershey (2001, 68) observed, for example, that Bush received "a free pass" from the media when he mistakenly claimed in the first debate in 2000 that he had been outspent by Gore. Fortunately for Bush, the media's postgame focus on that debate concerned Gore's audible sighs and aggressive demeanor. Gore's supercilious behavior fit into a news frame that the then–vice president was a major-league know-it-all, an image that was used in *Saturday Night Live* parodies of Gore (Paletz 2002). During the debates, Bush made a second significant error when he said that Texas was going to execute three people for the racially based murder of an African American in the state. (Actually, only two of the three men were to be executed.). But that misstep received less media attention than Gore's misstatements regarding the pricing of canine medications and the length of time a student in Florida had to stand up in a crowded classroom (Ceaser and Busch 2001; Sabato 2002). The latter two were seen as more newsworthy because of the "serial exaggerator" news frame that haunted Gore and worked to Bush's advantage throughout the 2000 campaign.

Bush should have known the facts better in both cases. His team had raised and spent record amounts of money during the 2000 campaign, an issue that had come up repeatedly during his primary campaign battles with John McCain, long a leading proponent of campaign finance reform. As governor of Texas, Bush had presided over the state perennially ranked first in number of executions, and Bush himself had aggressively defended the state's capital-punishment operations against many critics during his years as the state's governor.

Gore's behavior, so consistent with the "serial exaggerator" frame, simply proved more tempting to reporters who may have tired of the "Bush as dim bulb" media frame this late into the election year. Reporters had many opportunities to use this Bush frame during the Republican Party's much more contentious nomination process during the first third of 2000. Gore had a comparably easy time disposing of his Democratic rival in the 2000 primaries and so was out of the news throughout the spring of 2000. This may have made Gore particularly vulnerable to more aggressive media framing when the general election campaign began in earnest.

Reporters who search for the latest confirmation of an existing media frame take media time away from discussion of more substantive matters. In fact, policy proposals tend to be interesting to journalists mainly when reporters can attack them as unrealistic. When a candidate offers a new idea to the public-policy debate—be it George McGovern's plan in 1972 to develop a new income-assistance program, Ronald Reagan's Star Wars missile defense plan in 1984, Walter Mondale's observation in 1984 that the massive federal deficits of the Reagan years would require new taxes, or Bob Dole's 1996 tax cut plan—reporters always seem to find sources who will bury the idea or, in some cases, do the grave digging themselves (Patterson 1994, 158–59). Such a "kill on sight" media approach to new initiatives hardly encourages candidates to offer new ideas to try to solve old problems.

As poet Robert Frost once observed, the world may end in fire or in ice. "Either," Frost wrote, "would suffice." This is how candidates must feel about media treatment of their new policy ideas. Reporters may tear apart a new policy idea like hungry jackals, or they may ignore it entirely until it dies for lack of exposure. Although journalists often claim that candidates are shirking substance, our content analysis of campaign speeches during 1992 shows that the opposite is true. The journalists themselves, not the politicians, were the ones doing the shirking.

Fully 44 percent of the 1992 campaign speeches made by Clinton, Bush, and Perot focused on policy-issue stances, and another 33 percent focused on policy records. These speeches were divided roughly equally between economic matters (key lines of attacks on Bush by both Clinton and Perot during the lumbering 1992 campaign season) and other domestic policy issues, including Social Security and health care. Television newscasts and national newspaper stories focused mostly on candidate assessments and viability, which together comprised 35 percent of the media coverage. These topics were the focus of only 7 percent of the candidates' speeches that year. Issue stances and candidate records were the focus of 77 percent of the speeches made by the three candidates, but they were only the focus of 24 percent of the media coverage (Lichter and Noyes 1995, 111). With results like these, it is no wonder that candidates forced to campaign in sound bites a few seconds at a time look for another way to reach the voters.

Some observers think new technologies may be the answer. Candidates tried to take the 2008 presidential nomination campaigns online as much as possible, hoping that these resources would help them reach voters in a less-mediated way. There were some notable successes via online efforts, particularly in identifying and connecting with activists, donors, and would-be supporters (Goldfarb 2007). This positive aspect of online campaigning was clear during the rise of Howard Dean in 2004, and it became an even more powerful force during the 2008 cycle (Goldfarb 2007; Trippi 2004). New media also allowed for unmediated communication with voters for high-profile matters. Barack Obama answered questions about his views on race relations, a controversy triggered by the release of online clips of his radical Chicago pastor, via a thirty-seven-minute speech posted online in March 2008 and viewed over five million times (Owen 2009).

Unilateral disarmament is never a good idea, not even in the virtual world. Never again will a candidate likely be as outpaced online as was McCain during 2008. The Obama campaign placed 1,982 videos online, as compared to 376 posted by the McCain campaign (Owen 2009). Obama's videos, which included speeches, interviews, advertisements, and debate clips, had roughly nine hundred million hits during the campaign, far beyond the roughly five hundred million hits of McCain's online videos. McCain's difficulty in mastering the newer technologies made it harder to reach younger and more technologically savvy voters (Owen 2009). To make a difficult year even worse for the Republican candidate, the GOP's lackluster online efforts helped to draw further attention to the fact that McCain was a generation older than Obama.

But these new technologies were not entirely helpful to candidates seeking to define themselves. This new media environment can empower critics as well as supporters, as a number of candidates quickly and painfully discovered. Consider, for example, the case of former U.S. senator George Allen (R-Va.), an early favorite for the GOP's presidential nomination in 2008. As 2006 dawned, Allen looked to be in great political shape: his résumé included a term as governor, Christian conservative voters loved him, and he was raising huge amounts of money for his Senate reelection campaign and the presidential contest that seemed certain to follow. That Senate contest looked to be little more than an easy jog once around the track after every Democratic candidate who had ever waged a statewide race in Virginia declined to take on Allen (Toner 2006).

The trouble began during the summer of 2006 when Allen said one little word, *macaca*, which was captured on video and distributed worldwide via YouTube (Stout 2006). The grainy, amateur video showed Allen at his most harsh, "welcoming" an Indian-American campaign worker for Democratic rival James Webb to largely white rural Virginia. (It turned out that the campaign worker, unlike Allen, was a Virginia native.) The uncommon word, at least to American ears, was a racial epithet used in North Africa, where Allen's mother had lived before coming to the United States (Toner 2006).

Unfortunately for Allen, the gaffe did not go away in a few news cycles, as it almost certainly would have in pre-YouTube days. In a new example of how the public can also shape a campaign agenda, YouTube viewers kept the video front and center, creating a long-running crisis for Allen that helped draw sustained media attention. To make matters worse for Allen, subsequent news reports brought forth other allegations about Allen's racial insensitivity, and he clumsily handled the question of whether he had Jewish ancestry. His campaign never regained its stride, and he was defeated by Webb, a political novice (Hulse 2006; Kirkpatrick 2006; Toner 2006).

Few campaigns collapsed as completely as Allen's as a result of the new online news environment, but others have also been hurt. A clip of Hillary Clinton's off-key rendition of the national anthem at an Iowa rally was a top YouTube clip during the week the rally took place. A video clip of John Edwards fussing with his hair and otherwise getting ready for his televised close-up to the tune of "I Feel Pretty" suggested extreme vanity from the "son of a mill worker" candidate seeking to portray himself as a populist tribune

(Farnsworth 2009; Healy 2007). Old video footage of a 1994 debate between Mitt Romney and Senator Edward Kennedy (D-Mass.), in which Romney declared his support for abortion rights and gay rights, nearly derailed the former Republican governor's presidential campaigns. Romney had subsequently renounced those positions, but his earlier support did not endear him to the party's conservative primary voters (Cillizza and Balz 2007). Even Barack Obama faced regular assaults by conservative websites and others that alleged he was a Muslim, that he attended an Islamic school as a boy, and that he was not a U.S. citizen. These unfounded claims continued to reverberate long after his election (Etheridge 2009; Kurtz 2007a, 2007b).

Conclusion

Viewed from a variety of perspectives, it seems evident that reporters and editors increasingly believe that they have more to say about elections than do the candidates whose names appear on the ballot. Candidate sound bites in recent elections have shrunk to bumper-sticker slogans, making the direct dissemination of any but the simplest message problematic. Candidate comments represent only a tiny fraction of the total time spent covering the campaign. In fact, a whole election season of one candidate's comments on a nightly news show could be played back in the space of an hour.

Reporters could respond to these time pressures by spending more time on the candidates and the issues that the candidates—and the voters—think are important. Less time could be spent trying to demonstrate how smart reporters are and on placing candidates in oversimplified frames to telegraph the cast of characters appearing on the campaign trail. More time could be spent on those issues that the next president will likely face. These are not revolutionary ideas. In fact, reporters and anchors say much the same thing every four years.

But they do not follow their own advice. In election after election, campaign news on network television, on cable, online, and in the newspapers offers up horse-race-saturated coverage in which even policy discussions are often framed in terms of a candidate's election strategy or prospects. When reporters do step away from horse-race reporting, much of what remains is self-referential reporting. That reporting does little to illuminate the differences among candidates. Thirty minutes of news goes by very quickly—and without much public benefit—if the time is spent talking about such things as how many reporters came to hear Jerry Brown deny unsubstantiated allegations of marijuana use while governor of California.

As might not be surprising for people who seem to think campaigns are largely about them, reporters often give themselves high marks for their role in campaigns. A 1992 postelection survey of reporters, for example, found that four out of five rated their own 1992 coverage as "good" or "excellent," and nearly all considered it far better than the coverage of 1988 (Lichter and Noyes 1995, 225).

Ordinary citizens, who might be considered more objective evaluators than the journalists themselves, reach very different conclusions. Only 36 percent of those surveyed after the 1992 election were willing to give the press an A or a B grade (Lichter and Noyes 1995, 226). This is an illustration of why professors do not let students grade their own exams. Since then, CMPA data demonstrate repeatedly that television news is not getting any better, and the grades are falling along with the performance.

The online campaign news environment offers some advantages, but the more-open communication environment can hurt candidates as easily as it can help them. In the 2008 election cycle, some campaigns received an added boost for their online efforts, while others received a virtual punch in the gut from YouTube.

The next chapter addresses other important areas to consider when assessing news content: questions of media negativity, accuracy, and fairness. It is here that many of the candidates and the campaigns make some of their loudest criticisms about the performance of contemporary journalism. Using content analysis, we will consider whether those complaints—or whether the reporters' protestations that they are objective chroniclers of campaigns—have more merit.

4

A Plague on (Almost) All Your Houses: Fairness, Negativity, and Accuracy

WITH THIS CHAPTER, WE TURN to the most controversial aspect of campaign news. To be sure, the declining amount of coverage, the heavy mediation of news content, and the shrinking sound bites are all serious problems. But candidates and voters focus most frequently on questions of media negativity, unfairness, and inaccuracy. Partisans of both parties regularly charge the media with bias against their side, often without justification. But our scientific content analysis shows that the 2008 general election campaign was notable for the one-sided nature of news coverage. It represents the most uneven coverage we have seen in the six election cycles we have examined. Reporters on ABC, CBS, and NBC gave Barack Obama the most favorable coverage of the twelve major-party nominees who have run for president since the start of this analysis in 1988. Results for the larger range of media studied by the Project for Excellence in Journalism likewise found evidence of 2008 campaign coverage that was substantially more favorable toward Obama than McCain.

While news coverage of previous presidential elections was less one-sided than it was in 2008, there were serious problems with the negativity, fairness, or accuracy in all six campaigns we studied.

A major problem with the news coverage of recent presidential elections is the media's sometimes-cavalier approach to accuracy. The astonishing series of media blunders that marked the election in 2000 represents the worst errors of judgment that hurt the credibility of the news media and made a bad situation in deadlocked Florida far worse. The race among reporters to be first to report, which has intensified as media technologies have improved and use of the Internet has increased, has led to a growing recklessness in calling elections. The Florida blunder of 2000 was not the only mistake the networks made in their rush to report winners and losers on November 7, 2000, although it was by far the most visible and important. The *60 Minutes II* debacle regarding Bush's alleged National Guard records during the 2004 campaign suggests that the failures in 2000 did not mark an end to the media's accuracy problems (Kurtz 2005).

The Tide of Media Negativity: Past Research

More than a quarter century ago, Americans generally, and journalists in particular, were rocked by a pair of scandals involving governmental deceit: Vietnam and Watergate (Gergen 2000; Halberstam 1979; Haldeman 1994; Lowi 1985; Neustadt 1990; Sabato 2000; Woodward 1999). In a televised moment eerily similar to President Bill Clinton's finger-wagging denial of any sexual relationship with Monica Lewinsky more than twenty years later, President Richard Nixon boldly declared that he was "not a crook," while the Watergate scandal swirled around him (Gergen 2000; Haldeman 1994). President Nixon, and President Lyndon Johnson before him, repeatedly misled the country about the failed U.S. military intervention in Vietnam.

When the magnitude of their deceit became apparent, investigative reporters who doubted the government, such as Bob Woodward and Carl Bernstein of the *Washington Post*, became folk heroes and best-selling authors (Bernstein and Woodward 1974; Woodward and Bernstein 1976). The brightest of Hollywood's stars—Robert Redford and Dustin Hoffman—portrayed these enterprising reporters in a hit film replaying the Watergate break-in and ensuing scandal (Ryan and Kellner 1988). Reporters ever since have viewed government pronouncements with suspicion and governmental figures with contempt. For two generations now, reporters have resolved never to be fooled again (Kurtz 1998; Sabato 2000).

Or maybe it has been more than two generations. Some political scientists argue that today's aggressive reporting is a continuation of the "muckraking" journalistic trends of a century ago. "If television newspeople have any prevailing political outlook, it is not the liberalism of Edward Kennedy or the Americans for Democratic Action, but rather a revised and updated version of the 'progressive' outlook that dominated American politics from the 1890s to the 1920s" (Ranney 1983, 52).

However old the journalistic antecedents, it is clear that in today's political environment reporters are not the only ones who think the worst of politicians. Citizens became similarly cynical of government as the events of the

1960s and 1970s unfolded, and they remained negatively disposed in the decades that followed (Craig 1993, 1996; Farnsworth 1999a, 1999b, 2000, 2001; Hibbing and Theiss Morse 1995). In the 1964 American National Elections Study, 78 percent of the people surveyed said they believed that the government in Washington could be trusted to do the right thing just about always or most of the time. That percentage fell to 54 percent in 1972, when the magnitude of the government's deceits in Vietnam had become quite apparent. In 1980 only 26 percent of citizens surveyed believed the government did the right thing at least most of the time, an increased cynicism that followed President Jimmy Carter's struggles with the economy and with the Iranian hostage crisis (Farnsworth 1997; Woodward 1999).

Not until after the terrorist attacks on September 11, 2001, did this trust in government measure fully rebound. And even this gain had more to do with a "rally 'round the flag effect" that often occurs in times of political crisis than with any long-term renewed faith in governmental officials (Adams et al. 1994; Lowi 1985; Nincic 1997). By 2004, it became clear that the post–9/11 rebound was only temporary (Hetherington and Globetti 2006). Although many Americans said they were optimistic following Obama's 2008 election, the new president faced heavy opposition from Republicans in Washington and around the country over his proposed economic and health care reforms (Balz and Cohen 2009; Nagourney and Thee-Brenan 2010). The partisan rancor that marked Obama's first year, coupled with the rise of the "Tea Party" antigovernment movement, show that cynicism regarding Washington and the nation's leaders remains a perennial feature of American politics (Barstow 2010; Shear 2010).

The high levels of media negativity during the post-Watergate years pushed campaign news coverage in a more critical direction for the presidential campaigns that followed. A content analysis of news coverage of the 1980 presidential campaign found that all four major candidates—President Carter, Senator Edward Kennedy (D-Mass.), Ronald Reagan, and John Anderson—received more negative than positive press on CBS, the television network that was the subject of extensive scrutiny that year (Robinson and Sheehan 1983).

In his study of favorable and unfavorable references to major-party nominees in *Time* and *Newsweek*, Thomas Patterson (1994) found a dramatic trend toward negativity in recent decades. The study, which excluded horse-race evaluations, found that, in 1960, 75 percent of the references in America's two leading weekly news magazines were positive and that as late as 1976 over 60 percent of the coverage was positive. A majority of references were negative in 1980, and by 1992 reporters' evaluative references of the candidates were negative 60 percent of the time (1994, 20).

Struck by this negative coverage, political scientist Patterson asked reporters why the candidates are so often portrayed as liars. "'Because they are liars' was the most common response, which was usually followed by an example, such as Bush's 1988 pledge not to raise taxes ('Read my lips') and Clinton's description of his marijuana experience ('I didn't inhale')" (Patterson 1994, 8).

Once a few reporters develop a frame that is negative with respect to the candidate being covered, a media consensus may develop as to how an event should be portrayed or an individual's character presented (Fitzwater 1995; Kurtz 1994, 1998). Our content analysis of recent presidential elections has shown that reporters for the Big Three television networks consistently approach news stories from very similar perspectives. So when the news is good for a candidate on one network, it is usually good on the other networks as well. And when the news is bad, the candidate faces a simultaneous barrage of criticism from many news outlets, as this example from the 1992 Bush campaign suggests:

> On ABC, President Bush is in the cabinet room, dismissing "crazy rumors" that he is about to drop Vice President Quayle from the ticket. Democratic nominee Bill Clinton is addressing a huge crowd in St. Louis, drawing cheers when he contrasts his choice of Sen. Albert Gore with Bush's selection of Quayle. On CBS Dan Rather says Bush "had to put down talk that his reelection campaign is in retreat and in disarray," while Richard Threlkeld announces that "Bill Clinton's campaign is now off to the best start of any Democrat in sixteen years." On NBC, Tom Brokaw says Bush is "a distant second and fading," while Andrea Mitchell says Clinton's crowds have "exceeded anyone's expectations." (Kurtz 1992c)

Howard Kurtz, media critic for the *Washington Post*, has argued that reporters tend to avoid writing stories that are very different from what other reporters are writing. When the poll numbers are good, as they were for Clinton in mid-1992, there is a flood of positive stories. When the poll numbers are bad, as they were for President George H. W. Bush throughout the year, there is a flood of negative stories (1992c).

Previous research suggests that tonal coverage alternates in different years between balanced coverage and more favorable treatment of Democrats, a pattern detected by comparing the presidential campaigns of 1980 and 1984. Michael Robinson and Margaret Sheehan conducted the first large-scale content analysis of print and broadcast election news, which focused on the tone of coverage during the campaign in 1980. By controlling for horse-race evaluations, this landmark study provided the template for later studies of this type. They concluded that in 1980 Ronald Reagan and Jimmy Carter "both did about equally badly on television" (Robinson and Sheehan 1983, 138).

When Maura Clancey and Michael Robinson reprised this study four years later, however, they found that Walter Mondale received balanced coverage, while Reagan's was predominantly negative: "Our measure of candidate spin shows that [Reagan and Bush] lost the battle for the network news and lost it badly" (Clancey and Robinson 1985, 27). This finding was replicated by Doris Graber (1987), who pioneered the use of content analysis to code pictures as well as words in television newscasts. She concluded, "In both words and pictures, the Democrats were favored" (137–38). In an analysis of the words and images found in media coverage of the 1992 presidential campaign, the pictures tended to be kinder than the words for all candidates (Just et al. 1996).

Overall, the evidence from content analysis in recent decades suggests there has been more bad news than good news for most presidential candidates on the nightly newscasts and elsewhere in the world of journalism (cf. Germond and Witcover 1989, 1993; R. Simon 2001). The perspective of reporters is reflected in the comments of Jack Germond, a longtime political writer for the Baltimore *Sun*, who remarked after the 2000 election:

> You couldn't find anybody who would walk through a wall for Al Gore. Bush was even more superficial. His candidacy was based primarily on the money he raised for his campaign. . . . George Bush has a lack of knowledge of the world around him, and Gore was too programmed. I find it very hard to describe why I was spending my dotage on these two people. (quoted in Owen 2002, 129)

The Tone of Presidential Campaign Coverage

If academic criticism has concentrated mainly on the superficiality and negativity of campaign news, the candidates and their supporters are most attuned to the fairness issue. Historically, this complaint has been raised most often by Republicans, who see the national media as presenting the perspectives of liberals and Democrats (Bozell and Baker 1990; Dionne 1992; Rusher 1988). The Democratic voting patterns and relatively liberal personal perspectives of national media journalists are well documented, particularly on social and cultural rather than economic issues (Lichter 1996; Schneider and Lewis 1985). In recent years, however, Democrats have increasingly joined the chorus of media criticism. President Clinton's resentment of the media for its treatment of his personal life, beginning in the 1992 campaign, is well known. And in the waning weeks of the 2000 campaign, several prominent liberal commentators charged that the media coverage was favoring George W. Bush, stemming from either journalists' personal antipathy toward Al Gore or their efforts to lean over backwards to avoid charges of partisanship (Kurtz 2000b).

In response to such criticism, journalists typically argue that their professionalism prevents their personal politics from influencing their coverage in any overt or systematic fashion (Deakin 1983; Hunt 1985). Some scholars have reached the same conclusion by pointing to economic and social constraints as counterweights to personal opinion in the news product (Epstein 1975; Gans 1979). But this position should be treated as an empirical question rather than an article of faith. CMPA's content analysis system was designed to examine this question with greater depth and precision than it usually receives. The system identified the tone as well as the source and topic of each statement about a candidate or issue—that is, who said what about whom. This procedure allows for a more detailed and nuanced analysis than is possible when the entire story is treated as the unit of analysis.

Our coding procedure differentiated between the source and the object of each evaluative statement. We separated evaluations of candidate viability (horse-race assessments) from those of candidate desirability (assessments of a candidate's qualifications, policies, personal character, or conduct). Only the latter were included in our definition of tone or valence, which is concerned with the merit of each candidacy rather than its likelihood of success. (Judgments of candidate viability have already been addressed in chapter 2.) Second, we differentiated between evaluations made by (or attributed to) partisan and nonpartisan sources. In this case, "*partisan*" refers to sources identified as being affiliated with a particular candidacy; "*nonpartisan*" refers to all other sources. In practice, the majority of partisan evaluations in election stories come from the candidates and their campaign staffs. Nonpartisan sources of evaluative statements are most frequently journalists themselves, voters, experts (such as an economist commenting on a candidate's economic policies), and various pundits.

We followed the lead of Robinson and Sheehan's pioneering work in restricting our measure of tone to statements by nonpartisan sources (1983, 94ff). This was done for two reasons: First, they are more influential in the sense of predicting opinion change (Page et al. 1987), presumably because voters give less credence to identifiably partisan opinion. Second, they represent the more discretionary portion of election news, the value-added element of a journalist's (and media organization's) particular news judgment. So news accounts of partisan evaluations are more closely linked to the campaign trail give-and-take, whereas nonpartisan evaluations give more latitude to journalists' own judgments in selecting sources and topics. Examples of "positive" and "negative" evaluations by our definitions are as follows:

POSITIVE: "I think [Obama] brings a freshness to Washington" (voter, CBS, October 14, 2008).

NEGATIVE: "Even McCain's own focus group didn't buy [his tax policy]" (Andrea Mitchell, NBC, October 16, 2008).

Other examples from the 2008 campaign are found in table 1.3.

Tone in the 2008 General Election

As far as news coverage of presidential candidates goes, Barack Obama was treated extraordinarily well. The Democratic nominee received highly positive coverage between August 23 (before the start of both conventions) and election day—68 percent positive in tone. John McCain, the Republican nominee to succeed George W. Bush, received coverage that was only 33 percent positive (i.e., 67 percent negative) in tone. In other words, Obama won the battle for good press hands down. (Again, this was calculated by tallying every positive or negative on-air evaluation of a candidate's record, policies, personal character, and behavior on the campaign trail by nonpartisan sources.)

As shown in table 4.1, Obama's network news coverage was the most positive recorded by any general election candidate during the past twenty years, well above the 59 percent positive coverage of 2004 Democratic nominee John Kerry, the previous leader in the race for positive press. McCain's two-to-one negative margin was the second worst of the twelve major party nominees,

Table 4.1
General Election News: Tone of Coverage, 1988–2008

Presidential Candidates	2008EP	2004	2000	1996	1992	1988
Democratic nominee	68%	59%	40%	50%	52%	31%
Republican nominee	33%	37%	37%	33%	29%	38%
Difference in tone	35% (D)	22% (D)	3% (D)	17% (D)	23% (D)	7%(R)

2008 EP Vice Presidential Candidates

Joe Biden (D)	50%
Sarah Palin (R)	34%
Difference in tone	26% (D)

Data based on campaign news stories from ABC, CBS, and NBC evening newscasts between Labor Day and election day for 1988–2004. The 2008EP (extended period) included here adds the party conventions, which occurred on either side of Labor Day. To include both conventions, the 2008EP covers the evening newscasts starting on August 23 through the day before election day. 2004 data based on campaign news stories between September 7, 2004, and November 1, 2004. 2000 data based on campaign news stories between September 4, 2000, and November 6, 2000. 1996 data based on campaign news stories between September 2, 1996, and November 5, 1996. 1992 data based on campaign news stories between September 7, 1992, and November 3, 1992. 1988 data based on campaign news stories between September 8, 1988, and November 8, 1988.

behind President George H. W. Bush's coverage during the 1992 campaign, a time when Republicans also suffered electorally for poor economic conditions. This overall tonal pattern differed little among the networks, as Obama bested McCain by at least twenty-five percentage points on ABC, CBS, and NBC during the fall campaign season.

Network television tends to treat candidates better during their respective national conventions, and once again Obama was treated better than McCain in this subset of campaign news, by a margin of 80 percent positive to 46 percent positive. (This thirty-four-percentage-point tonal gap in coverage during the convention period mirrored almost exactly the tonal gap in coverage during the entire 2008 campaign period we analyzed to create the results found in table 4.1). And unlike the 2000 and 2004 campaigns (see below), the presidential debates produced no shifts in the tone of coverage—Obama led from post to post. Given the frequent leads in the polls for Obama, particularly in the weeks after the financial crisis hit in mid-September, horse-race evaluations of the Democratic ticket were nearly three times as positive as horse-race evaluations of the Republican ticket (91 percent positive versus 31 percent).

McCain, who was something of a media darling during his failed 2000 Republican nomination campaign, did not receive negative notices only because he was behind in the polls and struggled to respond to the economic crisis that hit in September 2008. McCain's network television news coverage also fell short of Obama's on the subset of news reports that focused on policy areas (27 percent versus 52 percent positive comments respectively). Unfortunately for McCain, the 2008 campaign did not revolve around foreign policy matters. International policy is his strong suit—and a topic that often helps Republicans, the party voters frequently expect to be tougher on military matters (Abramson et al. 2002, 2010; Campbell 2009; Entman 2005). Iraq was the focus of only ten network news discussions between August 23, 2008 and the eve of the election, part of a total of twenty-eight discussions of foreign policy matters during the campaign. By contrast, there were 174 economic discussions during the campaign period, seventy-two of them focusing on economic conditions, forty-four addressing the bank bailout legislation, and forty-three dealing with taxes. Even the eleven stories devoted to health care made that issue more a focus of media attention than the Iraq War, perhaps the defining issue of the George W. Bush's presidency (cf., Crotty 2009).

One Republican issue that drew significant media attention in 2008 was McCain's selection of then-governor Sarah Palin of Alaska as the party's vice presidential nominee. Palin was a first-term governor and was selected for her "maverick" temperament, her appeal to the party's evangelical Christian base, and her potential to change the campaign's dynamics (Abramson et al. 2010; Ceaser et al. 2009; Leibovich 2010; Owen 2009; Spitzer 2009). Palin

received an extraordinary amount of campaign coverage for a vice presidential nominee, but as table 4.1 demonstrates she did not dramatically alter the
tone of the GOP ticket's news coverage. Overall, coverage of Palin was 34
percent positive, only one percentage point more positive than the coverage
of McCain. She did, however, provide fodder for *Saturday Night Live*, where
actress Tina Fey drew record audiences for her imitations of Palin struggling
to express herself on the campaign trail. (We'll talk more about the comic
aspects of the 2008 campaign in chapter 5).

Biden's coverage, at 50 percent positive, was roughly in line with the tone
of most Democratic presidential candidates over the past six election cycles.
But Biden's sometimes awkward demeanor helped explain why his coverage
was less positive than Obama's record-breaking news treatment. (Early in the
2008 presidential campaign Biden praised Obama as an "African American
who is articulate and bright and clean" [Ceaser et al. 2009, 25].)

Tone in the 2004 General Election

Throughout the final weeks of the 2004 campaign John Kerry coasted on
network news. The Democratic nominee received highly positive coverage
between Labor Day and election day—59 percent positive in tone. George W.
Bush, in contrast, received coverage that was only 37 percent positive in tone.
In other words, Kerry easily won the battle for good press that year. This
overall pattern differed little among the networks, as Kerry bested Bush by at
least nineteen percentage points for all three. (Ironically, given its National
Guard documents scandal, CBS was the least positive in treatment of Kerry of
the three networks—54 percent positive in tone.)

During the two months between Labor Day and election day, when citizens
pay the most attention to the candidates, Kerry received better press than
Bush on overall policy matters (42 percent positive to 25 percent positive),
with a particular advantage in the domestic policy arena (50 percent positive
to 24 percent positive). In the two leading domestic issue areas, Kerry received
64 percent positive coverage for health care topics (versus 27 percent positive
for Bush) and 56 percent positive coverage on the economy (versus only 11
percent positive for Bush).

In the foreign policy arena, by contrast, the candidates received about
equally negative press: 25 percent positive coverage for Bush and 27 percent positive for Kerry. A difference this small across two months on three
networks is far too meager to be detectable by anything other than content
analysis. But that rough parity obscured significant differences within this
category. Bush received his most upbeat media assessment in any issue area

with respect to terrorism—65 percent positive versus a mere 9 percent posi-tive for Kerry. Kerry had an advantage with respect to campaign coverage re-lating to Iraq—21 percent positive versus 11 percent positive for Bush. But what is most striking about these numbers is how negative they are for both men. This may help explain the growing public and elite sentiment during the election year that Iraq was turning into a no-win situation (cf., Nagourney and Elder 2004; Wright 2004). Nearly 80 percent of the statements on these newscasts about Kerry's plan for Iraq and nearly 90 percent of the things said about Bush's plan for the occupied nation were negative.

Kerry was also favored with respect to comments on news reports regard-ing leadership abilities: more than 68 percent of the assessments of Kerry on this dimension were positive, as compared to 47 percent of Bush leadership assessments. Bush actually was covered somewhat more favorably on network television during September, when he bested Kerry by a margin of 36 percent to 27 percent positive evaluations. But after Kerry's strong showing in the first debate, his good press skyrocketed, creating an immense gap between the two. During October, coverage of Kerry was 73 percent positive, while coverage of Bush remained stable at 38 percent positive. In effect, the networks turned thumbs down on both candidates in September, but they gave Kerry a big boost in October.

Tone in the 2000 General Election

Throughout the 2000 campaign, the tone of the coverage was predominantly negative for both candidates. That is, Bush and Gore fared about equally poorly in the battle for good press. (Evaluations of Ralph Nader and Pat Bu-chanan were too rare to permit meaningful analysis—only eleven assessments for Nader and none for Buchanan.) Gore's substantive evaluations were 40 percent positive and 60 percent negative, while substantive evaluations of Bush were 37 percent positive and 63 percent negative (analysis of tone ex-cludes horse-race evaluations, which are discussed separately). This overall pattern differed little from network to network or according to the aspects of their candidacies that were most frequently addressed—their policies, their political skills, and the way they conducted their campaigns. Comments about their policies and performance, for example, were most positive overall—45 percent favorable for Gore and 39 percent for Bush. Evaluations of their po-litical skills were slightly less favorable, with Gore receiving 41 percent and Bush 34 percent positive comments.

But the main repository of candidate criticism lay elsewhere. By far the most negative on-air judgments were reserved for the ways both men conducted their campaigns. An overwhelming 96 percent of candidate evaluations linked to events on the campaign trail were negative, leaving a mere 4 percent that were positive—fewer than one in twenty assessments. For example, in response to a GOP commercial that briefly flashed the word "*rats*" on-screen, a voter told CBS on September 15, "When I heard about that 'Rat' thing the first thing that came to my mind was Nixon and Watergate." Thus, both candidates received almost unanimously bad reviews for their actual behavior on the campaign trail, including the speeches they gave, the ads they ran, and their raising and expenditure of campaign funds (Farnsworth and Lichter 2005b).

The tonal quality of the 2000 election news varied significantly along only one dimension that we measured—that of the campaign calendar. From Labor Day to the end of September 2000, Gore's coverage was almost evenly balanced between positive and negative evaluations (48 percent versus 52 percent, respectively), while the negative judgments of Bush outweighed the positive by a two-to-one margin (33 percent versus 67 percent). During the latter half of the campaign (October and early November), however, this pattern was reversed. Gore's proportion of positive comments dropped to 36 percent during this period, while Bush's evaluations improved to 39 percent positive. The only other instance of such a midcourse adjustment was in 2004 (discussed above). In 1988, 1992, 1996, and 2008, the tonal pattern that was established by Labor Day prevailed with only minor variations throughout the entire campaign.

Reversals of fortune like those in 2000 and 2004 have been far more characteristic of primary campaigns than of general elections. During the frenetic primary season, it is not unusual for a dark horse to receive a burst of favorable attention after either a surge in the preference polls or a better-than-expected showing in a primary. Meanwhile, the media's heaviest fire is often concentrated on the frontrunner. However, such bursts of good press are usually self-limiting, as the media begin to treat the new contender's presidential prospects seriously enough to warrant closer scrutiny, which usually brings more criticism (Arterton 1984; Lichter et al. 1988; Noyes et al. 1993; Orren and Polsby 1987). Thus, Gore experienced a wave of good press as he surged ahead of Bush in the preference polls during and after the Democratic convention. Having replaced Bush as the front-runner, however, Gore fell victim to the build-them-up-break-them-down cycle of election news that is so familiar from primary contests. The next turning point corresponded almost precisely with the first presidential debate on October 3. Thereafter, most polls showed an increase in voter support for Bush. However, Bush's relative advantage in the race for good press during the second half of the campaign owed less to his own slight increase in favorable notices than to Gore's sharp decline in supportive sound bites.

Tone Imbalances: Changes from Year to Year

Ever since Vice President Spiro Agnew complained publicly about "nattering nabobs of negativism" in 1969, Republicans and conservatives have voiced the loudest complaints of bias by the "liberal media." During the 2000 campaign, journalists might have been justified in treating complaints from both parties as evidence of balanced coverage. Their evaluations of both candidates' ideas and behavior were consistently downbeat. But they could at least lay claim to being equal opportunity naysayers. However, this balanced coverage has proved the exception rather than the rule.

As table 4.1 shows, in the presidential elections of 1992, 1996, 2004, and 2008, CMPA studies found a significant imbalance in the tone of network news toward the major party candidates. The 2008 campaign was marked by the largest partisan tonal gap, but several others years were pretty one-sided as well. In 1996, Democrat Bill Clinton enjoyed 50 percent positive evaluations versus only 33 percent positive commentary for Republican Bob Dole. In 1992 candidate Bill Clinton bested then-president George H. W. Bush by an even wider margin of 52 percent to 29 percent positive evaluations (Perot's coverage that year was 45 percent positive). Clinton's 1992 twenty-three-percentage-point advantage in tone was the second-greatest difference, behind the Obama versus McCain campaign of 2008. During his two campaigns for the presidency, a slight majority of Clinton's on-air evaluations were positive, while over two out of three evaluations of his Republican opponents were negative. Clinton's advantage in election news coverage has also been independently replicated by other media scholars (Just et al.1996; Kerbel 1998). Conversely, George W. Bush's coverage was only 37 percent positive in both 2000 and 2004. In the first run, his bad press was nearly matched by Al Gore. But in the second, John Kerry's average was twenty-two percentage points better.

The only time the Republican candidate fared any better than his Democratic opponent was in 1988, when coverage of George H. W. Bush, who was then Ronald Reagan's vice president, was slightly more positive than that of Michael Dukakis, by the margin of 38 percent to 31 percent favorable assessments. As in 2000, this was a case of both candidates receiving mainly bad press. Thus, in four out of the past six elections that CMPA has analyzed, the Democratic presidential candidate received substantially better coverage than his Republican opponent. In the other two races, both major-party candidates got mainly bad press. The Democrat received at least 50 percent positive evaluations in four of the six elections; no Republican ever received as many as 40 percent positive evaluations. In fact, since 1992 the Democratic candidate has averaged 54 percent favorable comments, compared to 34 percent for the Republican candidate—a twenty-percentage-point average margin of difference.

The CMPA findings demonstrating tonal advantages that favoring neither party in some years and favoring the Democrats in others are consistent with the results of the tonal analysis of the two presidential elections that occurred before our studies began in the 1988 campaign. Content analysis revealed relatively evenhanded tonal news coverage of the 1980 campaign (Robinson and Sheehan 1983), while analysis of the media essages in the 1984 campaign found the tonal news discussion favored Mondale over Reagan (Clancey and Robinson 1985). Clancey and Robinson (1985) accounted for the good-press gap between Mondale and Reagan by positing a general anti-front-runner bias termed "*compensatory journalism.*" With this bias, reporters are thought to be toughest on the candidates who are most likely to become president, in effect compensating those who are trailing with better press than the leaders. However, this hypothesis has since been contradicted by data from subsequent general elections. Clinton got far better press than both Bush in 1992 and Dole in 1996, despite his wire-to-wire leads in the polls. Bush led Dukakis in good press in 1988, albeit by a slight margin, despite his front-runner status in preference polls throughout the fall. And apart from a brief period in September, Obama led McCain in both the preference polls and the race for good press in 2008.

In sum, a general pattern of negativism on network news has coincided with an intermittent tendency toward more favorable press for Democrats than Republicans in presidential elections. In three of the past eight elections for which exhaustive systematic content analysis data are available (1980, 1988, and 2000), both sides received mainly negative notices. In the other five (1984, 1992, 1996, 2004, and 2008), Democrats fared substantially better on the evening news programs than did the Republicans.[1]

It appears that negativity and political ideology represent separate dimensions that contribute independently to the tone of election news. Patterson (1994) has traced the rise in network negativism back to 1960, based on changes in the aggregate tone of both parties' coverage. To paraphrase George Orwell, however, journalists may see all candidates as evil, but some as more evil than others. Democratic candidates did not always get better press than Republicans, but Republican candidates never got much better press than Democrats. To be sure, any difference in tone seems less pro-Democratic than anti-Republican. Nonetheless, these data suggest that allegations of ideological tilt in election coverage cannot be dismissed entirely as the special pleading of partisans. At the same time, neither negativity nor partisanship alone can fully account for the variation in the valence of campaign news.

It is important to note that positive media coverage during the general election does not always help the candidate who receives it. For the elections in which the Democrats received significantly better coverage (1984, 1992,

1996, 2004, and 2008), the party was three-for-five at the polls. Bill Clinton won his two presidential campaigns, but Democratic presidential nominee Walter Mondale was trounced in 1984, winning only his home state of Minnesota and the overwhelmingly Democratic District of Columbia. Kerry lost narrowly in 2004, and Obama won the White House for the Democrats four years later.

By contrast, the three elections where the coverage was about equally negative for the two presidential candidates (1980, 1988, and 2000) all produced Republican victories. Ronald Reagan won easily in 1980, and George H. W. Bush won the presidency in an easy victory in 1988, securing nearly 54 percent of the popular vote and the electoral votes of forty states (Pomper 1989). In 2000, of course, the presidential election ended in a virtual deadlock that was settled by the U.S. Supreme Court in the GOP's favor after a five-week struggle involving partisan activists, lawyers, and Florida ballot counters.

The mixed results suggest that the fear of an all-powerful media is overblown. In cases both of equally negative media and of more one-sided coverage, the results offer no evidence in support of the hypodermic effects model of media influence. The media don't tell us—or at least they don't tell us in a consistently decisive and effective way—for whom we should vote. Positive media coverage didn't win the White House for Mondale in 1984 or Kerry twenty years later.

But this doesn't mean television news coverage is unimportant. The media have powerful agenda-setting effects—particularly with respect to framing the story—and those agendas tell us what issues to think about and in what ways those issues should be thought about. The media negativity of our content analysis reveals that what we are told to think about by television—the horse race, candidates who seem to be scheming at every opportunity, and the human failings of those candidates—are not matters likely to make us more-informed citizens or public-spirited voters. Nor does the declining amount of coverage we have found on all networks remind us about the importance of presidential elections for us as citizens. We will return to these issues later in this chapter.

Tonal Imbalances on Cable, in Print, and Online during the 2008 Campaign

We turn now to the Project for Excellence in Journalism content analysis of a wider range of media for a shorter timeframe than the CMPA data analysis. At the outset it is important to note some differences in how good and bad news reports were calculated for the two studies. Unlike the CMPA studies, the PEJ study included judgments of the campaign horse race as part of the tone of the coverage. PEJ also included statements by members of the two political parties and their campaigns, while CMPA's analysis was limited to nonpartisan sources. Finally, PEJ used the entire news story as the unit of analysis, while CMPA analyzed individual statements within each story.

This difference was the most consequential in presenting the results. Because CMPA only coded evaluative statements, the total of positive and negative statements summed to 100 percent, that is, when we report that Obama received 68 percent positive press, that means the sound bites that evaluated him were also 32 percent negative. Neutral statements were not coded. By contrast, when PEJ encountered a story with no evaluative content, or one with a nearly equal number of positive and negative comments, that story was placed into a "*neutral*" category. By PEJ's count, 32.8 percent of all the stories they examined were neutral in tone. However, our aim in using the PEJ data was to provide evidence from a broader media landscape with which to compare our findings for network television news. Therefore we reevaluated the PEJ data on tone by deleting the neutral stories from the analysis. This renders the PEJ data in tables 4.2 (and later in table 4.3) more comparable with the CMPA data in table 4.1. In all these tables, the percentage of positive cases plus the percentage of negative cases sum to 100 percent.

Despite the differences in both the coding systems and the methods of calculating the results, the evidence suggests that there are fewer differences between network television and other news sources than one might expect. As shown in table 4.2, the same tonal advantages enjoyed by the Obama campaign on ABC, CBS, and NBC were also found in the PEJ content analysis of broadcast and cable news, Internet news, and newspapers. As a whole, these media outlets provided news coverage that was positive to Obama 55 percent of the time, as compared to 20 percent of the time for McCain. When examining the subset of stories relating to the horse-race (which was the largest single category in the PEJ sample), or to policy (the second largest), McCain fell far short of Obama, by better than two-to-one margins in both cases. Obama, who set fundraising records during his presidential campaign (cf., Boatright 2009), enjoyed his largest tonal advantage over his rival (nearly five to one) in the advertising/fundraising category.

In the 2008 campaign, the PEJ sample once again suggests Palin did not generate a dramatic improvement in the media fortunes of the Republican ticket. The tone of her coverage was 42 percent positive, better than McCain's but once again far less than Obama's. Biden's coverage in the PEJ study, as with CMPA's examination of network television, was more positive than Palin's but less positive than Obama's. Reporters did credit Palin with improving McCain's chances—the tone of her horse-race coverage was 50

Table 4.2
Tone of Candidate Coverage by Frame, 2008

Percent positive tone, September 8–October 16, 2008

	Obama	Biden	McCain	Palin
Overall tone*	55	44	20	42
N	(379)	(64)	(424)	(183)
Political horse race	55	54	18	50
N	(236)	(43)	(272)	(118)
Policy	58	33	27	***
N	(93)	(12)	(101)	(08)
Advertising/fundraising**	63	***	13	20
N	(40)	(04)	(31)	(20)
Public record	***	***	***	10
N	(04)	(01)	(06)	(20)

Note: To reduce differences with the CMPA content analysis data, PEJ tone is calculated here as percent-
    age of positive tone divided by percentage of positive and negative tone. Nevertheless, some differences
    remain. The PEJ sample measures tone at the story level rather than at the sound-bite level used by CMPA,
    and it includes comments by partisans, which are excluded from CMPA data.
* Overall tone measure for each candidate includes all tonal measures. In addition to those listed in this
    table, overall tone includes the personal and other categories used in table 2.6.
** This category also includes stories about the treatment of candidates by the press, the electoral calendar,
    and endorsements.
*** Too few tonal evaluations to calculate reliably (n < 10).
Source: Project for Excellence in Journalism content analysis of 2,412 campaign news stories from broadcast
    and cable television, newspapers, radio, and online during a portion of the presidential campaign. Tone
    measures include only those stories where a given candidate was in at least 25 percent of the story. Further
    details regarding the PEJ sample are found in appendix A.

percent positive, more than twice as positive as McCain's own coverage in this
category—but again she lagged the Democratic candidates.

Other coverage of Palin was withering, however. Only Palin received a
notable amount of coverage relating to her public record, and the coverage in
that category was only 10 percent positive, the most negative issue area for any
of the national candidates in 2008. Palin, a virtual unknown nationally when
named to the GOP ticket, suffered from a barrage of stories that alleged her
brief time in office had been marked by cronyism, frequent absences from the
State Capitol, personal vendettas, and a secretive style of governing that was
in sharp contrast to McCain's long-time support for maximizing transpar-
ency in government (Spitzer 2009). While one would have expected greater
background coverage of the relatively unknown Palin after she emerged on
the scene—the other three national candidates in 2008 had all been highly

visible senators in Washington for several years—the lack of coverage of the public record of the other three candidates in that election remains striking. For every story offering an assessment of Obama's public record in the PEJ sample, there are 50 horse-race stories. For McCain, the ratio is even worse, with a margin of more than seventy-to -one. Without more extensive discussion of what candidates have accomplished or sought to accomplish in public life, the online and offline media shortchange voters who are trying to figure out which candidate to support.

When the PEJ sample is broken down by media format, somewhat larger differences emerge for a few outlets. As shown in table 4.3, MSNBC was the most positive in its treatment of Obama during this mid-September to mid-October period, with 76 percent positive coverage. Fox was most critical, with only 39 percent positive coverage, and CNN was found in the middle with 48 percent positive coverage. CNN's figure, though, was below the average for all the PEJ media outlets, and was more critical of Obama than network television, newspapers, and online outlets, all of which ranged from 56 percent to 62 percent positive in their treatment of Obama.

But the bad news for Obama on Fox did not lead to positive treatment for McCain. McCain's coverage on Fox during this portion of the campaign was even slightly more negative than that of Obama, with only 36 percent positive stories. On CNN, which was less positive than all the other media outlets

Table 4.3
Tone of Candidate Coverage by News Outlet, 2008

Percent positive tone, September 8–October 16, 2008

	Total	Online	Print	Net work**	MSNBC*	CNN*	FOX*
Obama	55	56	62	60	76	48	39
Biden	44	40	***	53	***	42	30
McCain	20	12	08	19	12	17	36
Palin	42	41	36	45	24	42	58
All candidates combined	38	35	36	40	34	34	40

Note: To reduce differences with the CMPA content analysis data, PEJ tone is calculated here as percentage of positive tone divided by percentage of positive and negative tone. Nevertheless, some differences remain. The PEJ sample measures tone at the story level rather than at the sound-bite level used by CMPA, and it includes comments by partisans and tonal evaluations of candidate standings, both of which are excluded from CMPA data.
* Includes daytime and evening news reports and commentary.
** Includes morning and evening newscasts on ABC, CBS, and NBC.
*** Too few tonal evaluations to calculate reliably (n < 10).
Source: Project for Excellence in Journalism content analysis of 2,412 campaign news stories from broadcast and cable television, newspapers, radio, and online during a portion of the presidential campaign. Tone measures include only those stories where a given candidate was in at least 25 percent of the story. Further details regarding the PEJ sample are found in appendix A.

(except Fox) in table 4.3, McCain's coverage was only 17 percent positive. Other outlets were very harsh on McCain, with newspaper coverage during this period standing at only 8 percent positive, as compared to 12 percent positive online and on MSNBC.

Part of the explanation for McCain's poor showing may be a matter of the time period studied. The period examined by PEJ started roughly a week before the bank crisis and the deep stock market declines that transformed the 2008 election. McCain's uncertain responses to the financial shocks did not inspire much confidence—at one point he said that the troubles were not severe, and then a few days later he briefly suspended his campaign and wanted to cancel the first debate so that Washington could focus on saving the economy. The period of time examined in this study also included the presidential debates, where the plainspoken McCain faced one of the best orators in contemporary politics. Even so, McCain lost to Obama in terms of tone of coverage in every single media outlet during this period, and the margin was at least two to one favoring Obama on every outlet but Fox.

Fox, though, did like Sarah Palin. Their coverage of the Republican vice presidential candidate during this period—which also included the vice presidential debate—was 58 percent positive, more positive than any other national candidate on that cable network. (Palin, it should be noted, returned the favor. After the 2008 election, she resigned from her job as governor of Alaska in mid-term, went on a nationwide book tour, and eventually landed as a pundit on Fox [Balz 2010].)

Palin did better than McCain by a two-to-one margin on all the outlets examined here, but that is not necessarily saying much. Her 42 percent positive coverage on CNN tied with Biden's coverage and was only six percentage points behind Obama's. Her best coverage, after Fox, was the 45 percent positive coverage she received on the network news morning and evening programs, but she lagged behind both members of the Democratic ticket on ABC, CBS, and NBC.

Taken as a whole, the PEJ content analyses in tables 4.2 and 4.3 suggest that the same problems identified in network news occur across much of the new and old media alike. Regardless of where we turn, there is a heavy focus on the horse race at the expense of issues. There is uneven coverage, where one candidate—or one party—is singled out for extremely positive treatment across much of the media landscape. Ironically, the outlet most supportive of McCain was also the least likely to provide one-sided coverage during this phase of the 2008 presidential campaign. Like the broadcast networks in 1980, 1988, and 2000, Fox achieved tonal balance through negative coverage of both parties' candidates. Overall, the coverage gaps seen in table 4.3 are roughly in line with the tonal coverage gaps for network news, suggesting that seeking alternative sources of news may not lead one to more substantive and/or more even-handed coverage.

Tone in Primary Elections

The tone in coverage of presidential candidates during the nomination stage has varied far more widely than in general elections. The 2004 Democratic primary campaign set three records for positive news coverage. John Kerry, who received 81 percent positive comments from nonpartisan sources on network news, had the most positive treatment of any eventual presidential nominee since the start of this analysis in 1988. But John Edwards, who ended up as the party's 2004 vice presidential nominee, had the most upbeat coverage of any major candidate—96 percent positive—bar none.

The third record for most positive nomination coverage was set by the tone of the news about all the Democratic candidates in 2004: the 75 percent positive overall coverage was the most positive coverage of a nomination contest during the five election cycles examined here. And it wasn't even close—no other evaluations for any other group of party competitors received even 60 percent positive combined evaluations going back to the 1988 nomination contests.

Even Barack Obama, who also basked in highly favorable coverage throughout 2008, couldn't compete with the 2004 results. Obama's primary season campaign coverage was 75 percent positive in tone, which made him the fifth most positively treated Democratic candidate for president over the past twenty years, behind Edwards and Kerry in 2004, Jerry Brown in 1992, and Bruce Babbitt in 1988. As for the Democratic candidates who eventually became their party's nominees, Obama had the second-best tonal treatment behind Kerry.

Of course, not all major Democratic competitors were treated this well. Hillary Clinton, who finished a close second to Obama in the 2008 nomination campaign, lagged considerably behind him in the race for good press, though her 53 percent positive coverage was better than average for Democrats in past election cycles. Clinton, who had been viewed as the front-runner throughout 2007, received roughly as much positive coverage as had former Vermont governor Howard Dean, another front-runner who fell short. Even when Clinton was doing well—including after her victory in the New Hampshire primary—her coverage was less positive than her chief rival's. The same thing happened in 2004 when Dean was doing well in the polls prior to the Iowa caucuses—his coverage was far more negative than that of Kerry and Edwards.

Reporters were roughest on Clinton in their discussions of her campaign behavior. Some stories focused on her efforts to build up support among working-class whites by suggesting that Obama, the first viable African American presidential candidate, did not understand their concerns (Ceaser et al. 2009; Simien 2009). Despite his working-class roots, Obama did not help himself with comments he thought were being made privately about the "bitter" feelings some working-class whites harbored (cf., Owen 2009; Simien 2009). Former President Bill Clinton also got into the act and attacked Obama's viability as a candidate in a general election. But the strategy appeared to backfire, costing Hillary Clinton support among younger voters and African Americans (cf., Abramson et al. 2010; Ceaser et al. 2009; Simien 2009).

Four years earlier, reporters were roughest on Dean during the week following the Iowa caucuses, where he finished third. He was the subject of heavy coverage of the "Dean Scream" controversy (cf. Ceaser and Bush 2005). Dean's loud and frenzied-sounding exhortations to his supporters, which were frequently replayed on the broadcast and cable networks, were thought by some to illustrate a temperament that made him unsuitable for the high-pressure job he sought—even though Dean claims the media created an inaccurate image because of the noise-canceling microphone used on stage (Eggerton 2004).

The only time Dean received more positive coverage than Kerry was after Kerry's victories in Iowa and New Hampshire made him the odds-on favorite for the nomination. Meanwhile, Edwards had more positive coverage than both Kerry and Dean during every segment of the nomination period. In other words, even before his poll numbers sank, even before the infamous "Dean Scream," the media had turned on the former Vermont governor in a way comparable to that of other frontrunners for the nomination.

In the same way that disparities in the 2004 and 2008 general election coverage favoring the Democrats raise questions of fairness, so too does the very different coverage Dean received when compared to both Kerry and Edwards and the coverage Hillary Clinton received when compared to Obama. In 2000, the Democratic candidates received somewhat fewer positive assessments than did the Republicans. When combined, the two candidates for the Democratic nomination that year received a total of 43 percent positive reports. But that figure masks a very distinct difference: Bill Bradley's network-news coverage was 62 percent positive in tone, as compared to Al Gore's coverage, which was only 40 percent positive. This is powerful evidence of the compensatory coverage identified in past media research. As table 4.4 shows, Bradley won the battle for the press, but Gore won the Iowa caucuses, the New Hampshire primary, and every nomination contest that followed.

The compensatory coverage so apparent in 2000 was also found in 1992, the year Bill Clinton won the Democratic nomination and ultimately the presidency, after overcoming scandals involving Gennifer Flowers and questions over how he evaded military service during the Vietnam War (cf. Farnsworth

Table 4.4
Primary Election News:
Tone of Coverage for Democratic Candidates, 1988–2008*

Tone of Coverage (% good press)		
2008	Barack Obama	75%
	Hillary Clinton	53%
	Democratic candidates	66%
2004	John Edwards	96%
	John Kerry	81%
	Howard Dean	48%
	Democratic candidates	75%
2000	Bill Bradley	62%
	Al Gore	40%
	Democratic candidates	43%
1996	Democratic candidates	N/A
1992	Jerry Brown	82%
	Paul Tsongas	56%
	Bob Kerrey	52%
	Tom Harkin	52%
	Bill Clinton	37%
	Democratic candidates	50%
1988	Bruce Babbitt**	91%
	Jesse Jackson	70%
	Al Gore	48%
	Michael Dukakis	45%
	Richard Gephardt	43%
	Gary Hart**	38%
	Paul Simon	36%
	Democratic candidates	49%

* 2008 data is from December 16, 2007, through March 22, 2008. The campaign season in other years runs from January 1 through the eve of Super Tuesday primaries on March 1, 2004; March 7, 2000; March 12, 1996; March 10, 1992. 1988 data is from January 1 through the eve of the Illinois primary on March 15, 1988. Only candidates with ten or more evaluations are reported individually, but all candidates are included in party totals.
** Gary Hart and Bruce Babbitt good press only through February 26, 1988.

and Lichter 1999). Coverage of Bill Clinton was far more negative in tone than the coverage of his four major rivals for the Democratic nomination that year (Bill Clinton was re-nominated by his party without opposition in 1996).

In 1988, the most favorable evaluations of candidates were also saved for those candidates who had no realistic chance of being their party's nominee. In the 1988 Democratic nomination contest, for example, former Arizona governor Bruce Babbitt received an amazing 91 percent positive evaluations (second only to Edwards sixteen years later), and civil rights activist Jesse Jackson received 70 percent positive evaluations. Both were far ahead of the 45 percent positive evaluations received by Massachusetts governor Michael Dukakis, the eventual nominee.

Candidates who were seen as having a reasonable chance of securing the nomination received scores similar to Dukakis's. Congressman Richard Gephardt (D-Mo.), who won the 1988 Iowa caucuses, received a 43 percent positive tone. Then-senator Al Gore (D-Tenn.), who emerged as a serious contender in 1988 when he won five upper South and border states on Super Tuesday, received 48 percent positive press.

Of course, being unlikely to win did not guarantee a positive tone to one's coverage. Senator Paul Simon (D-Ill.) finished second in Iowa but third in New Hampshire, all but dooming his nomination hopes. (All the major-party nominees of the six presidential elections examined in this book finished either first or second in the pivotal New Hampshire primary.) But Simon's coverage was only 36 percent positive in tone, lower even than Gary Hart's. Hart, who had waged a strong but ultimately unsuccessful campaign in the 1984 Democratic contest against Walter Mondale, was an early casualty in the race for the 1988 nomination following reports of infidelity and the subsequent derision he faced from the press pack and from the late-night comedians (Pomper 1989).

Table 4.5 shows the tone of network news coverage received by candidates for the Republican presidential nominations in 1988, 1992, 1996, 2000, and 2008. (Since Bush was unopposed for the nomination in 2004, there was no analysis of that primary season.) John McCain, the Republican nominee in 2008, received 46 percent positive coverage, considerably less than the 63 percent positive press he received in losing the nomination to George W. Bush in 2000.

Of course, any candidate would prefer to win the nomination rather than the race for positive press. Mike Huckabee, the former governor of Arkansas, was well received by the party's evangelical Christian voters and also received 58 percent positive press on ABC, CBS, and NBC during the 2008 campaign. Huckabee, who had been a relative unknown when the campaign began, parlayed his increased visibility into regular appearances on Fox, where he and Sarah Palin and former U.S. speaker of the House Newt Gingrich (R-Ga.) provide news analysis. Former Massachusetts governor Mitt Romney was third in the race for positive press among Republicans in 2008, just behind McCain, with 44 percent positive coverage.

What a difference eight years made for John McCain. Of course, the Arizona Republican's more-positive coverage in early 2000 did not seem entirely well founded. CBS anchor Dan Rather, for example, described McCain as "a reformer and a hero" and "a shrewd politician . . . stirring up voters [with]

Table 4.5
Primary Election News: Tone of Coverage for Republican Candidates, 1988–2008*

Tone of Coverage (% good press)

2008	Mike Huckabee	58%
	John McCain	46%
	Mitt Romney	44%
	Republican candidates	44%
2004	Republican candidates	N/A
2000	John McCain	63%
	George W. Bush	53%
	Republican candidates	50%
1996	Richard Lugar	88%
	Phil Gramm	67%
	Bob Dole	44%
	Pat Buchanan	43%
	Lamar Alexander	39%
	Steve Forbes	36%
	Bob Dornan	0%
	Republican candidates	43%
1992	Pat Buchanan	34%
	George H. W. Bush	24%
	Republican candidates	27%
1988	Bob Dole	60%
	George H. W. Bush	49%
	Pat Robertson	48%
	Jack Kemp**	46%
	Republican candidates	52%

* 2008 data is from December 16, 2007, through March 22, 2008. The campaign season in other years runs from January 1 through the eve of Super Tuesday primaries on March 1, 2004; March 7, 2000; March 12, 1996; March 10, 1992. 1988 data is from January 1 through the eve of the Illinois primary on March 15, 1988. Only candidates with ten or more evaluations are reported individually, but all candidates are reported in party totals.
** Jack Kemp good press only through February 26, 1988.

his style and a heroic bio" on March 1, 2000. Although McCain, a former prisoner of war in North Vietnam, is unquestionably a hero, Rather's comments about his political savvy seemed ill timed. The night before Rather's comments, McCain had finished second to Bush in both the Virginia primary, by 53 percent to 44 percent, and the Washington primary, by 58 percent to 39 percent (Stanley 2001). A few days before those contests, McCain had criticized the "evil influence" of the Christian conservative movement on the

Republican Party, a curious approach to take in Virginia, the home state of two leading Christian conservatives: Pat Robertson and Jerry Falwell (Mayer 2001). Several days later, on March 7, the allegedly politically savvy McCain lost crucial contests in California, New York, and Ohio to Bush, though he did win four less-significant New England primaries (Stanley 2001).

In 1996, the most positive tone again was lavished on the candidates with little chance of winning the GOP nomination. Senator Richard Lugar (R-Ind.), a soft-spoken foreign-policy-oriented moderate unlikely to appeal to the conservative Republicans who dominate the party's primary electorate, received 88 percent positive coverage. Senator Phil Gramm (R-Tex.), who basically committed nomination suicide by suggesting that some state other than New Hampshire should hold the first primary, received 67 percent positive press. Senator Bob Dole (R-Kans.), the eventual nominee, was further back, with 44 percent positive press. Pat Buchanan, who emerged as the leading challenger to Dole after winning the New Hampshire primary, received similarly lukewarm press, only 43 percent positive in tone. Political novice Steve Forbes, a wealthy magazine publisher who could remain in the race thanks to his willingness to spend down his immense personal fortune, received the lowest rating of any remotely viable candidate, with 36 percent positive press.

The 1992 Republican nomination contest was remarkable for its very negative media tone. President George H. W. Bush's 24 percent positive evaluation was one of the lowest recorded for any candidate. Buchanan's more positive showing—34 percent positive—was not a great deal better, but the relative advantage enjoyed by this outsider candidate is consistent with the idea of compensatory journalism.

The tone of George H. W. Bush's campaign coverage was more favorable in 1988, when the then-vice president won his party's presidential nomination. Dole, the main Republican obstacle to Bush's plan to succeed Ronald Reagan, received the most positive press that year, again consistent with compensatory journalism. The GOP field received an average of 52 percent positive press that year, the party's highest average score on the network news in our study.

Tables 4.4 and 4.5 can be used to compare the tone of coverage of the two parties' candidates during the nomination stage. In 2008, the Democrats had a twenty-two-point advantage during the primary season, about the same as the 23 percent advantage they enjoyed in 1992. The Republicans had a 50 percent positive to 43 percent positive advantage in 2000, and a 52 percent to 49 percent advantage in 1988. There were also two years (1996 and 2004) in which there can be no comparison because there was no party opposition to incumbent presidents' renominations. The pattern seen here with respect to primary coverage is consistent with that found for network news tone in general elections, where some years are fairly balanced and other years favor the Democrats.

Blaming the Victim?

Reporters often criticize candidates for being too tightly managed and too uninteresting. Many journalists say that the candidates, not the reporters, are responsible for many of the complaints over campaign coverage. They say they are only reporting the facts about the candidates, which can get ugly (Shogan 2001). If readers and viewers have a problem with what they see and read, the politicians are largely to blame. "The politicians provide us with a campaign that's superficial, deceptive, dishonest. It's hard for reporters to change that," lamented Robert Shogan, long-time political correspondent for the *Los Angeles Times* (quoted in Owen 2002, 129).

News routines create certain unavoidable demands on reporters. The first of these, a particularly powerful one for television reporters, is the need to condense available information into a brief news segment. A day's campaigning cannot be repeated verbatim on the evening news. The whole program lasts only half an hour—just over twenty minutes once the commercials are subtracted. Reporters who want their stories to make it past the producers will choose the most interesting, exciting, controversial, and revealing material for their segments, which usually run two minutes or less. Presidential candidates and their campaigns hire media experts who can help their candidate get on the air, and, if they are lucky, sometimes even convince a reporter to portray the candidate in a way the candidate wishes to be portrayed. The central question here is how well the picture that emerges reflects the actual campaign.

To examine this question, we analyzed televised candidate interviews during the 1996 campaign and compared them to network evening news presentations of the candidates. This involved 164 nationally televised interviews with presidential candidates during the primary season (January 1 through March 26) and the general election (September 2 through November 5). The interviews were broadcast or cablecast on more than twenty different programs, including the morning, evening, and Sunday news shows for all three major networks, the *NewsHour* on PBS, and a variety of CNN programs, including *Larry King Live, Late Edition with Frank Sesno, Talkback Live,* and *PrimeNews.* These 164 interviews totaled twenty-six hours and thirty-eight minutes of questions and answers, led by *Larry King Live,* which had five hours and nineteen minutes of interviewing and twenty-two interviews.

In the 1996 general election, Bill Clinton received 50 percent positive tone on network television's nightly newscasts during the general election period, and Bob Dole received 33 percent good press (reported in table 4.1 above). Dole had far more positive reviews in the talk-show interviews, with 62 percent positive evaluations. In contrast, Clinton fared worse, with only 37 percent positive evaluations in the interviews. Clinton's low score resulted from his decision to give only one TV interview during the entire fall campaign. During a September 23 interview on PBS's *News-Hour*, Clinton was asked a series of questions about Susan McDougal's imprisonment for her refusal to cooperate with Kenneth Starr, the Whitewater independent counsel. Clinton's intimation during the interview that he believed Starr had a personal vendetta against him led to considerable criticism from normally friendly media sources. In the wake of this experience, Clinton did not schedule another interview during the remainder of the 1996 campaign.

Dole also did not grant many interviews, apparently because of concerns that he would face allegations (which first surfaced in the *National Enquirer*) that he had committed adultery during his first marriage many years earlier. Dole granted just four television interviews in the fall. A Dole aide told a *Washington Post* reporter after the election that the allegations "froze our ability to do a number of things, most importantly to have the candidate commit to television interviews" (Kurtz 1996b). Despite his positive treatment in these venues during 1996, Dole's reluctance to participate in more interviews demonstrates that the media's search for scandal can discourage candidates from participating in communication environments that are both friendly to them and useful to citizens. By sometimes scaring candidates away from these more open venues, journalists take away from voters a useful source for policy information that citizens are not likely to receive through a sound bite and horse-race-oriented evening newscast.

Most Republicans did not do badly on these interview shows during the 1996 primary campaign either. Overall, the Republican candidates in the 1996 primaries received 43 percent positive press on the network news, and three of the four leading candidates had far more positive evaluations on the interview shows. Lamar Alexander received 85 percent positive coverage on the interview programs, Pat Buchanan 74 percent, and billionaire publisher Steve Forbes 61 percent. The tone of the coverage on the evening news programs for these three candidates was 39 percent, 43 percent, and 36 percent positive, respectively. Only Dole, the GOP front-runner who stumbled in New Hampshire and struggled to win his party's nomination, faced particularly negative treatment on the interview shows, with only 31 percent positive evaluations there. The tone of his network news coverage was 44 percent positive, making him the only one of the four leading candidates to do better on the evening news shows than on the interview shows.

What sets these interview shows apart from traditional television news coverage, of course, is that the candidates themselves control large portions of the discussions. Nearly nine out of ten evaluative statements (88 percent) from these 164 interviews came from the candidates rather than the hosts or callers. Of course, candidates would not be expected to undermine their own campaigns, but they concentrated far more on their own virtues than on their opponents' vices. These much-less-filtered venues also allowed for far more discussion of issues than the more horse-race-dominated coverage of the network nightly newscasts.

CMPA also analyzed campaign speeches given and campaign ads aired nationally by Clinton and Dole from Labor Day to election eve, a total of 131 speeches and 110 different commercials. Clinton's top four campaign issues were (in order) education, children, the state of the economy, and crime. Dole's leading campaign issues were taxes, drugs, the state of the economy, and Medicare. The news media agenda, however, focused on (in order) Dole's strategy, taxes, Clinton's strategy, and the state of the economy.

This comprehensive analysis shows clearly that both candidates ran issue-dominated campaigns in both their speeches and their advertisements. But their issue-dominated campaigns were heavily mediated—and distorted—by reporters, who focused far more intensely on campaign strategy than did the candidates themselves. In their ads and speeches, both the front-running incumbent and the increasingly desperate challenger offered voters far more valuable information with which to evaluate their candidacies than did the reporters covering them.

Journalists often express dismay over the negativity of candidates during the primaries, when candidates need to distinguish themselves from the pack clearly and quickly. Yet our content analysis of speeches and ads during the 1996 Republican primaries again found a positive and issue-oriented message. Contrary to the conventional wisdom, the 1996 primaries, like the general election that followed, were marked by positive and informative candidate messages, which were undermined by network news coverage that selectively focused on the most negative elements. Despite Dole's overwhelmingly positive stump speeches during the primaries (78 percent positive, to be precise), a majority of Dole's sound bites (56 percent) that ran on the evening news were negative. Similarly, Dole was 56 percent positive in his advertising during the primary campaign, but reporters portrayed his advertising as being positive only 11 percent of the time. A dominant media frame for Dole was that he was ill-tempered, and this may account for these dramatic gaps between what Dole said and what the networks said Dole said (Kerbel 1998).

Buchanan saw somewhat less dramatic but nevertheless significant gaps between what he said and what the network reporters said he said. The CMPA content analysis found him to be 70 percent positive in his speeches and 45 percent positive in his advertising, but he was portrayed in the media as only 46 percent positive in speeches and a mere 13 percent positive in his advertising during the primaries. Both Alexander and Forbes were also more than 70 percent positive in their speeches, though the media portrayals of their speeches fell to 48 percent and 51 percent positive, respectively.

Once again, the news media were equal-opportunity naysayers. The pattern here is clear: television news portrayed the 1996 primary and general elections far more negatively, and as far less issue-oriented, than they actually were. The 1996 results raise general questions about the accuracy of the mediated "reality" of presidential campaigns. The evidence in chapter 1 demonstrates that voters want issue-oriented campaigning, and our comparative content analysis indicates that candidates try to give citizens just that. But the reporters choke off much of that substantive communication through shrinking sound bites, negativity, reduced coverage overall, and their focus on the horse race rather than substance. You can't help but wonder why candidates continue to offer up hearty portions of positive, issue-oriented campaigning when they will be served to so few people. Even some reporters are starting to realize they may be getting in the way of issue-based public discourse during campaigns, as demonstrated by Cathleen Decker's article in the June 11, 2000, edition of the *Los Angeles Times*.

> It is one of the strange ironies of politics: candidates expound on issues, and people assume they are angling for votes. Politicians try hard, only to have people believe them less—even when they are speaking from the heart. Rarely does a candidate emerge with that trait that neither charm nor money can buy: the assumption that one wholly means what one says. (Decker, quoted in Kerbel 2001, 125)

The results here again point to the utility of the media effects model. As reporters present their cynical views of candidates, citizens are being encouraged to consider candidates in that same negative light.

The Scandals of the 2004 Presidential Election (Or Was That 1972?)

During the summer and fall of 2004, Democratic presidential nominee John Kerry of Massachusetts and President George W. Bush both faced renewed questions concerning what they did more than three decades earlier, when both were young men staring into the void that was Vietnam (Seelye 2004; Wilgoren 2004). Kerry, a naval officer, had been awarded several medals for bravery and for being wounded while patrolling the waterways of Vietnam.

After Kerry locked up the Democratic nomination, a group of Kerry opponents began raising money to pay for advertisements arguing that the senator did not deserve his medals, and that he had impugned his fellow veterans when he later descried war crimes allegedly committed by U.S. soldiers in Vietnam and led an antiwar group called Vietnam Veterans Against the War (Bumiller 2004; Rutenberg 2004b; Zernike and Rutenberg 2004).

The controversy reopened old wounds endured by the Vietnam-era generation, a time that split the nation like few others in American history (Egan 2004). Although investigations by news organizations failed to validate the allegations that Kerry did not deserve his medals, the news media gave the controversy extensive coverage. Network news carried eighty-nine sound bites on Kerry's military records between June 2 and September 2, when the Kerry controversies were prominent in the news. A slight majority of 54 percent of them were positive in tone, in part because a number of Kerry's former naval comrades rose to his defense. One fellow veteran, Jim Rasmussen, even traveled with the Kerry campaign to tell audiences how the young naval officer risked his life to pull him out of a river under enemy fire (Rasmussen 2004). Nonetheless, the Kerry campaign's failure to respond promptly and effectively to the charges by an organization called the Swift Boat Veterans for Truth cost him considerable support among veterans, and probably contributed to his eventual defeat (Easton et al. 2004; Nagourney 2004; Wilgoren 2004).

Bush got his turn in the spotlight for a Vietnam-era scandal that fall. Critics argued that he had used family connections to secure a place in the National Guard to avoid being sent into combat overseas (Rimer et al. 2004). Once in the Texas Air National Guard, the *New York Times* reported, Bush failed to undergo a required physical or show up for required training for at least five months after transferring to an Alabama guard unit (Rimer et al. 2004; Seelye and Blumenthal 2004). The spotty records that have survived and been released show that Bush left the guard with an honorable discharge (Rimer et al. 2004).

During the election-year controversy, no one came forward to vouch publicly that Bush had served his time as required in Alabama. But, in the end, the Bush campaign did not need to produce character witnesses from the Alabama base. Questions over his activities in 1972 and 1973 were eclipsed by a larger controversy—an erroneous report on the CBS News program *60 Minutes II* that used documents later revealed to be forgeries to question Bush's guard service (Rutenberg 2004a; Rutenberg and Zernike 2004). The documents, which allegedly came from the personnel files of one of Bush's commanders in Texas, claimed that high-ranking officers wanted Bush's immediate supervisors to "sugar-coat" the young man's record (Rutenberg 2004a).

Internet bloggers quickly pounced on the memos used by CBS, claiming they were fakes that had not been produced on a 1970s-era typewriter as indicated by the font used, and because of the abbreviations used, which did not conform to standard military practice (Rutenberg and Zernike 2004). After nearly two weeks of withering controversy, the network retracted the story, and CBS News apologized (Rutenberg and Zernkie 2004).

In January 2005, after a lengthy independent investigation, CBS News fired three top executives, including the producer of the September article. The investigators also concluded that Dan Rather, who reported the story, exercised bad judgment in pursuing it so aggressively and in doggedly defending it even after serious questions about its authenticity were raised (Kurtz 2005).

The Big Three network evening news programs aired a total of forty-seven sound bites on Bush's military record between September 7, the day before the story broke on *60 Minutes II*, and November 1, the night before the election. The coverage was 81 percent negative in tone, far more negative than the coverage of Kerry's war record. (Like Kerry, Bush did not vigorously defend his Vietnam-era record during the peak of this controversy.)

To conservative critics, what some wags dubbed "Rather-gate" demonstrated the liberal bias long thought to exist at CBS News (cf., Goldberg 2002). To other critics, the incident demonstrated the declining standards of mainstream news organizations that cut corners in the rush to be the first to air an explosive investigative report. The success of bloggers in monitoring the mainstream media may lead reporters to be less reckless in the future. There are too many people out there who can draw attention to their mistakes after all. But because the media environment is in great flux, the long-term consequences of the changing media environment illustrated by "Rather-gate" are still playing themselves out.

Poll-Coverage Miscues during Campaign 2000

Of course, distortion is one thing, while simple inaccuracy is quite another, as an examination of television's treatment of campaign polls during the 2000 general election campaign shows. Ironically, although news coverage is dominated by horse-race concerns, reports of campaign polls suffer from an apparent confusion over such basic matters as proper sampling techniques, effective question design, and the uncertainty represented by the polls' margins of sampling error (Larson 2001; Owen 2002).

> The wide variation in the type of polls made it difficult for news consumers to gauge the quality of information. Polls were being conducted in quick succession, and many did not use proper sampling techniques and question design. "Instant

polls" conducted overnight to gauge people's reactions to dramatic events, such as the announcement of vice presidential candidates, proliferated. These polls, often fielded using auto-dialers with recorded messages, are notoriously inaccurate, as they average a 2 percent acceptance rate of homes dialed. (Owen 2002, 128)

In her study of network evening news coverage of polls during the 2000 election, media scholar Stephanie Larson (2001) found that fewer than one-quarter of the 192 stories that included reports of public opinion showed or mentioned the surveys' margins of error, a key component of the reliability of any survey. The stories that did include some reference to the margin of error often mangled the discussion. Larson observed:

> Word choice indicated that reporters were not sure how to talk about sampling error. On November 3, Peter Jennings claimed, "It's as close as ever. Take a look— Mr. Gore and Mr. Bush are within *shall we say* the margin of error—48 percent support for Mr. Bush and 45 percent for Mr. Gore." Dan Rather also seemed confused when he reported on September 12: "The latest CBS News/ *New York Times* poll out tonight suggests Al Gore may have a very narrow edge over George Bush, but it's so small it is within the poll's *possible* margin of error." (Larson 2001, 12, emphasis in original)

When results are within a survey's margin of error, as any student of public opinion knows, the determination of who is ahead or behind cannot be determined with any acceptable level of confidence. If the poll numbers for the two candidates are close enough to be within the survey's margin of error, it is appropriate to describe the results as "too close to call" or some other way of saying that we do not know for sure who is actually ahead (or, more precisely, that we are not 95 percent certain that the candidate with the higher number in the poll actually is ahead of the candidate with the lower number).

If reporters do not understand margins of error, they could turn to public opinion professionals or academics to explain such matters. Reporters often do so when reporting on other complicated issues, such as economics, health care issues, and the military. But reporters rarely turn to polling experts, at least not on air. Larson (2001) found that 87 percent of network news stories featuring poll results did not use experts to interpret the polls on-air, an obvious way for reporters to provide viewers with an interpretation for something that the reporters themselves apparently do not understand.

Further, some of the experts who were used to answering questions of public opinion were not always being fair and objective. NBC was censured by the National Council of Public Polls for using Republican pollster Frank Luntz as an allegedly objective public-opinion analyst: "This stuff is rough and ready and would hardly pass anyone's test of gauging a representative sample of voters. I don't know what purpose it serves journalistically or in terms of research,"

Andrew Kohut, director of the Pew Research Center for the People and the Press, said of Luntz's appearances on NBC (quoted in Owen 2002, 128).

In a finding consistent with the horse-race orientation of network news coverage, Larson (2001) found that few news reports included references to questions other than who was ahead and who was behind. Only 1 percent of the reports she examined included discussion of responses to a question related to which candidate would make a better leader, for example.

The difficulties news programs had in interpreting the polls during the fall campaign should have made reporters and editors doubly concerned about how their limited ability to make sense of survey research might be further compromised in the high-pressure, uncertain, and anxious environment of highly competitive election night reporting. Indeed, there was some concern early on that evening that television reporters should be careful. But that concern was soon brushed aside in the rush to be first to "call" a state for one of the candidates. The result was the most irresponsible and error-ridden night in the history of television news.

The Election Night 2000 Mess

For months, the candidate preference polls had moved back and forth between George W. Bush and Al Gore. For part of the 2000 campaign, Bush was ahead; at other times Gore held the lead. The surveys conducted in the final days before the first presidential election of the twenty-first century indicated that the contest had become too close to call. Pundits began to speculate that one candidate might win the popular vote, while the other would win in the Electoral College, something that had not happened in more than a century. Election day was marked by early-morning campaign rallies and feverish get-out-the-vote drives in closely contested states. As the polls began to close in the Eastern states, the network news teams settled in for what many expected would be a long night. But no one expected that the hours of uncertainty would ultimately stretch into days and then weeks (Ceaser and Busch 2001).

Rather than wait for the votes to be counted, a process that can take many hours to determine a winner under normal circumstances, many news organizations rely on exit polls to forecast winners. Workers ask people in selected precincts whom they voted for as a way of perceiving larger trends in a state. Every state has towns or counties that are overwhelmingly Democratic, others that are overwhelmingly Republican, and still others that could tip either way, depending on the candidates and the issues in a given election. In Florida, for example, Democratic candidates are likely to prevail in places like Broward and Palm Beach counties. Republicans are likely to do very well in many of the northern-tier counties of the Florida Panhandle, jurisdictions like Oka-loosa and Clay counties (Fiedler 2002). Still other counties are *"swing"* counties, meaning they swing back and forth from one party to another, depending on the particulars of a given election.

By sampling precincts in counties with different voting patterns, exit pollsters can get an indication of such things as whether turnout is high in normally Democratic jurisdictions, whether a Republican candidate isn't keeping pace with past Republican patterns in overwhelmingly GOP counties, and whether groups of swing voters, like the so-called soccer moms, are trending Republican or Democratic. Put a number of these factors together, combine them with early official returns, and polling experts may be able to predict a winner in an election long before all the votes are counted.

Of course, making a prediction is not the same as making a correct count. There are things that exit polls cannot do, such as determining the significance of the absentee ballots (which in Florida in 2000 didn't even need to have arrived at state election offices by election day), or whether voters actually cast their ballots in a valid, countable manner. Both of these matters turned out to be highly significant to the outcome of the presidential election in Florida.

Large numbers of absentee votes for Bush were received by election officials in the days following the election, primarily from military personnel on duty outside the United States. A *New York Times* investigation subsequently concluded that some of the absentee ballots were counted as legitimate despite having no postmark and in some cases despite having been cast after election day, in violation of Florida law (Barstow and Van Natta 2001). In addition, thousands of voters in Palm Beach County—a county with large numbers of African Americans and Jewish Americans—apparently mistakenly invalidated their ballots or accidentally cast a vote for Reform Party nominee Pat Buchanan, whose opposition to affirmative action and criticism of U.S. aid to Israel would hardly have made him an appealing choice to large numbers of voters in that jurisdiction. Experts believe many of the 3,400 votes Buchanan received in Palm Beach County were the result of a poorly designed "butterfly ballot" that generated considerable attention in the days following the election (Fiedler 2002; Pomper 2001).

In addition to the bizarre factors that undermined the legitimacy of the exit polls in Florida in 2000—factors that even cast doubts in many minds about the legitimacy of the actual vote count in the state—exit polls are not immune from the normal sources of error that are a fact of life for any survey. No matter how carefully designed, a survey that asks some people how they will vote or did vote as a proxy for determining how everyone in a group voted will always have risks: one side may be oversampled while the other side is undersampled. This basic factor should lead to caution on the part of anyone calling elections on the basis of exit polls, as is done routinely in American news programming. Exit polls may be particularly prone to bias because of who would and would not participate—it may be much easier to answer questions over the phone at home in the evening than to fill out a survey while rushing back to work or to pick up the kids at day care. Finally, voters who refuse to cooperate may skew the sample.

During the afternoon of election day, while the entire country was still voting, the first early and erroneous returns were trickling in to the television networks affiliated with the Voter News Service (VNS). Before 2 p.m., network executives had in their hands exit-poll results suggesting that Gore was going to lose Pennsylvania, a key state in Gore's Electoral College strategy. Those results, soon determined to be erroneous, were withdrawn by VNS before 5 p.m. (Greenfield 2001; Mnookin 2001). Although not released to the public that day, those results offered a powerful, early warning sign to journalists that the VNS models had major problems, as Jeff Greenfield of CNN noted:

> At 4:47 p.m., VNS sent out a reassuring alert to subscribers: "The problems with the [Pennsylvania] survey weighting are cleared up. We have cleaned out the bad precinct problems." This was not all that reassuring to CNN co-anchor Judy Woodruff, who was openly uneasy about a vote-gathering operation—the only vote-gathering operation—deciding in the middle of election day that its model might have a bug or two in it. It was, said another colleague, like looking out the window of a jumbo jet ten minutes before departure time, and noticing a group of mechanics huddling around engine number four, shaking their heads and flipping through the maintenance manual. (Greenfield 2001, 56)

Gore, by the way, ended up winning Pennsylvania by a 51 percent to 47 percent margin, with a plurality of more than 204,000 votes (Nelson 2001). When the evening campaign coverage began, the network anchors promised to be very careful as they sorted through the exit polls and the election returns that would be coming in during the subsequent hours. As Dan Rather of CBS offered: "Let's get one thing straight from the get-go. . . . We would rather be last in reporting returns than to be wrong. . . . If we say someone has carried a state, you can pretty much take it to the bank" (quoted in Sabato 2002, 112).

The Voter News Service was hired by ABC, CBS, NBC, CNN, Fox News, and the Associated Press to be their collective exit pollster in the 2000 election. Dozens of other media outlets, including some of the nation's largest newspapers, also paid to use the VNS data. Ironically, the networks pooled their resources in the 2000 election, as they had in the 1992 and 1996 presidential contests, to improve the quality of the exit polling beyond a level that would have been affordable for any one news outlet (Sabato 2002). What actually happened was that this collective arrangement, together with the normal journalistic fears of being beaten to the story by competitors, led all the networks to make the same mistakes at the same time. The limitations of polling may not make much difference in one-sided elections, but there is a world of difference between a first-place finish of 51 percent and a second-place finish of 49 percent.

There was one other reason for the reporters to be highly cautious in their use of VNS estimates. The networks had already learned that the Voter News Service could make mistakes. In 1996, for example, the VNS provided exit-poll data that indicated that Senator Bob Smith (R-N.H.) had been defeated in his bid for reelection. Television anchors called the contest in favor of Dick Swett, but when the votes were counted, Smith emerged victorious (Greenfield 2001; Mnookin 2001).

Everyone expected Florida to be one of the most important states in the close presidential contest, and an early call that one candidate had won Florida's twenty-five electoral votes would have a dramatic impact on the overall election. Early on, Clinton adviser-turned-media-pundit George Stephanopoulos told ABC's viewers to watch three states: Pennsylvania, Michigan, and Florida. "Whoever wins two of those three states should be in the driver's seat tonight," Stephanopoulos said (quoted in Sabato 2002, 112).

By 8 p.m. all six media outlets behind the VNS had officially placed Florida's electoral votes in Gore's column. All relied on the same faulty VNS data, which seemed more and more questionable as the actual precinct-by-precinct returns came in (Owen 2002). During the next two hours, a number of Republicans started criticizing the networks for what they claimed were faulty calls on the state (Greenfield 2001). By 10 P.M. or so, all the networks reported computer problems, returned this crucial state to the "undecided" column, and said they were sorry. "To err is human, but to really foul up requires a computer," Rather said during one of his election night mea culpas on CBS. "If you're disgusted with us, frankly, I don't blame you" (quoted in Owen 2002, 123). Humility was likewise the order of the day in the following CNN exchange concerning Florida:.

> BERNARD SHAW: Stand by, stand by—CNN right now is moving our earlier declaration of Florida back to the too-close-to-call. . . .—
> JEFF GREENFIELD: Oh, waiter . . .
> SHAW: —into the too-close-to-call column.
> GREENFIELD: One order of crow.
> BILL SCHNEIDER: One order of crow, yes.
> (quoted in Mnookin 2001, 150)

In the undecided column was where the state remained until shortly after 2 a.m. Wednesday morning. At that time, a cousin of George W. Bush, working as a vote counter at Fox News, declared that the Republicans had taken that crucial state, containing the electoral votes that would decide the next president. The other television networks followed suit immediately, with the same sense of security with which they had proclaimed a Gore victory several hours earlier. The networks' sense of certainty was back, despite having been so powerfully humbled a few hours before. As Rather said shortly before 2:30 a.m., "Bush wins. . . . That's it. . . . Sip it. Savor it. Cup it. Photostat it. Underline it in red. Put it in an album. Hang it on a wall" (quoted in Sabato 2002, 113).

The networks' certainty during those early- morning hours was sufficient to trigger a telephone call from Gore to Bush to concede. The dejected Gore team began to make their way to a campaign rally to deliver a concession speech. But something happened on the way to the rally: the supposed Bush lead in Florida vanished, and VNS and the networks were shown to have missed the Florida call once again. Gore then called Bush to retract his concession and canceled his planned public appearance (Owen 2002).

Over at the networks, doubts also began to resurface. As the minutes ticked by, the actual returns continued to show that Gore and Bush remained locked in a neck-and-neck race, and Gore was not making the concession speech that everyone had been told to expect. "Good grief," Tom Brokaw said on NBC at 3:27 a.m. on November 8, as the returns suggested no one had clearly won Florida. "That would be something, if the networks managed to blow it twice in the same night" (quoted in Sabato 2002, 113).

As the hours of uncertainty passed, and as Florida was pulled back once again into the undecided column, the comments from the weary and repeatedly humbled anchors became increasingly strange. "Frankly, we don't know whether to run, to watch, or bark at the moon. We just don't know what to do under these circumstances," said CBS's Rather at 4:10 a.m. on November 8 (quoted in Mnookin 2001, 98).

Things were even more bizarre at the ABC News studio an hour or so later, as Peter Jennings and Stephanopoulos had the following "heated" exchange at 5:30 a.m. on November 8:

> JENNINGS: Okay, I hate to tell you, we're also on fire here at the moment. . . . Yes, please, go ahead. We're not always right, but we're very efficient. Thanks, gentlemen, very much. You know, it's a very—I mean I realize at this late hour of the night we're probably broadcasting to ourselves in many respects, but it's a very good time for me to say thank you to the local fire department.
> STEPHANAPOULOS: Wow, the smell.
> JENNINGS: You talk, I'll check the fire.
> (quoted in Mnookin 2001, 98)

There actually was an early-morning fire in the ABC studio, one that was put out relatively quickly. But what the election night of 2000 actually incinerated was the networks' credibility, their most precious but highly flammable asset (Jamieson and Waldman 2002). Television news was not alone in its media malpractice, however. Overall, the media's handling of this story was a widespread "Dewey Beats Truman" failure, to quote the famously erroneous 1948 *Chicago Tribune* headline that Truman never tired of ridiculing (Karabell 2000). The *New York Times* released one hundred thousand papers stating that Bush "appears to have won," while the *New York Post* boldly proclaimed "Bush Wins!" Many other newspapers also prematurely called the election for Bush, including the *Miami Herald, San Francisco Chronicle*, and *Atlanta Journal-Constitution* (Owen 2002, 141).

Although the morning-after focus was on the miscalls in Florida, VNS and the networks also bungled a number of other projections on election night. Early reports that Virginia—a reliably Republican state that at that time had not given its electoral votes to a Democrat since 1964—was too close to call proved terribly wrong as Bush ultimately carried the state by a comfortable 52 percent to 45 percent margin (Owen 2002; Sabato 2002). VNS and the networks also called New Mexico for Gore too soon, and the networks had to recall that early finding as well (Sabato 2002). They also prematurely called the Washington State U.S. Senate race for Democrat Maria Cantwell, even though the race was finally decided by absentee ballots that took several days to count (Mnookin 2001). Although Gore did in the end win New Mexico by a narrow margin— well under one thousand votes—and although Cantwell was eventually found to have defeated incumbent Slade Gorton narrowly, these contests clearly were too close to have been called on election night (Owen 2002; Sabato 2002). That, after all, is why the calls based on insufficient evidence were retracted later on during that chaotic evening. Writing in 2001 for *Brill's Content*, media analyst Seth Mnookin surveyed the wreckage of network television news had made of the election night in 2000, concluding, "These mistakes combine to paint of picture of VNS' model as seriously flawed. On the basis of about thirty close races nationwide—senatorial, gubernatorial, and statewide presidential races that were decided by five percentage points or less—VNS fumbled three calls, or 10 percent of those it was hired to make" (Mnookin 2001, 151).

In fact, Mnookin was generous in his analysis, counting only Florida, New Mexico, and the Washington Senate races as clear mistakes. He neither included the early-afternoon mess in Pennsylvania, nor the erroneous first reports of "too close to call" in the races in Virginia, North Carolina, and Ohio (all easy Bush wins). Nor did Mnookin count Florida as two separate mistakes, since VNS and the networks called the presidential race in the state incorrectly twice in the same night.

We should mention, in fairness, that political scientists who try to determine presidential election outcomes on the basis of macroeconomic statistics also turned out to be poor prognosticators in 2000. The average forecast for a Gore victory among the seven most-cited academic models predicted Gore would get 56.2 percent of the two-party vote; in the end he received 50.2 percent of the votes cast either for himself or Bush. Political scientists tended to blame Gore's campaign blunders, not the mathematical models themselves, for the poor predictions (Campbell 2001; Lewis-Beck and Tien 2001; Wlezien 2001).

As the day after the 2000 election dawned, armies of campaign lawyers and partisan activists were making plans to go to Florida to monitor recounts and perhaps prepare legal arguments. Even in the early morning hours of "the day after," it was clear that this was going to be a postelection like no other in American history (Klain and Bash 2002; Tapper 2001, 2002; Terwilliger 2002). Ironically, television's coverage of the weeks that followed deserves considerable credit, particularly in comparison to the election night (and morning after) fiasco. Reporters immediately recognized the magnitude of this story: the 2000 election deadlock produced 183 network newscasts during the first week (November 8–14, 2000) alone. That exceeded the first week's coverage of such megastories as the 1999 death of John F. Kennedy, Jr. (148 stories), the 1995 Oklahoma City bombing (146 stories), the 1999 Colorado high school killings (142 stories), and the Clinton/Lewinsky scandal (142 stories).

The resources devoted to the 2000 postelection allowed for extensive network news coverage of the complicated and rapidly changing scandal. Without a full-fledged horse race to report on—though there was of course some jockeying for an advantage in public opinion—the coverage moved in a more responsible and factual direction in the weeks following the election night. It may come as no surprise that the 2000 election was the top network-news story of 2000, with 2,420 stories on the evening news programs of the Big Three networks. But who could have predicted that the coverage *after* election day (812 stories) would be more copious than that of either the primary season (550 stories) or the general election (462 stories)?

In a February 14, 2001, congressional hearing called to examine the networks' performance on November 7 and 8, 2000, television executives pronounced themselves deeply embarrassed by their election night coverage (Kurtz 2001a). They said that though they would continue to use exit polls in their coverage, they would try to fix the problems before the next election. The executives called for a law that would require all national polls to close at the same time, in part to reduce the possibility that the early returns reported from early poll-closing Eastern states would depress turnout in Western states, which have later closing times (Kurtz 2001a).

Fox News came under considerable criticism for allowing John Ellis, a first cousin of both George W. Bush and Florida governor Jeb Bush, to make Fox's pro-Bush call in Florida, a move rapidly followed by the other networks in those early-morning hours. Ellis—who talked to both of his cousins on election night—was also harshly criticized by political writer Robert Shogan of the *Los Angeles Times*: "The opportunity he eagerly granted his cousin to influence his judgment was a manifest betrayal of those Americans who watched Fox on election night in the innocent belief that its projections would be made by someone who was not personally involved with one of the protagonists" (2001, 264).

Ellis, and the network's decision to place him in such a prominent role, was defended by Fox News president Roger Ailes, who described Ellis as "a consummate professional" who acted "as a good journalist talking to his very high-level sources" (quoted in Kurtz 2001). The hearing offered one final caution to network news organizations planning to rely on exit polls in the future. Whatever limitations in terms of reliability these surveys now have may increase in the future, at least if citizens follow the advice of Congressman Billy Tauzin (R-La.), then chairman of the House Energy and Commerce Committee. "Americans don't like exit polls," Tauzin remarked at the hearing. "Perhaps they ought to adopt a simple strategy, and that's to lie about how they voted" (quoted in Kurtz 2001).

Consequences of Negativity: Cynicism and Apathy

It is clear from past research that today's television and newspaper reports concerning government and politicians are far more negative than they once were (cf. Kerbel 1995; Patterson 1994; Sabato 2000; Sabato et al. 2000). The research in this chapter likewise documents considerable negativity in the media coverage of recent presidential elections (though the Obama and Kerry campaigns represent key exceptions).

But scholars disagree over what this increased negativity means for American government and politics. A key problem is the inability to demonstrate consistently that media impacts are as powerful or as destructive as many scholars expect. As political scientist Larry Bartels observed: "The scholarly literature has been much better at refuting, qualifying, and circumscribing the thesis of media impact than at supporting it" (1993, 267). But Bartels attributed many of the problems to measurement error and research-design difficulties, not to a lack of media effects. He was not advocating a return to the days of minimal effects. Instead, he was worried that scholars would try to morph the "more-than-minimal" media effects model back into the "hypodermic effects" perspective, the once influential model that is not supported by most contemporary research.

The pervasive media negativity found in coverage of recent presidential elections can trigger dire consequences for the polity, cutting to the heart of our democratic traditions, according to some media researchers. "For most men [and women] most of the time, politics is a series of pictures in the mind, placed there by television news, newspapers, magazines, discussions. The pictures create a moving panorama taking place in a world the mass public never quite touches, yet one its members come to fear or cheer, often with passion and sometimes with action" (Edelman 1985, 5).

Media scholar Michael Robinson (1976), a leading early researcher of how news programs relate to public opinion change, developed the concept of "*videomalaise*" to describe how media exposure can increase citizen cynicism and negativity. Subsequent researchers also found that the downbeat coverage offered by jaded post-Vietnam, post-Watergate reporters leads to heightened citizen frustration, which can bring about an increase in the number of citizens "tuning out" from news and perhaps from politics entirely (cf. Putnam 2000; Jamieson 2000). And the anti-Washington Tea Party movement that arose during Obama's first year in the Oval Office seems to have a lot in common with disaffected voters of previous years (cf. Barstow 2010).

Thomas Patterson (1994) found that rising citizen dissatisfaction with candidates tracks the increasingly negative coverage those candidates have received from journalists. In the 1960s, a period of far more positive press evaluations of candidates, the only major-party nominee who received negative public marks was Barry Goldwater, the highly controversial 1964 GOP nominee. But by 1980, half the people polled said that they were unhappy with the major-party nominees; in 1988 more citizens said they felt negatively than positively about Michael Dukakis and George Bush; and in 1992, 40 percent of those surveyed wished they had someone else to choose from besides presidential candidates Ross Perot, Bill Clinton, and George W. Bush. "Politicians are not saints, but when the balance of coverage tilts so strongly in the negative direction, the election cannot serve as it should to raise the quality of public life," wrote Patterson (1994, 202).

Political scientist Russell Neuman (1986) said that the news media—particularly television—contribute to a fragmentary, haphazard understanding of issues through their generally entertainment-oriented (and superficial) coverage. Media critic Neil Postman (1985) says we are "amusing ourselves to death" as we watch what he considered to be the insultingly trivialized reporting found in television news programming. The harsh and sometimes simplistic news reports, these scholars (and others) have concluded, lead to increased citizen cynicism with politicians and may trigger greater alienation with respect to the government as well.

Experimental evidence supports this proposition. Citizens exposed to a heavier diet of strategic, or horse-race, campaign news generated higher levels of cynicism than those exposed to coverage that was less focused on the "game schema" of politics (Cappella and Jamieson 1997). When they consumed policy-oriented news about health care reform, citizens exposed to more strategic-oriented news showed greater cynicism about the political process than they had previously.

Indeed, the evidence that news activates cynicism is so strong that the researchers raise the possibility that at least some citizens exposed to years of negative coverage of government and politics are perceiving politics and policy through an overall negative frame that dominates one's thoughts about politics: "A public that has accepted the belief that officials are acting in their own self-interest rather than in the interest of the common weal can be easily primed to see self-promotion in every political act. When journalists frame political events strategically, they activate existing beliefs and understandings; they do not need to create them" wrote Cappella and Jamieson (1997, 208).

Above all, says political scientist Roderick Hart, today's horse-race-infused and negatively oriented media coverage of politics tends to suggest that elections and politicians are not worth much respect. "We tower above politics by making it seem beneath us," Hart wrote (1994, 8). But he noted that this erroneous public impression of politics as just another form of gossip is dangerous to us all: "[Democracy is] imperiled (1) when its people do not know what they think they know and (2) when they do not care about what they do not know. Television miseducates the citizenry, but, worse, it makes that miseducation attractive" (Hart 1994, 12).

The very act of watching television has come under suspicion of undermining democracy, according to Robert Putnam (1995a, 1995b, 2000), who is one of the best-known researchers on how citizen discontent may be undermining any sense of community in this country. In his widely read *Bowling Alone* (2000), Putnam blames the mass media for much of the disintegration of our sense of common purpose. He also blames the media for much of our declining interest in interacting with each other to achieve any collective end, even a relatively modest activity like operating a community bowling league.

To illustrate the magnitude of this media-abetted change, Putnam contrasts the sacrifices of the World War II generation—a group some have christened "the greatest generation"—with today's greater self-centeredness. Nearly seventy years ago those on the home front bought bonds, saved scrap metal, and accepted food and gasoline rationing to help defeat Hitler. Today, in contrast, many people cannot even be civil on the nation's highways or take the time to cast a ballot for president once every four years. Of course, the surge of patriotism that followed the September 11, 2001, attacks on the World Trade Center and the Pentagon revived a public-mindedness that had last been seen in America more than a half century ago. But the change was not long lasting.

Some scholars think that media critics like Putnam have gone too far in their condemnations. Studies show that heavy consumers of television news tend to have high levels of interest in politics and actually are more likely to vote than those who do not consume news (Norris 1996). Researchers have also found that critical coverage of specific issues, even of the highly charged Vietnam War, does not necessarily trigger declines in support for the political system (Hallin 1984). "Television news may be objective, but it is far from neutral. The production of news takes place within boundaries established by official sources and dominant values. . . . We see television news as a cautious and conservative medium, much more likely to defend traditional values and institutions than attack them" (Iyengar and Kinder 1987, 133).

Along the same lines, these researchers argue that media effects actually add up to political system-building activities, even as reporters may criticize individual politicians through episodic coverage (Iyengar 1991). Citizen reactions depend on the ways a given issue is framed. Television and newspapers can, for example, act as boundary-maintaining institutions that declare certain types of criticism off-limits, too threatening for mass dissemination (Ginsberg 1986). For example, the way scandals are framed can actually help political leaders remain in power. Although the nation's media outlets severely criticized President Clinton throughout the Clinton/Lewinsky scandal and the subsequent impeachment trial, many reporters and citizens came to view the incident as a personal failing, not as a reason to throw a still-popular president out of office (Owen 2000). The same incident could have been presented quite differently. It could have been used as evidence against the political system itself, painting it to be a flawed system that allowed such a self-centered and ultimately self-destructive man to rise to the pinnacle of power in America (Owen 2000; Sabato et al. 2000).

In addition, researchers at Harvard University's Vanishing Voter Project found a correlation between media coverage of the 2000 campaign and public interest in the contest. "The Vanishing Voter Project (VVP) discovered that public interest in and discussion of the campaign peaked when press coverage was high and diminished when it was low. Key campaign events, such as heated primary contests, conventions, and debates, can drive up civic engagement" (Owen 2002, 130). These results can be coupled with the work of a number of other researchers who suggest that recent trends in media coverage have exacerbated public cynicism (Jamieson 2000; Putnam 2000). Veteran

Washington Post political writer David Broder, who often spends a great deal of time interviewing ordinary citizens as he prepares his reports, likewise has long argued that media (and candidate) cynicism leads voters to turn away from civic involvement. And so he has urged journalists to become more "partisan . . . on behalf of the process" (Broder 1990).

These results suggest that more network television coverage of campaigns would not hurt, and might even help, overall voter turnout, one of the most important ways that America falls short of its ideals of a highly participatory democratic society. Low turnout is also a major way in which America lags far behind other Western democracies. But the trend is improving. Voter turnout in 2008—61.7 percent—was the highest since 1968, before eighteen-year-olds were given the right to vote (Abramson et al. 2010). Even so, the figure falls short of the turnout in Britain and Israel (over 70 percent), and in Denmark, Germany, and South Africa (over 80 percent) (Lowi et al. 2002, 425).

Conclusion

Over the past several chapters, we have demonstrated that television news does a poor job of telling the electorate what they need to know in order to effectively evaluate candidates for president. The amount of coverage has fallen since 1988, including the primaries, the general election, and even the primary "preseason," although the 2008 election proved an exception to this trend. This was due at least partly to the historic nature of Barack Obama's successful quest to become America's first African American president. The smaller amount of coverage that remains is focused on handicapping the horse race rather than considering matters of substance. Even in those instances when issues are discussed, they are often viewed in terms of their political impact. In Patterson's words, the politics-as-"game" frame dominates, leaving viewers with a sense of politicians as scoundrels.

Candidates get little opportunity to speak for themselves, as the average length of a sound bite has fallen to less than ten seconds in some election cycles. Anchors and reporters hog the reduced airtime that remains, even though they aren't running for anything, and they spend a lot of that time talking about themselves. In addition, reporters and producers air far more negative than positive assessments about most candidates, and reporters and anchors have a very unsatisfying record on that cardinal journalistic just getting the facts right and being fair to the candidates.

In 1964, media theorist Marshall McLuhan argued that "the medium is the message." But the evidence shows that in presidential campaigns the message matters a great deal to candidates and voters. So what messages does television news offer us? The short sound bites and reduced amount of election news coverage tell us that presidential candidates aren't worth listening to for long, and that presidential campaigns don't deserve much of our attention. The horse-race–dominated coverage tells us that issues don't really matter much either.

The embarrassing way the networks made mistake after mistake on election night in 2000, and the highly one-sided coverage of the two party nominees in 2004 and 2008, raise questions about how seriously they really take their central mission of being responsible, fair, and accurate transmitters of critically important information. The heavily mediated and negative coverage of the 2000 campaign told us that neither the Democratic liar nor the Republican lightweight deserved to be president. And the lack of coverage entirely of third-party candidates like Ralph Nader and Pat Buchanan tells us they don't even exist. (Ironically, the votes for both of these candidates turned out to be decisive in Florida in 2000. Gore would have won Florida with a fraction of either Nader's 97,000 votes in the state or less than one-quarter of the 3,400 apparently mistaken votes recorded for Buchanan in Palm Beach County.)

This multicount indictment of campaign news—which, as the 2008 PEJ study showed, applies to much of the mainstream media—is particularly troubling in light of the central role that the news media play in linking citizens to candidates. Since few of us ever meet presidential candidates in person, our views of Obama, Hillary Clinton, McCain, George W. Bush, Kerry, Gore, Bill Clinton, George H. W. Bush, and the rest develop largely from what we learn about them from the mass media. With the information provided by many news outlets, we are not in a position to learn much beyond intimations that candidates are not nearly as important as reporters, that the candidates' positions and records don't matter much, and that one or both of the major-party candidates don't deserve our vote. Of course, the networks' many inaccuracies during coverage on the election night in 2000 might also send an unintended message that the news industry doesn't deserve our confidence any more than the candidates do.

Although the media's performance leaves much to be desired, it is by no means impossible to do better, either in print or the electronic media. We examine alternative media approaches in chapter 5, which relies largely on case studies to compare campaign news coverage of network television with that of the many other alternatives that exist in today's multimedia environment. We also compare network news coverage to the campaign discourse of the candidates themselves and to the content of late-night comedy programming as well.

Note

1. Hofstetter (1976) found negative but balanced network news coverage in the 1972 race between Nixon and McGovern. Unfortunately his coding system conflated what we have termed the viability and desirability dimensions of evaluative content. Robinson and Sheehan cite this problem as a major drawback of this study, which "relied almost totally on references to success or failure as a measure of good press or bad" (1983, 311). This convinced them to separate the two dimensions in their analysis of the 1980 campaign.

5

"Nobody Does It Better"? Comparing Key Campaign News Sources

A FTER EVERY PRESIDENTIAL ELECTION, reporters promise to do better next time. They vow to offer more-substantive coverage less devoted to the horse race, coverage that will educate the public about what the candidates would do if elected. Journalists vow to provide more detailed coverage on what the candidates stand for and give them more of a chance to make their cases to the country in their own words. So they say, every four years.

Unfortunately, when these promises are put to the test of systematic analysis, we find that they have been broken just as regularly as they were made. By most measures, evening news coverage of the 2008 campaign was at best no better, and sometimes worse, than the coverage of the 2004, 2000, 1996, 1992, and 1988 campaigns

We are far from the first researchers to find fault with the news media's election coverage. But our empirical analysis is based on one of the deepest and most wide-ranging quantitative critiques ever applied to campaign news. By basing our analysis on each individual sound bite rather than entire stories, and by examining every story during an election season rather than looking only at samples, we can determine in a far more extensive and precise way just how poor a job reporters have done in campaign coverage in recent elections. Our comparisons, using the same measures across several elections, allow us to plot a clear trajectory of network television's coverage of presidential campaigns since the 1988 contest.

Most of the resulting trends are not encouraging for either television's potential or its past performance. The television networks do such a poor job on these important issues that even the self-interested candidates often offer more information about their policies, and sometimes provide that information with a less-negative orientation, than do the reporters' accounts of those same campaigns. The PEJ analysis of other campaign news outlets shows that cable television, online news, and newspapers did not do much better in 2008 on some of these key measures of media content. As this chapter demonstrates, we have come to a point in American journalism where the campaign speeches and candidate advertisements—so widely disparaged as the self-interested pleadings of the desperately ambitious—can be compared favorably to news media accounts.

To the extent that we have a national discussion about the future of the country during a presidential election season, it occurs largely through campaign news reports. The worse the performance of the mass media in covering the election, the worse stands our polity. Voters with better information can make more meaningful choices among the candidates and their issues. As it is now, much of the media offers little more than warped portraits of horse-race coverage framed by cynical media carping regarding candidates' hidden motivations.

While the mass media are vital links between citizens and presidential candidates, they are not the only politician-citizen links involving the news media. In this chapter, we use focused case studies to ask whether any other source of news or information does the job better.

In the following, we compare several news outlets in a more focused way than we have in earlier chapters. In addition to network news, we examine the reports of other major sources of news and information, including the Fox News's *Special Report with Brit Hume*; *NewsHour* on PBS; leading newspapers like the *New York Times*, the *Washington Post*, and the *Wall Street Journal*; CNN's *PrimeNews*; and even late-night comedy. Particularly during the 2008 election cycle, candidates sought out opportunities to sit opposite Jon Stewart, Stephen Colbert, and other late-night hosts, making that programming more important to campaign discourse than ever before. For one previous election campaign, we even analyzed the messages disseminated by the campaigns themselves. By examining different media sources in different election years, we can make broader comparisons than would have been possible if we had looked at a smaller number of news providers in every election or a larger number in only one election.

The Networks versus Fox News in Campaign 2008

During the 2008 general election campaign, we compared the network television newscasts with the main evening news program on the Fox News

Channel, an upstart cable news outlet that has seen a substantial rise in its audience in the past several years. We picked *Special Report with Brit Hume* because it is Fox's closest equivalent to the networks' evening newscasts. The program is broadcast live in the early evening (6 p.m. to 7 p.m. eastern time), heavily oriented toward political news, and in 2008 was anchored by Brit Hume, ABC's former chief White House correspondent. Like the network newscasts, the first half hour of *Special Report* consists mainly of taped news stories, interspersed with anchor leadins and discussions with correspondents. But the second half hour shifts to a debate format as regular and guest panelists discuss and debate the day's issues.

We analyzed the tone of all campaign news that appeared during the first half hour of *Special Report*. This is the key issue raised by many of Fox's critics, who sometimes view the conservative-oriented channel as "GOP TV." We compare the tone of Fox's coverage to that of the Big Three broadcast networks, in terms of the overall treatment of Obama and McCain as well as their positions on several key issues.

As we discussed in chapter 4, McCain's decision to name Palin to the GOP ticket did not help his campaign overall on network television news, since the tone of her coverage was almost exactly the same as McCain's. But when you examine the three broadcast networks separately, and compare them to Fox News, a very different picture of Palin's impact emerges.

As shown in table 5.1, the coverage Palin received differed greatly by media outlet, a sharp contrast to television's relatively consistent treatment of McCain. The GOP presidential candidate's coverage ranged between 31 percent and 36 percent positive on the evening newscasts of ABC, CBS, and NBC; on Fox McCain's coverage was not much better, at 40 percent positive. Palin was not treated all that much better than McCain on Fox—her coverage there was 43 percent positive, not significant enough a difference to have been detected by ordinary viewers.

But on ABC Palin mattered a great deal to how the ticket was represented. Of the four news programs examined here, ABC's evening newscast was by far the most positive in its treatment of Palin, with an Obama-like 68 percent positive tone of coverage. Palin's coverage on that network was nearly twice as positive as that of McCain, whose coverage was 36 percent positive. By contrast, coverage of Palin on CBS was 31 percent positive, roughly equivalent to McCain's 33 percent. On NBC Palin's coverage was even more critical—only 16 percent positive, while reports on McCain were 31 percent positive.

Clearly, Palin's debut on the national stage was not nearly as favorable as her supporters might have hoped. In the weeks after being named the GOP vice presidential nominee, Palin endured two painful and extensively aired one-on-one interviews with anchors Charles Gibson on ABC and Katie Couric on

Table 5.1
Fox News versus the Broadcast Networks: Tone of Coverage, 2008

Percent positive press on evening newscasts

	Republican ticket	McCain	Palin	Democratic ticket	Obama	Biden
Networks*	34%	33%	34%	66%	68%	50%
(N)	(284)	(173)	(111)	(223)	(197)	(26)
Fox News	41%	40%	43%	32%	37%	11%
(N)	(178)	(101)	(77)	(148)	(121)	(27)
ABC	46%	36%	68%	68%	68%	—
CBS	32%	33%	31%	69%	68%	—
NBC	22%	31%	16%	58%	73%	—

Note: The 2008 general election campaign period used here includes both party conventions and runs from August 23 through the day before election day. N refers to number of evaluations of the candidate by sources not identified by partisan loyalty in the newscasts.
* Network figures are for individual evaluations on ABC, CBS, and NBC evening newscasts.
A dash (—) indicates insufficient number of evaluations for analysis (ten or fewer).
Source: Center for Media and Public Affairs

CBS. Those two interviews offered an unflattering view of the vice presidential nominee; she stumbled over a question about which news media she read or watched and defended her foreign policy credentials with an observation of Alaska's geographic proximity to Russia, raising doubts among many voters as to whether or not she was sufficiently experienced or possessed the right temperament to be a replacement president should something happen to the GOP's elderly nominee (cf., Cohen and Agiesta 2008). In particular, the Katie Couric interview (which got heavy play on YouTube) echoed Howard Dean's troubling and politically devastating post-Iowa scream four years earlier.

There was a clear difference between Fox's treatment of the Democratic candidate Barack Obama and network television's. Fox coverage of Obama was 37 percent positive, while the *least*-positive broadcast networks overall—a tie between ABC and CBS—was 68 percent positive in its treatment of Obama. NBC, which gave McCain and Palin their most negative ratings of these four media outlets, was the most pro-Obama network, with coverage that was 73 percent positive.

Since these tonal measures exclude horse-race reports, the enthusiastic coverage for the Democrats and the negative numbers for the GOP are not a direct reflection of their respective standings in the polls. Rather these tone measures capture the comments that network correspondents and the sources they quoted offered regarding the candidates, their backgrounds, and their policies.

If campaign news coverage is supposed to be relatively evenhanded, then the frequently maligned Fox network's evening news program was the only one of these four outlets that passed the test. A three percentage point tonal difference between the two presidential candidates on *Special Report* is markedly more balanced than gaps of 32, 35, and 42 percentage points on ABC, CBS, and NBC, respectively. (This comparison, it should be noted, does not include the cable channel's talk programs, such as the highly partisan shows hosted by Bill O'Reilly and Glenn Beck. Nor does it include *Special Report*'s roundtable discussion, which takes place during the second half hour of that program.)

The Networks versus Fox News in the 2004 Campaign

We also selected Fox News for close comparison with network news during the 2004 general election campaign. The results that year cast a less favorable light on Fox than did its 2008 coverage, as seen in table 5.2.

As shown in the first row of figures in table 5.2, Fox was even more one-sided than the broadcast networks in its reporting on the 2004 presidential election. The difference was that Fox was tilted in the opposite direction. On Fox, Bush received campaign news coverage that was 53 percent positive

Table 5.2
Fox News versus the Broadcast Networks: Tone of Issue Coverage, 2004

Percent positive press on evening newscasts

| | Broadcast networks | | Fox News | |
	Kerry	Bush	Kerry	Bush
Overall	59	37	21	53
Total foreign policy	27	25	10	61
Terrorism	9	65	21	88
Iraq	21	11	5	54
Total domestic policy	50	24	33	43
Economy	56	11	40	40
Health care	64	27	33	43
Leadership qualities	68	47	34	63

Evening news election campaign comments by nonpartisan sources and reporters from September 7, 2004, through November 1, 2004.

versus Kerry's mere 21 percent positive coverage. That thirty-two-percentage point margin favoring Bush was even greater than the overall twenty-two-percentage-point gap on the three broadcast networks.

Readers of table 5.2 may wonder if the broadcast networks and Fox News were looking at the same election. While the networks' coverage of foreign-policy matters was relatively evenhanded (Kerry's coverage was only two percentage points more positive than Bush's), on Fox News Bush had a more than a six-to-one advantage in the tone of campaign foreign policy coverage. With respect to the subset of reports on Iraq, Bush had a ten-to-one positive coverage advantage on Fox. While Kerry had an advantage in terms of positive coverage regarding Iraq on network news, the gap was much narrower—21 percent positive versus 11 percent positive for Bush.

Both the networks and Fox were more positive toward Bush on terrorism. Fox News gave Bush his most positive treatment in that issue area, with 88 percent positive coverage, versus 21 percent positive coverage for Kerry. But the network coverage also favored Bush on terrorism, with 65 percent positive evaluations, versus 9 percent positive for Kerry. In fact, the margin of Bush's coverage advantage was greater on the broadcast networks (where the margin was seven to one) than on Fox (where it was four to one).

Domestic policy, thought by many to be Kerry's stronger suit, was the source of far more positive coverage for the Massachusetts Democrat. On the broadcast networks, Kerry's domestic policy coverage was 50 percent positive in tone, compared to 24 percent positive for Bush. On Fox, by contrast, Bush fared better than Kerry by 43 positive to 33 percent positive assessments on domestic policy matters. Fox's coverage on Kerry's domestic policy proposals, though, was three times more positive than its coverage of Kerry's foreign policy positions. On the economy, Kerry had a huge coverage advantage over Bush on network television (56 percent positive versus 11 percent), while the two candidates had equally negative economic coverage on Fox (each received only 40 percent positive evaluations).

As was the case in 2000, the first debate of 2004 marked an important transition point in the campaign news coverage. While Gore's coverage soured after his first sigh-filled debate, Kerry's soared in the wake of his unexpectedly crisp answers. In fact, Kerry's fortunes improved considerably following that debate on all four networks examined here. On the broadcast networks, Bush received coverage that was 36 percent positive in tone during September—that is, before the first debate—compared to coverage that was 27 percent positive in tone for Kerry. Bush also beat Kerry on Fox that month by a much greater margin, 58 percent to 9 percent (Kerry was also struggling to deal with questions raised by the Swift Boat Veterans for Truth during September.) During October, after the first debate, the tone of Kerry's coverage rebounded to an unprecedented 73 percent positive on the Big Three networks, versus 38 percent positive for Bush.

Thus, Kerry's overall coverage on the networks was almost twice as positive as Bush's during the final month of the campaign. Even on the Fox News Channel, Kerry's coverage rose to 30 percent positive in tone during October. But that was still more negative than the 50 percent positive evaluations Bush received on Fox News that month.

The Networks versus the *NewsHour* in Campaign 2000

For the 2000 campaign, we applied the CMPA method of content analysis to the *NewsHour*, the nightly evening newscast of the Public Broadcasting Service. Because public television does not have the commercial breaks throughout the broadcast found on the Big Three networks, the news hole (i.e., actual airtime apart from commercials and promotions) of the *NewsHour* is slightly less than that of the three commercial network evening news shows combined.

Despite the somewhat smaller news hole, PBS devoted 31 percent more airtime to election news during the 2000 campaign than did ABC, CBS, and NBC combined—sixteen and a half minutes versus twelve and a half minutes per night. Moreover, the PBS coverage included far more substantive discussion, with a substance rating of 67 percent for *NewsHour* stories to 40 percent for the networks. Horse-race coverage was far less concentrated on PBS, appearing in only 32 percent of all *NewsHour* stories versus 71 percent for the networks. The tone of PBS coverage was as balanced as that of the networks but far more positive overall—59 percent positive for Bush and 60 percent positive for Gore, for a combined 59 percent positive, compared to only 39 percent positive combined candidate evaluations on the networks.

Most striking of all the findings in table 5.3 was the difference in mediation. The *NewsHour* reversed commercial television's journalist-centered presentation style. Only 24 percent of airtime on PBS went to journalists, one-third the level of reporter discourse at the networks. Candidates accounted for 21 percent of the coverage, and other sources provided the remaining 55 percent. Total speaking time for the candidates on the *NewsHour* more than doubled the combined total of the three commercial networks (three hours and eleven minutes versus one hour and thirty-eight minutes).[1]

Other measures of mediation also showed that viewers can learn more of the candidates' perspectives directly on PBS. The average candidate sound bite on the *NewsHour* was fifty-two seconds, nearly seven times the average length allowed on the network newscasts, and about twice the length

Table 5.3
PBS versus the Networks, 2000

	PBS	Networks
Amount of coverage		
Minutes per day	16.5	12.5
Candidate airtime (minutes)	191	98
Average sound bite (seconds)	52	7.8
Locus (percentage)		
Journalists	24	74
Candidates	21	12
Other	55	14
Focus (percentage)		
Horse race	32	71
Substantive	67	40
Tone (percentage positive)		
Bush	59	37
Gore	60	40
Combined	59	39

News media based on 639 campaign news stories on ABC, CBS, NBC, and PBS between September 4 and November 6, 2000. A news story may have discussed substantive topics or the horse race, both topics, or neither topic. Thus percentages do not sum to 100 percent.

of an average commercial advertisement on network television. PBS's more candidate-centered and issue-oriented focus reflects a format in which an initial taped "package" allowed the candidates to speak at length on a campaign issue, followed by an in-studio live discussion among their surrogates or independent experts.

These findings are consistent with those found by most other researchers. Political scientist Marjorie Hershey is among those who are bothered by the consequences for democracy of inadequate network news coverage of issues.

> The emphasis on game and personality frames serves to construct a comforting illusion, just as entertainment programs usually do. In this case, the illusion is that an American presidential election in the twenty-first century—which has the potential to determine matters ranging from the composition of the Supreme Court to the state of our nuclear arsenal—*can be* about nothing more weighty than whether the gregarious chairman of the Inter-Fraternity Council will beat the earnest leader of the Science Club. (Hershey 2001, 70, emphasis in original)

In essence, the *NewsHour* gave voters reasons why they should support one or the other candidate, while the commercial networks gave them reasons to oppose both. Thus, public broadcasting offers a model of election news that is more thorough, more substantive, and more positive in tone than its commercial network counterparts. This is not to say that the Big Three could successfully emulate PBS, whose evening newscast is seen by a far smaller and more elite audience. Indeed, the notion that PBS coverage is relatively substantive and positive in tone might be regarded as a truism. (This conclusion, it should be noted, runs counter to a recent "revisionist" portrayal of PBS election news that depicted the commercial and public television newscasts as fundamentally similar in style, substance, and quality.[2])

Horse Race versus Substance, 1996–2008

For the 1988, 1992, and 1996 elections, we also broadened the comparisons to include a variety of additional outlets, depending on the year. During the 1996 general election, the year of the most extensive CMPA content analysis of campaign news content, we examined 2,360 news and editorial items from a wide range of television and print news outlets, including local as well as national news. To measure local news coverage, we examined campaign news from a sample of fifteen local newspapers, representing cities of varying sizes and from different geographic regions. During each fifteen-day period, a different newspaper was randomly selected for analysis.

Past research involving local news coverage has found some similarities between network and local news coverage, and some differences (cf. Farnsworth and Lichter 2004, 2005a). This sampling procedure, designed by political scientists Ann Crigler and Marion Just, yielded the equivalent of a single "composite" local newspaper without any consistent regional or local bias. The local newspaper composite included the *Las Vegas Review Journal, Dallas Morning News, Fargo Forum, Salem Statesman-Journal, Oakland Tribune, Manchester Union-Leader, Winston–Salem Journal, Chicago Tribune, Boston Globe, Tucson Citizen, Flint Journal, Shreveport Times, Harrisburg Patriot-News, Miami Herald,* and *Los Angeles Times.* A comparison of the various broadcast and print sources, including PBS, the networks, *New York Times,* and *Wall Street Journal,* as well as the candidates' own campaign discourse for 1996, is found in table 5.4.

Turning first to the 1996 results, the year of our most extensive comparisons, note that the three broadcast networks stand far above all the other media outlets in their focus on horse race and near the bottom in the amount of news content devoted to more substantive matters. ABC, CBS, and NBC ranged from 45 percent to 51 percent horse-race coverage in the 1996 election, a contest in which President Bill Clinton cruised to such an easy victory

Table 5.4
Substance versus Horse Race in General Elections, 1996–2008

Comparing Various Forms of Campaign Media

	*Percentage substance**	*Percentage horse race**	*Number of cases*
2008EP			
NBC *Nightly News*	42%	30%	231 stories
ABC *World News Tonight*	40%	37%	190 stories
CBS *Evening News*	35%	26%	261 stories
Fox *Special Report*	26%	24%	524 stories
2004			
CBS *Evening News*	52%	40%	136 stories
ABC *World News Tonight*	51%	49%	175 stories
NBC *Nightly News*	46%	52%	193 stories
2000			
PBS *NewsHour*	68%	30%	171 stories
ABC *World News Tonight*	42%	71%	180 stories
CBS *Evening News*	42%	69%	137 stories
NBC *Nightly News*	36%	72%	145 stories
1996			
Free candidate airtime	100%	0%	54 speeches
Campaign speeches	99%	4%	142 speeches
Campaign advertising	87%	1%	130 ads
Candidate debates	85%	0%	50 exchanges
Television interviews	70%	43%	42 segments
PBS *NewsHour*	68%	20%	256 stories
Internet websites	63%	6%	1,171 files
New York Times	51%	37%	821 stories
CBS *Evening News*	49%	47%	159 stories
Local newspapers	47%	32%	440 stories
Wall Street Journal	43%	32%	360 stories
NBC *Nightly News*	39%	45%	155 stories
ABC *World News Tonight*	27%	51%	169 stories

2008 data based on 1,206 campaign news stories from ABC, CBS, NBC, and Fox News between August 23, 2008, and November 3, 2008; 2004 data based on 504 campaign news stories from ABC, CBS, and NBC between September 7, 2004, and November 1, 2004; 2000 news media based on 639 campaign news stories from ABC, CBS, NBC, and PBS between September 4, 2000, and November 6, 2000; 1996 news media based on 2,360 campaign news stories and editorials from the *New York Times*, *Wall Street Journal*, a local newspaper sample compiled from fifteen local newspapers, ABC, CBS, NBC, and PBS between September 2, 1996, and November 5, 1996.

* Percent of cases. A news story, speech, commercial, etc., may have discussed both substantive topics and the horse race, or other topics. Thus, percentages do not sum to 100 percent

over Republican nominee Bob Dole that there was very little horse race to report. The newspapers examined here focused far less on the horse-race aspects of the campaign. The *New York Times* led, with 37 percent emphasis on horse-race matters, followed by the *Wall Street Journal* and the local newspaper sample with 32 percent each. Once again, there were dramatic differences in 1996 between the networks and PBS. The *NewsHour* carried the lowest proportion of horse-race news among mainstream news outlets, only 20 percent of its election coverage, compared to 48 percent for the Big Three.

A heavy diet of horse-race coverage not only crowds out more substantive coverage but can also give voters the impression that the outcome is preordained, so their own ballot doesn't matter. This isn't a question of accuracy. Most horse-race assessments these days are based on scientific polls, which make them much more objective than many other matters raised by journalists in news accounts. Candidates are far less able to question poll results than other areas of media mistreatment, even though reporters do not always understand the limitations of survey research. It is the consequences for democracy that are worthy of concern. Heavy horse-race coverage, particularly in a one-sided campaign year like 1996, can hardly help voter turnout. Nor does an emphasis on the sports aspects of politics encourage citizens to learn more about the candidates, their issue positions, or their personal characters.

In 1996, the media's horse-race conclusions were not controversial; even Dole's own supporters expected him to lose. A September 1996 Pew Research Center poll found that only 12 percent of voters believed Dole would be elected, even though 35 percent said they intended to vote for him (Pew 1996). "The question is not whether these are reasonable judgments, but whether the margin [between Clinton and Dole] has become the message. A constant media drumbeat that the election is all but over could drown out Dole's attempts to dramatize the differences between himself and President Clinton" (Kurtz 1996a).

Since the New Hampshire primary is a pivotal point in the nomination process, we also looked at the horse-race orientation of leading sources of news in that state during the 1996 primary season (cf. Farnsworth and Lichter 2002). We examined 1,103 stories and editorials in three leading New Hampshire media sources from January 20 to February 20, 1996 (the month before the primary). WMUR, the dominant New Hampshire television station, turned out to be much like the national television news, with 60 percent horse-race coverage. During this period, 56 percent of network news campaign coverage was devoted to horse-race matters, roughly the same percentage as that for the networks during the entire primary season. In contrast, the state's two dominant newspapers, the *Concord Monitor* (37 percent horse race) and the

Union-Leader of Manchester (32 percent) were the least horse-race oriented of any of the media outlets studied during the primaries.

The drawbacks of horse-race news are more significant in light of the reduction in overall coverage on the network evening news programs in recent years. When compared to the 1992 general election, the Big Three television networks each cut their coverage by more than 40 percent during the 1996 general election. Further, the nineteen hours and thirty-nine minutes of general election news on the *NewsHour* was 47 percent more than the thirteen hours and eight minutes aired by the three commercial networks *combined.*

This pattern of horse-race-oriented coverage was repeated in the elections that followed. With the exception of PBS's *Newshour* in 2000, throughout the three most recent presidential elections, the bulk of campaign coverage focused on the sports of politics—who was ahead and who was behind—with more substantive coverage in the best of times in the range of 50 percent of the news coverage. In 2008, the percentage of horse-race coverage generally was lower than four years earlier, but there also tended to be less discussion of substantive issues. And as we have seen in earlier studies from the Project for Excellence in Journalism, an obsessive focus on horse-race news is a common problem for a variety of media outlets, including cable channels, online discourse, and newspapers.

Is this just a media malady, or did the candidates also give short shrift to substance, campaigning in bland generalities or attacking opponents' records without offering detailed policy alternatives? To find out, we examined the candidates' campaign discourse, including campaign speeches, advertising, comments in candidate debates, and the campaigns' web sites. We evaluated these forms of campaign communication in 1996 with the same content analysis methodology that we applied to the news reports. In table 5.4 (above), the differences between campaign-generated election discourse and news media-generated election discourse stand out in sharp relief.

The distinctions among the messages the candidates themselves offer and the mediated messages offered by journalists could not be clearer. The more control the candidates have, the more substantive the discourse; the less control candidates have over the campaign message, the greater the devotion to the horse race. The candidate-controlled venues, including the free candidate airtime messages, campaign speeches, and campaign advertising, take the top three positions in the substance sweepstakes. All three offer at least 87 percent substance, and all three provide at most 4 percent coverage of the horse race. Another candidate-controlled venue, the campaigns' web sites, finished seventh, behind only the *NewsHour.* Other venues in which candidates have at least a share of the control over content—the candidate debates and the television interviews—rank fourth and fifth in the percentage of substance. The interviews, which are the most subject to media influence over content among the top five categories, had the greatest amount of horse-race coverage.

At the bottom of the rankings is ABC *World News Tonight*, which had less than one-third the percentage of substance found in the free candidate airtime statements and the campaign speeches. Both ABC and the NBC *Nightly News* had less than half the substance found in the top four candidate-controlled campaign discourse categories. CBS, the best of the Big Three, nevertheless finished fifth from the bottom, beating out the *Wall Street Journal*, the composite local newspaper, and its two sister broadcast networks. But even the best television network by this measure finished far back in the comparison of substantive content. (The relatively high performance of CBS was the result of the network's decision to include free-airtime statements during their evening newscasts in 1996. NBC aired them at other times in the evening, and ABC did not air them at all.)

This chasm between the campaign presented by the candidates and the campaign filtered through the media brings back into focus the questions we raised earlier about media fairness and objectivity. When audiences watch television news, they don't receive a fair and accurate representation of the election campaigns as they actually take place on the campaign trail and in the materials distributed by the campaigns. When the politicians talk, the discourse is almost entirely about matters of substance; when the reporters report, it is often about the horse race. While the prestige press is not the main focus of our inquiry, the results here suggest that major newspapers do better than the broadcast network newscasts on these matters. But that is a cold comfort, since our 1996 results demonstrate quite clearly that even the leading newspapers skew candidate discourse in a negative direction. (And for the print press to be declared superior to TV news is not much of a compliment.)

The comparisons found in table 5.4 for 1996 (above) open a window onto possible alternatives to improved campaign discourse. Any solution must involve less mediation and more candidate-controlled discourse. If those free-airtime remarks—sometimes in the form of two-and-a-half-minute speeches by Clinton and Dole, sometimes in the form of sixty-second remarks—are on network television where they can be seen widely, so much the better. The free candidate remarks in 1996 were carried by CBS, NBC, PBS, CNN, C-SPAN, some Paramount-owned stations, and National Public Radio. CBS put the speeches on the *Evening News* broadcasts, NBC used the news magazine *Dateline*, and CNN used its *Inside Politics* program (Lichter and Noyes 1998). Each of the fifty-four free-airtime speeches, according to the CMPA content analysis, focused primarily on issues, with taxes (fifteen speeches), children's issues (twelve), and education policy (eleven) the most common topics.

The following economic policy exchange, aired on Fox News on October 6, 1996, demonstrates how substantive the candidates can be, even in brief remarks that are unmediated and considerably longer than the average network news sound bite, now under nine seconds.

> CLINTON: Our strategy is to raise incomes by growing the economy, creating more high-wage jobs, giving people the education they need to hold those jobs. It's working—wages are rising for the first time in a decade; we have the lowest unemployment in seven and a half years; ten-and-a-half-million new jobs; a 60 percent cut in the deficit; lowering interest rates on car loans, home mortgages, business loans; a minimum wage increase for ten million families. Now we have to help more people get ahead by balancing the budget without undermining Medicare, Medicaid, education, and the environment. We need targeted tax cuts for child rearing, home ownership, health care, and especially for college costs because education is the key to higher-paying jobs.
>
> Our opponents have a risky $550 billion tax scheme that independent experts say would balloon the deficit, slow the economy, raise taxes on nine million families. My plan will keep our economy growing, building our bridge to the twenty-first century.
>
> DOLE: My economic plan will help millions of Americans who are working harder to make ends meet. We will provide the average American family with a $1,600 tax cut. That's $1,600 to save, spend, or invest as they see fit. We'll also cut the capital gains tax in half, which will increase jobs and opportunities. And I will expand Individual Retirement Accounts to increase savings and investments.
>
> My tax-relief plan is based on a simple theory: it is your money, not the government's, and you should be able to keep more of it. That's a principle President Clinton simply doesn't understand. The average American family is now spending nearly 40 percent of its income on taxes, thanks to the president's tax increase, the largest tax increase in history. I would also put America on a path to a balanced budget, which, with low interest rates, would put more money in the pockets of Americans who borrow money to buy a home, a car, or send a child to college. The president's vetoed two balanced budgets, and he did everything in his power to defeat a balanced-budget amendment to the Constitution.
>
> (quoted in Lichter and Noyes 1998, 96–99)

In these brief remarks, each candidate describes in some detail his economic plan. As would any incumbent presiding over good economic times, Clinton stresses the improvements that occurred during his term, and he offers a clear set of economic policy goals for a second term. He does take a swipe at what he described as "a risky $550 billion tax scheme," but on balance Clinton's remarks are far more focused on what he has done and would do in the economic arena than on negative attacks. Dole, like many Republicans, makes a clear appeal to voters' pocketbooks. His tax-cut plan is front and center, and he takes a swipe at Clinton, whom he intimates is mainly interested in raising taxes.

In both cases, the negative remarks are part of the candidates' efforts to illuminate what they consider to be the substantive differences between their approaches. Attacks on opponents are in the background, not the foreground. Further, the discussion of horse race that is so dominant on the evening newscasts is not in evidence here. The thoughtful, issue-oriented discussion offered by these competing statements is simply not supported on network newscasts, with their constant references to campaign strategy and horse-race calculations, and with the candidates able to speak in their own words for only eight seconds at a time. Paid candidate advertisements, as well as the major-party-candidate debates, offer additional venues for citizens to learn about candidate policy preferences and plans, and the evidence suggests that citizens do learn more about candidates' positions in less-mediated formats such as debates (Drew and Weaver 1991). One of the most interesting new developments in the 1996 election was the increasing use of the Internet by campaigns as a source of political communication (Owen 1997). At that time the numbers of citizens using the Internet remained quite small—78 percent of those surveyed by the Pew Research Center that year said they never went online for news or information about the election, and another 10 percent said they went online no more than once a week (Farnsworth and Owen 2004).

But these numbers did not stop candidates, campaigns, news organizations, and other interested parties from developing extensive campaign web sites. On his site, Dole provided lengthy position papers of at least several pages on twenty-five different issues, while Clinton's site contained thirty-five major issue discussions, and Perot's site presented his point of view on fourteen major issues. These lengthy position papers provided far more detail than would be provided in a debate response or a thirty-second commercial, and of course far more than could be expressed in a television sound bite.

As was the case in other candidate-controlled venues, the bulk of the material presented on web sites (71 percent) was devoted to promotion of the host candidate rather than criticism of other candidates. In sum, in many ways, candidate-controlled communication is an entirely different campaign from that seen by television viewers, and one that may be more appealing to citizens than the negative, horse-race-obsessed, scandal-driven politics of recent presidential elections as presented by network television news.

Campaign Tone, 1996–2008

Perhaps even more controversial than the focus of campaign news is its tone. In earlier chapters, we found that network news coverage was often negative toward both major-party presidential candidates. In some years the network news coverage was about roughly equally harsh during the general election period (1988 and 2000), and in some years the networks were more negative in tone with respect to the Republican presidential nominee (1992, 1996, 2004, and 2008). How do the candidates, and other media outlets, stack up against the networks in this respect? Table 5.5 compares the tone of network and other news media coverage with the tone of candidate-controlled discourse venues, including free candidate airtime, campaign speeches, and campaign websites.

Once again, the candidate-dominated-discourse venues scored well, demonstrating high percentages of positive discourse. The news media outlets dominated the bottom of the table, indicating a far more negative tone to their coverage. When candidates control the campaign discourse environment, as they do with respect to free candidate airtime, campaign speeches, and campaign web sites, the result is an overwhelmingly positive discourse (cf., Alliance for Better Campaigns 1999, 2001). These top three venues in 1996 were all more than two-thirds positive. A fourth venue that involves some candidate control, the campaign debates, was also about two-thirds positive. Another venue in which the candidates have some control, the television interview programs, were 62 percent positive, and campaign advertising was 60 percent positive in tone.

The mainstream media sources were again found at the bottom of the table, mired in the depths of negativity. The *Wall Street Journal* was the most negative outlet of all, at only 34 percent positive coverage, below ABC *World News Tonight* and the NBC *Nightly News*, with 39 percent and 41 percent positive coverage, respectively. The *NewsHour* on PBS again finished at the top of the media outlets, with 60 percent positive tone, followed by the CBS *Evening News* at 46 percent positive. Between CBS and the other networks came the *New York Times* and the composite local newspapers sample, both with 43 percent positive coverage.

These findings deepen our concerns regarding the fairness and accuracy of network news coverage. The 1996 findings suggest a campaign that was though relatively positive in tone, but was skewed toward its most negative snippets when mediated by the country's leading news outlets. Since few voters attend campaign rallies or watch C-SPAN regularly, the electorate relies primarily on the news media to present the facts. If the news media suggest that the campaigns are more negative and the candidates more critical of each other than they actually are, then the news media are doing the country a considerable disservice. Many researchers (see chapter 4) suggest that citizen discontent with government is at least partially the result of media negativity, and our findings do little to allay those concerns.

Although some years offer more positive network news content than others, these overall figures may obscure the fact that most of the positive news was focused on one party's candidate. In fact, 2008 marked the second conservative

Table 5.5
Tone of General Election Discourse, 1996–2008

Comparing various forms of campaign media

	Percent positive	Percent negative	Number of cases
2008EP			
CBS *Evening News*	57%	43%	698 statements
NBC *Nightly News*	54%	46%	587 statements
ABC *World News Tonight*	51%	49%	547 statements
Fox News *Special Report*	46%	54%	1,023 statements
2004			
NBC *Nightly News*	51%	49%	277 statements
ABC *World News Tonight*	46%	54%	260 statements
CBS *Evening News*	42%	58%	393 statements
Fox News *Special Report*	40%	60%	560 statements
2000			
PBS *NewsHour*	56%	44%	171 stories
ABC *World News Tonight*	43%	57%	180 stories
CBS *Evening News*	38%	62%	137 stories
NBC *Nightly News*	39%	61%	145 stories
1996			
Free candidate airtime	80%	20%	54 speeches
Campaign speeches	78%	22%	142 speeches
Websites	71%	29%	1,171 files
Candidate debates	66%	34%	50 exchanges
Television interviews	62%	38%	42 segments
Campaign advertising	60%	40%	130 commercials
PBS *NewsHour*	60%	40%	256 stories
CBS *Evening News*	46%	54%	159 stories
New York Times	43%	57%	821 stories
Local newspapers	43%	57%	440 stories
NBC *Nightly News*	41%	59%	155 stories
ABC *World News Tonight*	39%	61%	169 stories
Wall Street Journal	34%	66%	360 stories

Note: The data here exclude all ambiguous or neutral comments and all references to the candidates' status in the campaign horse race.

The 2008 results are based on 2,855 statements from news stories about Barack Obama and John McCain from ABC, CBS, NBC, and Fox News's *Special Report with Brit Hume* between August 23, 2008, and November 3, 2008. Data include all explicitly positive and negative evaluations. The panel discussions during the second half hour of the newscast on Fox are excluded.

The 2004 results are based on 1,463 statements about George W. Bush and John Kerry from ABC, CBS, NBC, and Fox's *Special Report with Brit Hume* between September 7, 2004, and November 1, 2004. The panel discussions during the second half hour of the newscast on Fox are excluded.

The 2000 results are based on 639 campaign news stories from ABC, CBS, NBC, and PBS between September 4, 2000, and November 6, 2000. Data include all explicitly positive and negative evaluations of Al Gore, George Bush, and Ralph Nader.

The 1996 results are based on 2,360 campaign news stories and editorials from the *New York Times*, *Wall Street Journal*, a local newspaper sample compiled from fifteen local newspapers, ABC, CBS, NBC, and PBS between September 2, 1996, and November 5, 1996. Data include all explicitly positive and negative evaluations of Bill Clinton, Ross Perot, and Bob Dole.

election in which the Democratic presidential candidate received relatively favorable press, while the Republican candidate continued to receive the critical treatment that the media had typically parceled out to both sides. That one-sided treatment does not seem to us the best way to make campaign discourse less negative. (Fox News, of course, proved the exception to this pattern.)

Thus, despite the revolutionary developments in news and information delivery, the problems of less-than-evenhanded campaign coverage and generally negative treatment of politics remain. Both the CMPA and PEJ content analysis demonstrate that despite all the changes in information dissemination, the quality of the information disseminated remains more or less the same. That's not good news for voters, regardless of which party they prefer.

Talk Shows and Late-Night TV as Sources of News

The 1992 election marked the first appearance of talk shows as an alternative source of information for those frustrated with the mainstream media (Kurtz 1994; Owen 1996; Davis and Owen 1998). Independent presidential candidate Ross Perot launched his candidacy via appearances on *Larry King Live*, and throughout the election Perot and Bill Clinton tried to use these venues for making their cases to the country in a more direct way than by going through the campaign press corps. The legacy of that year for entertainment news remains with us, as the 2008 presidential candidates were in the greatest competition ever to share a laugh with Jay Leno or sit at the table with Jon Stewart or Stephen Colbert—and as a result reach their audiences (Jones 2010).

The hosts of these talk and entertainment shows—and the callers who ask questions of the candidates—are often seen by reporters as too soft on the candidates. In 1992 Michael Kinsley, then with the *New Republic*, said that the mainstream media could learn something from the issue-oriented focus of citizen and talk-show-host questions. But Kinsley nevertheless felt uneasy about having candidates campaign in this way:

> First . . . untrained amateurs are no match for skilled professionals in exposing a candidate's flaws and weaknesses. And second, that semi-journalists like [Phil] Donahue and [Larry] King, not to mention nonjournalists like Arsenio [Hall], unhealthily—or at least surrealistically—muddy the distinction between serious politics and trivial show biz. There is, no question, something eerie about the same show discussing men-who-would-be-president one day and women-who-hate-their husbands the next. (Kinsley 1992)

Conversely, Bill Clinton, a leading practitioner of talk-show campaigning in 1992, portrayed the mainstream press as the source of triviality:

I think the watchdog function is fine. But it's often carried to extremes in a search for headlines. For instance, the missing pages from my State Department file—here was a deal where *Newsweek* bit on a rumor. So you had these serious reporters who just wanted to grill me about that—when the economy is in the tubes, when one hundred thousand people a month are losing their health insurance. . . . And I'm supposed to take these people seriously as our sole intermediaries to the voters of this country? Sure, they should do their watchdog function, but anyone who lets himself be interpreted to the American people through these intermediaries alone is nuts. (quoted in Lichter and Noyes 1995, 261)

So what does the evidence say? CMPA's content analysis of thirty-four national TV talk shows in 1992 found that this format actually did a far better job of focusing on the issues than any of the journalist-centered media outlets. Based on the same criteria we used to evaluate the content of newscasts, we found that 74 percent of the segments on TV talk shows focused on substantive matters (primarily policy issues and candidate qualifications). By way of comparison, CNN's *PrimeNews* was only 53 percent substantive, PBS's *NewsHour* was 48 percent substantive, and the Big Three television networks ranged from 26 percent to 34 percent substantive. The somewhat higher rating for CNN may be the result of a $3.5 million grant from the Markle Foundation designed to improve the quality of campaign news coverage (Kerbel 1998, 132). It appears that the news media *can* be more substantive in orientation, at least if you pay them to!

The focus of discussion was also quite different on the talk shows in 1992. The top four topics of candidate discussion on the traditional news media (the three networks, CNN, the *Wall Street Journal*, the *New York Times*, and the *Washington Post*) were general candidate viability (22 percent), poll standings (14 percent), general candidate assessments (13 percent), and issue stances (13 percent). The top four topics on the television talk shows were candidate records (23 percent), campaign conduct (20 percent), issue stances (19 percent), and general candidate assessment (12 percent). Once again, the evidence shows that the less-mediated formats do a better job of focusing on issues. Even though some programs in this group are not news shows, policy issues received a more-extensive hearing on the television talk-show circuit than on the nightly newscasts.

Late-Night Programs: Candidates' New Best Friends?

Daytime talk shows are not the only unlikely places where citizens dissatisfied with network television news coverage have turned in recent years for more information about presidential candidates. A 2004 Pew Research Center survey found that 61 percent of those under thirty years of age said they sometimes learned something new about the campaign from late-night comedy programs like *The Daily Show with Jon Stewart* on Comedy Central, and *Saturday Night Live* on NBC, or from traditional late-night talk shows like *The Tonight Show with Jay Leno* on NBC and *Late Night with David Letterman* on CBS (Pew 2004a).

Most candidates badly want to appear on these programs. The audiences for the late-night programming on Comedy Central are younger than the audiences for other late-night cable fare. Since young voters may be more persuadeable than older voters accustomed to voting for a particular party—and because these younger voters are more likely to eschew traditional news sources—late-night programming has considerable appeal for candidates (Jones 2010).

Since younger voters trend Democratic by a roughly two-to-one margin (Abramson et al. 2010), Republicans want to persuade them to give the GOP a try, and Democrats want to make sure these voters show up at the polls. According to a 2007 Pew survey, 42 percent of the *Daily Show*'s audience is between eighteen and twenty-nine years of age, and another 37 percent is between thirty and fifty. For *The Colbert Report*, the numbers are almost identical: 43 percent young adult and 34 percent in their thirties and forties (Pew 2008b). For the O'Reilly *Factor*, one of the most popular programs on Fox, the comparables are 15 percent and 29 percent in those two age groups (Pew 2008b). Overall, 21 percent of the U.S. voting-age population is between eighteen and twenty-nine years of age, and 36 percent are between thirty and forty-nine years old.

Where the gaze of young voters' turns, ambitious politicians are quick to follow. On November 11, 2003, John Kerry sought to revive his sagging electoral fortunes and refashion his political persona with an appearance on *The Tonight Show with Jay Leno* (Rich 2004). He arrived atop a Harley-Davidson, sporting a leather jacket and jeans, wisecracking to Leno that the sarcastic, foulmouthed puppet "Triumph the Insult Comic Dog" might be a good choice as a running mate (Rich 2004). In August 2004, Kerry became the first major-party presidential nominee to appear on *The Daily Show*; Bush was routinely invited on-air to appear on the show but declined to do so (Johnson 2004). Without suggesting cause and effect, one might note that although Kerry lost the 2004 election, he won the under-thirty vote by a margin of 54 percent to 45 percent (Pomper 2005, 48).

Four years earlier, when neither major-party candidate was an incumbent, both nominees demonstrated the importance of this venue by appearing on the Jay Leno and David Letterman shows and engaging in some serious discussion of political issues as well as the usual banter. Researchers have started to consider these entertainment venues as important areas for at least some citizens to receive political cues away from the stuffier—and, for many, less entertaining— news programs (Jones 2001; Media Monitor 2000).

Things really exploded for late-night television during the 2008 campaign season. To put it simply, many politicians couldn't get enough of the late-night comics and their talk shows. In all, political figures made four times as many appearances during the most recent presidential election than they did during the 2004 campaign. *The Tonight Show* had the largest number of political guests during the campaign season (twenty-two), followed closely by *The Daily Show* (twenty-one).

As shown in table 5.6, Republicans were particularly aggressive in their outreach efforts during 2007 and 2008. John McCain was the unlikely king of late night, with a total of 17 appearances during the campaign season. If you add appearances by his wife and eldest daughter, the McCain family made twenty-one appearances on late-night television during that campaign cycle. In fact, so focused was McCain on the importance of these programs—and

Table 5.6
Candidate Appearances on Late Night Television, 2007–2008

From January 1, 2007, through November 3, 2008			
	Total	*2008*	*2007*
John McCain	17	13	4
Mike Huckabee	16	11	5
Barack Obama	15	11	4
Hillary Clinton	7	6	1
Joe Biden	6	1	5
Ron Paul	6	2	4
John Edwards	5	1	4
Dennis Kucinich	4	1	3
Fred Thompson	3	—	3
Christopher Dodd	3	1	2
Mike Gravel	2	—	2
Rudy Giuliani	2	—	2
Mitt Romney	2	1	1
Tommy Thompson	2	—	2
Bill Richardson	2	—	2
Sarah Palin	1	1	—
Duncan Hunter	1	—	1
Ralph Nader	1	1	—
Bob Barr	1	1	—

Source: Center for Media and Public Affairs analysis of ten late-night talk and comedy shows: *Tonight Show, Late Show with David Letterman, Late Night with Conan O'Brien, Late Late Show with Craig Ferguson, The Daily Show with Jon Stewart, The Colbert Report, Jimmy Kimmel Live, Last Call with Carson Daly, Real Time with Bill Maher,* and *Saturday Night Live.*
Dashes (—) mark the absence of a candidate on talk shows during that year.

the potential voters that they reach—that he even announced his campaign for president on the *Late Show with David Letterman*.

But the hosts are not always all that grateful. Letterman, for example, turned on McCain after the GOP nominee cancelled an appearance on Letterman's show at the last minute. McCain said he urgently needed to return to Washington to deal with the economic crisis, but Letterman showed footage of McCain getting make-up applied to his face for an interview with CBS News anchor Katie Couric that same day.

In terms of number of appearances on late-night television, McCain was first, followed closely by former Arkansas governor Mike Huckabee, who ended up losing the GOP nomination to McCain that year. The only other candidate in double digits was Barack Obama, who appeared fifteen times on late-night television during 2007 and 2008.

Next in line came Hillary Clinton, who lost the nomination to Obama after an unusually long nomination campaign but eventually became his choice for secretary of state. She ranked fourth, with seven appearances during the time she was competing for the Democratic presidential nomination. Joe Biden, the Democratic nominee for vice president, tied for fifth place in the rankings, appearing six times as a candidate on these late-night programs.

The programs also offer far more opportunity for candidates back in the pack. Congressman Ron Paul (R-Tex.) ran for president with a libertarian vision for the GOP. He wasn't very successful in drawing media attention, but he did get to appear on late-night shows six times during the 2007–2008 campaign season. Congressman Dennis Kucinich (D-Ohio), a candidate from the left wing of the Democratic Party, likewise did not draw large numbers of votes or news reports, but he made his case during four late-night comedic appearances. Consumer advocate Ralph Nader, an independent candidate for president in 2008, received almost no media attention but finished third with 0.6 percent of the vote. But he was given his say once on late-night TV. So too did former Congressman Bob Barr (R-Ga.), who finished fourth with 0.4 percent of the vote as the nominee of the Libertarian Party.

In terms of number of appearances, the numbers do not point to a clear partisan bias. While the Republicans ranked first and second, and tied for fifth, the Democrats were third and fourth and tied for fifth. Of the nineteen candidates listed in table 5.6 (above), ten were elected as Republicans (though one of them ended up running for president as a Libertarian), and eight were elected as Democrats. (The other was Ralph Nader.)

Arguably the most famous candidate appearance on late-night television during the 2008 campaign was the highly promoted and top-rated appearance of Sarah Palin on *Saturday Night Live* shortly before election day. Throughout the fall of 2008 comic Tina Fey had offered viewers a dead-on impersonation of the then–GOP vice presidential nominee, mocking her folksy manner and dubious grasp of policy matters. Palin's one late-night appearance on the show's "Weekend Update" segment suggested she could take a joke. (But what a harsh joke it turned out to be, as she sat through what one observer described as a "damning rap song" that included shooting a moose [Jones 2010, 10]).

When McCain also appeared on the show shortly before election day, he was forced to watch Fey do her Palin imitation, talk about "going rogue" and secretly try to sell "Palin in 2012" tee-shirts behind his back.

If the candidates run the risk of being ridiculed so intensely, why do they appear in such venues? One answer, of course, is that they hope to reach voters who don't pay that much attention to the news. Such potential voters might not care that much about issues, but they might be persuaded to vote for a candidate who appears to have a healthy sense of humor. Self-deprecating humor is of particular value in U.S. politics, as the country has a highly skeptical view of politicians and can appreciate a more "human" presentation of the candidate than the tightly controlled campaign appearances that are the norm.

In addition, candidates on these shows at a minimum can be the center of attention in a way that may not be available to them in more conventional formats. Ironically, at a time when candidates are relegated to the briefest of sound bites in the mainstream media, they can present themselves to viewers and voters in extensive give-and-take sessions in that fluffiest of entertainment formats, the variety show. For example, George W. Bush was on screen for thirteen minutes during his October 19, 2000, appearance on Letterman's show, which exceeded his entire speaking time on all three network news evening shows that month. Similarly, Al Gore received more time on his September 14, 2000, appearance on Letterman's show than he got on all three network newscasts during the entire month of September. Several other candidates, including Green Party candidate Ralph Nader and Democratic vice presidential nominee Joe Lieberman, also made appearances on the late-night talk-show circuit. Nader was rarely covered by network news reporters during the campaign, even though his candidacy proved to be of historic significance, dealing a fatal wound to Gore's hopes for the White House in 2000.

When they told jokes about the 2008 presidential campaign, the late-night comics created a tough environment for politicians, particularly for Republicans. A CMPA analysis of the comics' targets between August 23 and election eve, shown in table 5.7, found that McCain was the subject of 658 jokes during the fall campaign season, while Palin inspired an additional 566 jokes. Third place was held by President George W. Bush, another Republican, who was the target of 244 jokes. Bush finished ahead of his successor Barack Obama, who finished in fourth place with 243 jokes. Joe Biden, the Democratic vice presidential nominee, was far back in fifth place with 87 jokes. Hillary Clinton

Table 5.7
Jokes about Leading Public Figures during the 2008 Campaign

From August 23, 2008, through November 3, 2008

1. John McCain	658
2. Sarah Palin	566
3. George W. Bush	244
4. Barack Obama	243
5. Joe Biden	87
6. Hillary Clinton	84
7. Bill Clinton	68
8. O. J. Simpson	45
9. Dick Cheney	43
10. Joe "The Plumber" Wurzelbacher	32
11. Larry Craig	25
12. Henry Paulson	24
13. Joe Lieberman	20
14. Kim Jong Il	19
15. John Edwards	18
16. Ralph Nader	18
17. John Kerry	15
18. Bristol Palin	13
19. Regis Philbin	12
20. Mahmoud Ahmadinejad	10

Source: Center for Media and Public Affairs analysis of five late-night talk and comedy shows: *Tonight Show, Late Show with David Letterman, Late Night with Conan O'Brien, The Daily Show with Jon Stewart,* and *The Colbert Report.*

finished in sixth place, and Bill Clinton, who holds the all-time career record for inspiring late-night humor (cf., Farnsworth and Lichter 2006a), was close behind in seventh place.

Most of McCain's jokes were about his age (202 jokes), followed by cracks about his intelligence (twenty-nine jokes) and personality (twenty-nine jokes). Most of the comics' barbs directed at Palin made fun of her intelligence (105 jokes), her physical appearance (sixty-one), and her folksy demeanor (sixty). Jokes about Obama lacked a clear focus, with comments about his "rock star" status during the campaign (twenty-four jokes), his infomercial appeal the week before the election (nineteen jokes), and his ability to handle the economic crisis (thirteen jokes). Biden was mocked for his physical appearance (fifteen jokes), particularly his lack of hair, followed closely by his personality quirks (fourteen jokes).

Overall, though, the partisan disparity in political humor was dramatic. There were nearly four times as many jokes about the Republican ticket as there were about the Democratic ticket—1,224 versus 330.

During other campaign years, one also would not be advised to look to the late-night comedians for evenhanded treatment of candidates. CMPA tabulations of Leno and Letterman monologues found that Bush was the target of 261 jokes during the 2004 election season, as compared to 135 for John Kerry. Four years earlier, Bush was the target of 254 jokes during the general election campaign, while Gore was the subject of 165. The 1996 contest produced a split decision, with a more balanced result of 242 jokes by late-night comedians skewering Clinton and 228 targeting Dole. Over the past four election cycles, in other words, there have been more jokes told about Republicans than Democrats and in no year was the disparity greater than it was in 2008.

Conclusion

After watching his ragtag New York Mets blow yet another game in their miserable first season as an expansion team, manager Casey Stengel famously lamented, "Can't anybody here play this game?" More and more viewers—and voters—seem to be asking, "Can't anybody here cover this election?" Something is very wrong with election coverage when the one-liners are on the evening news and the serious discussions are on Leno and Letterman.

Throughout this book, we have tried to determine whether anybody can cover campaigns better than television news, which has dominated the field for over four decades. From the volume to the substance to the tone of the coverage, we can find somebody who does it at least as well, if not better. Over six presidential elections, and through many different comparisons among information sources, we found few instances where television networks did a better job of covering the presidential election than the other news sources we examined. This was the result when we compared the flagship network evening newscasts to the PBS *NewsHour*, to CNN *PrimeNews*, to the major newspapers, and to a composite local newspaper. (The networks did do better than Fox on some measures, but not on others.)

Even more troubling, considering the role that the news media play in building links between the government and citizens, was that the networks did not even do a better job of allowing candidates to speak to voters than did the entertainment-oriented talk shows. Our content analysis found that the networks consistently focused on the horse race, shortchanged matters of substance, and accentuated the most negative aspects of the campaign trail, and in so doing failed to provide an accurate and fair reflection of the presidential campaigns. This litany of failure nears the point of absurdity when it is possible to hear more from a candidate during one night with a late-night comedian than from a month of television newscasts.

Despite the emergence of several new sources of political information in recent years, the evidence here suggests that a lot of the news produced in 2008 reflects some of the same problems found in the past. The single most troubling finding of this analysis is the massive chasm between what the campaigns say in their various unmediated forms—including candidate free-airtime segments, paid campaign ads, candidate speeches, and candidate websites—and what citizens learn about those campaigns from the networks' nightly news programs. That the chasm narrows somewhat when we compare the campaigns' unmediated discourse with other media outlets is hardly a cause for rejoicing, particularly when one considers the size of the gap that separates the campaign communication from the print outlets and even from CNN and PBS.

In recent years, as intensified partisan strife began to suggest a "civility gap" in politics, the news media often make campaign messages seem more negative and less substantive than they really are. Reporters often argue that they are far better interpreters of campaigns and elections than the candidates and their handlers because people connected to the campaigns are anything but objective in the information they put out. Their goal, after all, is to win an election, not to tell the truth.

That is true enough in theory, but our findings show that even these self-interested politicians sometimes are more informative and useful sources about the campaigns than the news organizations that claim to improve upon them. Candidate speeches, advertisements, and websites were far more issue-oriented in their substance and more positive in their tone than any of the television and print outlets we examined, even outdoing the generally high-scoring PBS.

It is difficult to imagine a more damning indictment of mainstream media than this fact: even the obviously biased campaigns sometimes do a better job of informing citizens about candidates and issues than do the armies of highly trained and supposedly dispassionate professionals who spend years following the candidates from Iowa to New Hampshire, through Super Tuesday, the nominating conventions, and the general elections, and ultimately on to the White House.

At its best, American politics represents a marketplace of ideas, an area where truth and the most appealing public policies can emerge from the muscular democratic competitions waged by candidates, their campaigns, and other political actors, including voters. Even the Founders, who had anything but an elevated view of human nature, nevertheless ultimately trusted citizens' abilities to sort out the wheat from the chaff. Reporters don't have to be self-appointed guardians of a gullible public, protecting citizens from the candidates they think we should not elect. Nobody asked Washington correspondents to do this job. Their efforts to place an imprimatur on campaigns—or more precisely, to cut every candidate down to size—diminishes everyone concerned. Journalists have descended into a mode of reporting that is notable for its negativity, for its near-silencing of the candidates themselves, and for its obsessive pursuit of the trivial.

As a result, reporters are less likely to be listened to and respected by citizens. Voters turn away from all the candidates in disgust, or if they do venture to the polls, they cast their votes while figuratively holding their noses. Even if they find a candidate they can feel good about voting for—like the many voters who embraced the Obama campaign's themes of "hope" and "change" in 2008—they tend to lose their enthusiasm in the months after the votes are counted (Balz and Cohen 2009; Murray et al. 2010; Nagourney and Thee-Brennan 2010). America's elections, the nation's central marketplace of ideas, are being stocked by the mainstream media with junk food that slowly rots our political discourse. Today's high-fat journalism doesn't make for a healthy democracy.

The *NewsHour* content analysis for Campaign 2000, together with the comparative analyses from CMPA and PEJ involving PBS, MSNBC, CNN, Fox News, newspapers, and even entertainment media outlets, show there is more than one way to cover presidential elections. Our trivialized news coverage is not simply a reflection of either reality or of the structural limitations of news programming. Of course, even if this critique of election news coverage were to be embraced by journalism, it would not necessarily stimulate substantial changes in news practices and content. To paraphrase Marx, the scholars have interpreted the news; the point, however, is to change it. Nonetheless, there are two external factors whose interaction may yet substantially alter the broadcast news format. The first is the growing disaffection of the viewing audience. The second is the rise of new methods of obtaining information, which provides alternatives for those disaffected viewers. We now turn to the prospects for change.

Notes

1. The *NewsHour* candidate totals were eighty-five minutes for Gore, seventy-seven minutes for Bush, fifteen minutes for Ralph Nader, and fourteen minutes apiece for Joe Lieberman and Dick Cheney. In addition to the overall totals for the major-party tickets, this indicates the attention that PBS gave to the vice presidential and minor party candidates who received almost no airtime on the networks.

2. Kerbel et al. (2000) conducted a story-level "frame analysis" of a sample of the 1996 election coverage comparing PBS with ABC. The authors concluded that the PBS version was no more substantive, thoughtful, or "empowering" to voters than

its commercial counterpart: "The evidence points with few exceptions to the similar fashion in which the two networks portray the electoral process" (16). However, this conclusion may reflect methodological limitations of their research method, which applied a less precise content analysis system to a much smaller sample of stories.

Further data analysis of CMPA's election news demonstrated the robustness of our findings. First, the same pattern emerged whether the unit of analysis was the story or the message units that comprised it. Second, analysis of our PBS data from the expanded 1996 primary and general election data sets replicated the findings for 2000. Kerbel and his colleagues' conclusion derives primarily from a single variable (the "frame"), whose variates are not mutually exclusive and which was coded for a small sample (ninety PBS stories for the entire period from January 1 to election day, or about two stories per week), with the entire story serving as the unit of analysis. Thus, for example, a story might be coded as being framed in terms of the horse race and the political process but not in terms of issues or personal character. This coding system lacks the precision of a message-unit analysis that encodes each statement within a story for its source, object, and valence. These codes can be used as the individual building blocks for story-level analysis, rather than relying on a single code to represent an entire story, which contains numerous discrete pieces of information. As they note, "These classifications [frames] are meant to provide no more than a broad framework for understanding the various ways that the election story may be told." Thus, as a further check, we reanalyzed our data by building horse-race and substance variables out of individual message units. The results strongly reinforced the conclusions that were found on CMPA's story-level variables. In addition, the CMPA study coded the entire universe of general election news for all 218 stories on PBS and 462 stories on ABC, CBS, and NBC. And the same core instrument has been applied by the same researchers to four consecutive previous presidential elections with evidence of independent replication.

But the case for accepting CMPA's findings is not merely inferential. The expanded 1996 study included PBS data for both the primaries and the general election. We combined content categories related to policy issues and candidate qualifications into a story-level index of substantive news, in order to make our measure of substance more comparable to Kerbel et al.'s frames. By this measure, during the primaries the *NewsHour* offered 50 percent substantive coverage, compared to 42 percent for CBS, 37 percent for ABC, and 34 percent for NBC. During the general election a remarkable 68 percent of PBS coverage was substantive, compared to 49 percent on CBS, 39 percent on NBC, and only 27 percent on ABC. In light of this evidence, it would seem that the burden of proof for their counterintuitive interpretation of PBS election coverage rests with Kerbel and his colleagues.

6

Maybe Next Year?
The Future of Campaign Coverage

THE CONSEQUENCES OF THE MANY media failings we have cataloged in previous chapters are not trivial for our polity. Democracy depends on a free exchange of ideas and a fruitful discussion of issues among citizens and public officials through communication vehicles such as a vibrant, independent mass media. Yet our findings show that the mass media are far from being as helpful as they could be, with reporters and editors cutting the time devoted to politics and often focusing in what little time remains on horse-race standings rather than on the vital issues facing the nation's future leaders.

The First Amendment guarantee of a free press is one of our most sacred constitutional birthrights. Reporters have performed vital roles throughout our nation's history in exposing corruption and official misconduct, ranging from attacking the partisan political machines and the corporate trusts of a century ago to exposing the more-recent deceits surrounding Watergate and Vietnam. Democracy depends on a fair and critical news media to investigate public wrongdoing and to evaluate objectively the claims of the self-interested partisans who populate the fields of politics and government. That said, journalists have behaved irresponsibly in their reporting of recent presidential nomination and election campaigns, particularly regarding the heavy emphasis on the horse race (even for one-sided campaigns like 1996, where there was at most a "horse trot" to cover) and their generally negative orientation.

In many elections, reporters could have been more evenhanded as well. By using campaigns as opportunities for expressing little more than cynicism, today's media do not help, and sometimes may even hinder, democratic practices. Why should you as a citizen take the trouble to vote when, judging from what is reported, it looks as if there are no important issues and none of the candidates deserve your attention, much less your respect? Why surf the Web for the news if it doesn't consistently focus on the issues that will help citizens compare the candidates? With rights come responsibilities, and this is true not only for citizens but also for the Fourth Estate.

And so in this chapter we examine possible ways of improving the communication links between citizens and presidential candidates, with an emphasis on the media's vital role. We consider ways that television could improve its performance through such changes as hour-long newscasts; weekday editions of interview shows like *This Week, Face the Nation,* and *Meet the Press* (at least during presidential election years); and an expansion of the free-airtime-for-candidates initiative that has been tried sporadically in past elections.

But as Publius observed in 1788 in *Federalist* 51, "Experience has taught mankind the necessity of auxiliary precautions." Therefore we also consider a variety of reforms to enhance this link between presidential candidates and citizens in ways that do not directly involve television journalists. Despite the near-universal conviction among scholars and even many reporters that the television news should do better, its performance continues to decline. So we also consider the prospects for reforming the nomination and electoral process, as well as the potential uses of other news outlets to supplement the woefully inadequate coverage offered by network television news. The Internet is a particularly appealing alternative venue for additional information, at least in theory, as more people spend more time online in the years ahead.

Perhaps a newly competitive environment along the lines envisioned in this chapter will spur network television on to a higher-quality performance. But we must admit the media's response so far to the increasingly fluid news environment is not encouraging, regardless of the news format employed. As the PEJ content analysis shows, many media outlets chose in 2008 to offer a news menu that had many of the same problems CMPA found with the journalistic offerings of ABC, CBS, and NBC.

A Brief Review of the Content Analysis Evidence

The purpose of this research is to evaluate the degree to which the mass media have succeeded in their often-stated desires to produce serious, substantive, and evenhanded coverage of presidential elections. Unfortunately, the results have been disappointing. CMPA's initial study of the 1988 campaign documented the predominance of the horse race over substantive issues, the negative treatment of both major-party nominees, and a heavily mediated approach that lets journalists rather than candidates do most of the talking. After that campaign was widely criticized for its negativity and lack of substance, media companies introduced numerous reforms designed to produce coverage that was more serious, fair, and informative to voters. But CMPA's subsequent studies have shown little evidence of improvement and considerable evidence of decline over the past several presidential election campaigns on most measures. From the standpoint of a healthy public discourse, the PEJ evidence covering a variety of news outlets for 2008 was not encouraging either.

For television, the main focus of our attention here, the airtime devoted to campaign news has dropped sharply, candidate sound bites have continued to shrink, and candidate airtime has remained static. The proportion of horse-race to issue-based news declined in 1996, but in 2000 it shot back up to well above 1988 levels. While 2008's general election campaign marked a clear improvement over some years on the amount of horse-race coverage and candidate airtime, reporters were far less even-handed than they had been in any of the presidential elections held over the past twenty years. Because the total volume of election news has dropped over that time period, the amount of substantive information available to viewers has declined.

Election news coverage has been characterized in this analysis by declining volume, little substance, pervasive negativism, a sometimes-partisan tilt, and heavy mediation. Despite the good intentions announced by journalists anxious to improve the coverage after the 1988 campaign (and after subsequent campaigns as well), we seem to be getting the same approach, only less of it. As we have demonstrated, this pattern cannot be attributed mainly to manipulation of the coverage by candidates and their spin doctors. CMPA's 1996 study directly compared candidate discourse to media discourse and found the latter to be more negative and less substantive.

Of course, most voters experience the campaign through media images rather than direct contact with the candidates. One likely reason they perceive the process as lacking in substance and civility is that campaign news accentuates the least-attractive elements of electoral realities. One source of optimism is that polls indicate that citizens can see the differences among various sources of campaign news and information. Surveys show that most voters direct most of their ire at reporters, not at the candidates, the political parties, or even the much-maligned political consultants.

The Declining Network News Audience

Not only is the declining quality of network television's coverage of presidential elections bad for candidates and citizens, but it is hurting the media companies themselves. The rapid movement of viewers in recent years from network television to cable news, and, to a lesser extent, the Internet, is well documented. It ought to provide a significant incentive for the network newscasts to improve their coverage (cf. Farnsworth and Owen 2004; Norris 2001; Pew 2008a, 2008b, 2008c).

The sharp decline in citizen use of network television as a source of campaign news over recent years was illustrated in the first chapter of this work (table 1.1). Viewers' shifting attention demonstrates that the television companies have a sound financial reason for addressing some of the problems we have raised with respect to the trivial, negative, and skewed campaign material that dominates the nightly newscasts. Higher-quality outlets are increasing market share, or declining at a less-rapid pace than network television.

Noted political scientist V. O. Key once quipped, "Voters are not fools" (1966). The same appears to be true for news media consumers. Citizen evaluations of news sources demonstrate once again that the news media's effects are modest, not all-powerful—nothing along the lines projected by the old hypodermic effects model. The declining market share for network news seen in table 1.1 is consistent with the negative ratings citizens give the television networks after every presidential contest.

In 1992, 37 percent of the voters gave the news media a grade of A or B based on their performance during the campaign. This was seen as a vote of no confidence at the time, but in surveys conducted to assess coverage of subsequent elections the media have never equaled or surpassed the 1992 results (Pew 2000a, 2004c, 2008c). This demonstrates that the same public frustration with mainstream news sources seen through news source preferences is reflected in campaign information source evaluations.

Voters also seem to have identified the differences among information sources that we found in the course of our systematic content analysis. For example, the proportion of those surveyed that gave Barack Obama an A or B grade for his 2008 campaign (76 percent) was well above the percentage of good grades that the news media received (35 percent). John McCain, who did not run a particularly effective campaign, also received a higher percentage of good grades (40 percent) than those awarded the news media (Pew 2008c).

Four years earlier, Pew found a similar pattern. The proportion of those surveyed that gave George W. Bush an A or B for his 2004 campaign (56 percent) was well above the percentage of good grades that the news media received (38 percent). John Kerry, who ran an uneven campaign, also received a higher percentage of good grades (47 percent) than those awarded the news media.

And the same pattern of higher grades for the candidates was found in 2000, when Al Gore received 54 percent A and B grades and 53 percent of citizens gave George W. Bush these grades, again both markedly higher than the scores given reporters. The only presidential candidate to receive a lower grade than the press over the last six presidential elections was George H. W. Bush in 1992.

Even the much-maligned political parties usually outscore the media. In 2008, 70 percent of those surveyed gave the Democratic Party an A or a B, while only 28 percent gave the GOP similar grades (Pew 2008c). Those 2008 results for the Republican Party marked the first time since 1992 that a political party was viewed more negatively than the Fourth Estate. (The Democratic Party has not received a lower grade than the media over the past six presidential election years when Pew asked this question [Pew 2008c]). In 2004, a more-typical year, 37 percent gave good grades to the Democrats in 2004 and 51 percent for Republicans (Pew 2000a; Pew 2004c).

Thomas Jefferson once said he would prefer a vibrant press and no government to the reverse. Were he alive today he would find it quite difficult to make a similar observation regarding network television, as candidates offer far more relevant and informative campaign discourse than the supposedly consumer-sensitive network television news companies.

Voters also rate talk-show hosts higher than the news media, with 41 percent of survey respondents giving the talk shows A or B grades in 2008, 37 percent in 2004, and 41 percent in 2000 (Pew 2008c). Support for talk-show hosts was considerably more negative in 1996, when the percentage of good grades fell to 28 percent, about the same as the 29 percent score for the press. The low score registered by talk-show hosts in 1996 may be an exception caused by the political circumstances that year; partisan voters in 1996 were primed to focus on talk-radio hosts like Rush Limbaugh, who regularly attacked Clinton and who was among those voices supporting the Republicans as they engaged in the unpopular shutdown of the federal government a year earlier (Davis and Owen 1998; Laufer 1995; Owen 1996, 1997). The more-recent evaluations of talk-show hosts were far less likely to be colored by evaluations of talk-radio celebrities like Limbaugh, who in the mid-1990s was something of a lightning rod for liberals (Franken 1999).

These findings regarding citizen choices and media evaluations demonstrate that the corporate owners of the three television networks have sound financial reasons for improving the quality of presidential election coverage. So too do the cable companies and other media outlets that are following the networks' leads. People are moving away from junk-food journalism in the direction of more effective and informative media sources.

So far, though, the networks have responded to negative evaluations and declining viewer interest mainly by trying to improve the quality of their media offerings through expanding alternative news outlets. NBC uses its cable partner MSNBC to provide more-extensive evening newscasts beyond

its thirty-minute (before commercials) *Nightly News* program, and it promotes the cable offshoot heavily on its flagship news program. All three
network newscasts regularly refer viewers to their news websites for more
information than that provided on air. But these media modifications do not
seem sufficient, particularly when we consider that many citizens still do not
turn to the Internet for information about politics (Farnsworth and Owen
2004; Pew 2008b, 2008c).

Reforming Network News?

All this suggests that the most significant changes in the delivery of election news are originating less from conscious intentions than from rapid
market changes and technological innovations. Even as journalists struggle
to improve the news product from within, they find themselves adapting to
outside forces that are reshaping audience expectations as well as newsroom
norms and practices. The initial impact of these changes in recent years has
not always inspired confidence, to put it mildly (Kovach and Rosenstiel 1999).
Reporters have long been among the harshest critics of television news and
are among the most insistent in their demands for reform. Writing about
television's shortcomings in its coverage of the 1984 presidential election, for
example, Roger Mudd—formerly a top reporter and anchor for CBS—called
for the networks to establish a thirty-minute weekly segment to solely reporting the campaign (1987).

Now, as Mudd's thoughtful suggestion moves through its adult years, it is
long-past time to consider this modest proposal. One possible explanation
why television news is so fragmented and trivialized is that a thirty-minute
newscast is simply too brief a period of time to report on anything all that
well. The much-longer segments on PBS's hour-long *NewsHour* and on the
network-affiliated MSNBC's hour-long nightly newscast allow for more-
extensive treatment of issues than would be possible in the shorter format that
has long been the network newscast standard. CBS's *60 Minutes* has been one
of the most commercially successful and highly rated shows in the history of
broadcast television, demonstrating that being informative and being profitable are not mutually exclusive. In other words, success in televised news
delivery does not have to come in thirty-minute packages.

One possible reform along these lines, as Roger Mudd suggested, would be
for television to produce a weekly thirty-minute program during presidential-
election years, perhaps airing right after the news on a Tuesday night, cor-
responding with the day of the week that Americans go to the polls. This additional program could take a variety of shapes—perhaps a weeknight version

of the networks' Sunday news programs. Such interview shows, as the CMPA content analysis shows, offer far more information and less negativity than the nightly newscasts.

Alternately, the half hour could be spent going through an important issue or two, perhaps even with a deliberative public assembly convened to debate the issue on television (Fishkin 1991, 1995; Georges 1993; Harwood Group 1991, 1993; Janowitz 1983). There could even be mini-debates among the leading candidates, perhaps with extended versions of the free-airtime remarks by the candidates that have been used in the past (Taylor 2002). In addition to improved candidate discourse, free-airtime policies would reduce the pressure on candidates to raise vast sums of money needed for campaign advertising from special interests, an important reason for citizen distrust of government (Farnsworth 1997, 2001). Experimentation and diversity could mark this half-hour block in its early going.

These days, television content does not have to be a one-time-only affair. These information-rich programs could be aired on cable offshoot channels and loaded online, where a variety of online commentators and bloggers could link to them. Citizens can find substantial information about campaigns on the Web, but never have the words *caveat emptor* meant more than in the world of cyberspace. Professional news organizations producing quality journalism still possess the imprimatur, being well-known media brand names. With that advantage, they continue to be leading sources for reliable information (Pew 2008b, 2008c).

Only execution of these various proposals can determine what would be most appealing to the viewers, most effective for expanding the network-newscast audiences, and most reinvigorating for the political discourse. What the above ideas have in common is that the news programming should be expanded, since a lack of time for covering issues is a major impediment to serious discussion and analysis of campaigns on network television. Ross Perot's high ratings for his televised lectures on the economy demonstrate that a substantial number of citizens are interested in watching serious presentations of issues on television, a point similarly proved by the decades of commercial success enjoyed by *60 Minutes* and various imitators. Further evidence of such a public willingness for higher-quality news programming is found in the steady erosion of the influence of network news on election politics and the relative strength of those media outlets that our content analysis demonstrates offer far more substantial coverage—including print sources, CNN, and PBS.

Along these same lines, the media's exercise of their vital linkage functions between candidates and citizens, and between government and citizens, would be enhanced by doubling the length of the nightly network newscasts to an hour. The superficial treatment that is television's hallmark could be replaced

by extending discussions of the important issues of the day and of the differences between the candidates. Local television newscasts usually run for at least
an hour, and some last considerably longer than that. Are not the networks'
evening newscasts equally important? Since the evidence suggests that citizens
are deserting network news for more substantial media outlets, the best ways
for television to compete would be by offering more and better coverage. The
only real cost to an hour-long newscast would be that local stations would lose
some of the revenue from rerunning half an hour of *The Office* or *Friends*. The
local affiliates could be compensated with more advertising slots during the
newscasts or perhaps rebates to make the decision to move to an hour-long
newscast revenue-neutral to local stations. Democracy would be better off with
once-a-week news specials or hour-long network newscasts, and we believe the
networks would be better off under such a change as well.

Our argument in favor of voluntary increases in the amount of evening
news the networks provide rests on the free-market assumption that it is in the
rational self-interest of a profit-making corporation to respond to consumer
desires. To fail to take account of the evidence that suggests viewers want
more and better news is simply not a rational decision on the part of these
companies. The dramatically declining audience for network news translates
into lower advertising revenues for the television networks and local stations,
since advertisers pay rates based on the size of each show's viewing audience.

Indeed, the disproportionately older audience that watches television news
is not all that appealing to most advertisers (Mindich 2005; Pew 2004c). The
advertisers most interested in buying spots during evening news programs
sell insurance, arthritis pain medications, and other products of particular
interest to older viewers. Younger viewers are likely to have greater disposable
income and so are particularly appealing to many advertisers. But apparel
retailers, soft-drink makers, and other businesses most interested in younger
audiences hawk their wares elsewhere. The networks' failure to attract large
numbers of younger viewers—and the advertisers who court them—to their
evening news shows indicates that the audiences and revenues associated with
these network news shows will be even smaller in the years ahead.

Perhaps historical trends in network television explain this disconnect. The
broadcast industry has been heavily regulated in the past through such policies as the fairness doctrine and tight limitations on cross-ownership of media
properties (McChesney 1999). The old regulatory structures, in other words,
may not have prepared the news media to be all that responsive to current
citizens' wishes. But if these network news dinosaurs do not evolve into news
organizations capable of responding more effectively to the public's search for
higher-quality media sources, the nightly newscasts are unlikely to thrive in
the years ahead (Kurtz 2002a, 2002b).

Television's approach, an apparently consistent denial of market forces, may result from the fact that even well-watched newscasts do not have the potential to generate profits of the magnitude possible with prime-time evening entertainment programs. Network news exists in a world of limited resources, and the media acquisitions of recent years have deeply indebted many media outlets. Given such circumstances, it may be rational for a media company to focus its finite energies and resources on building a new *Survivor* or some other new reality show to replace the programming holes caused by the end of long-running hits like *ER* and *Friends*. What seems irrational from a news-oriented perspective may be rational when considered in the light of the network's entertainment-division priorities. Rational or not for the networks, decisions to close foreign bureaus, to keep the newscasts to thirty minutes, and to provide the news content that has been found wanting so often in this analysis clearly do not help build an informed citizenry. These trends don't help expand news ratings, either.

A news operation more responsive to public desires, our evidence suggests, would allow candidates to say more, offer more evenhanded commentary, provide a greater volume of information on air, and focus more on the country's key issues. One of the easiest ways to reduce the pressures that induce media companies to offer trivial, superficial, sound-bite coverage is for those news programs to be longer, at least once a week but perhaps every night. We believe it is in the news media's best interests, commercially speaking, to make these changes voluntarily.

There are other ways that today's media undermine their potential. To paraphrase Thoreau, the issue here is not so much that the news media are often negative; rather, the question is, what are they so negative about? Bruce Sanford, one of the nation's leading press lawyers, has argued that today's large media companies actually have backed away from the aggressive investigative reporting that tells people what they need to know. Rather, today's wary media companies prefer to offer trivial and largely litigation-proof distractions like the O. J. Simpson case, the Clinton-Lewinsky scandal, and a parade of missing young—mostly white—women (Sanford 1999).

The rush to get the news first—rather than worrying first about getting the news right—undermines the media's credibility, as does negative treatment of figures like Donna Rice, the overnight houseguest of 1984 and 1988 Democratic presidential hopeful Gary Hart (in media sex-scandal terms, Rice might be described as the Monica Lewinsky of the 1980s). The media's credibility is not being compromised by the lack of effective investigative reporting that was once a more significant part of network news; network news credibility is undermined by the focus on the trivial (cf. Kurtz 1994).

The change in focus is immense. Newspapers that not so long ago defied the government and published the Pentagon Papers in the midst of the

Vietnam War now write obsessively about the scandal of the week, whether it is John Edwards's illegitimate child, Tiger Woods's extramarital affairs, or Jessica Simpson's latest boyfriend. "It is not death or torture or imprisonment that threaten us as American journalists," Ted Koppel of *Nightline* remarked in 1997 when he received a lifetime-achievement award from the Committee to Protect Journalists. "It is the trivialization of our industry" (quoted in Sanford 1999, 116). Koppel's comments were prophetic: five years later his own show was in jeopardy as Disney tried to lure David Letterman by offering him Koppel's ABC time slot (Ahrens 2002; Rosenstiel and Kovach 2002). Although the late-night talk-show host decided in March 2002 to remain at CBS, the long-term future of the award-winning news show remains uncertain, particularly in the wake of Koppel's retirement from the program a few years ago.

The constant sniping and negativity found in much media campaign coverage undermine the ability of journalists to do the sort of effective investigative reporting that brings important matters to light. Readers and viewers see the silliness of what often passes for effective criticism with these reporters, and the credibility of the news business itself is compromised. If today's reporters were fairer in their treatment of campaigns and politicians, their news organizations would be more respected and reporters would have greater support to expose wrongdoing by corporations and public officials. They wouldn't need to fear huge damage awards from judges and juries turned off by trivialized media coverage (Sanford 1999). Today's Woodwards and Bernsteins may spend more time and energy writing clever put-downs of candidates and looking for the girlfriends or boyfriends of members of Congress than burrowing through government files to find the latest abuses of power or the latest cases of corruption.

If the news media remain unmoved by any sense of public purpose, and if they remain unmoved by the corporate self-interest argument presented here, some would argue that there is another—albeit highly unlikely—alternative to voluntary change: We, the people, own the nation's airwaves, and the broadcast television stations are permitted to use those airwaves without charge in exchange for providing public-service programming, including news and educational shows (Graber 2006). When the federal government says that a particular station has a license to broadcast on channel 3, for example, no one else can broadcast on channel 3 in that viewing area. Despite recent declines in viewership discussed here, the broadcast television business remains enormously profitable. Recent changes in telecommunications laws allow greater ownership concentrations that have made the television business even more valuable (Graber 2006; McChesney 1999). The Federal Communications Commission (FCC) has the authority to terminate broadcast licenses for poor performance, and it has done so in the past to punish stations that have engaged in discriminatory hiring practices (Graber 2006). Some media critics may observe that under existing law the FCC could more precisely define what is meant by "programming in the public interest," perhaps by saying that this phrase should be construed to require an hour-long nightly network newscast.

The thought that the government would establish an hour-long network newscast by demanding higher public-interest standards seems to us a vain hope. This proposal ignores the fact that the broadcasters' lobby is one of the most powerful in Washington and one not likely to be pushed around by a regulatory agency (West and Loomis 1999). The broadcasting industry is also not likely to be pressured in any meaningful way by lawmakers who want to stay in the good graces of television station owners from whom they will buy advertising time and from whom they will desire favorable news coverage of their next campaign (West and Loomis 1999). An aggressive stand by government to force expansion of the media's response to the industry's public-interest obligations would likely occur only in the wake of sustained citizen pressure for change, something that in a few instances has triggered FCC license nonrenewals in the past (Graber 2006).

Americans, of course, are not known for their aggressive demands upon governmental authorities, though we often mutter our complaints about governmental performance. The powerful cynicism most voters have toward the national government most of the time—together with America's constitutional traditions to keep the news media as far away from government control as possible—are highly effective barriers to government intervention even in the volume of news programming provided, regardless of how low the quality of those programs may sink. While others may call for greater government regulation in this area, we consider voluntary network news reform the best way—and the only politically viable one—for the news business to raise its standards of coverage.

A Miscast Institution?

More than a decade ago, media scholar Thomas Patterson (1994) described the news media as a "miscast institution." Reporters have come to replace the political parties as the overseers of the presidential nomination and election process, leaving a country focusing on images such as Michael Dukakis peering out of a tank like a cartoon character and the dueling he said/she said stories of Bill Clinton versus Gennifer Flowers, Paula Jones, and later Monica Lewinsky. The weakening of political parties over the past several decades through various political-reform efforts has created a power vacuum (Polsby 1983; Polsby and Wildavsky 2000). Reporters ended up filling that void, as in recent decades the citizens' role in selecting presidential nominees through primaries has increased greatly. Reporters did not particularly want to do this, Patterson argues. They are not very good at it either, but they just cannot stop.

In response to this observation of a miscast news media, Patterson proposed shortening the length of the primary season as a way of reducing media influence over the presidential-nomination process. Reporters would have less time to pound their horse-race messages into voters' brains and less time to dig up dirt from the candidates' distant pasts. The primary season has been compressed (though not shortened) over the past several elections—states want to hold their primaries while the partisan outcomes remain in doubt and therefore have crowded near the front of the nomination contest line—but the influence of the news media has hardly been reduced in the days since Muskie cried (or, by some accounts, had his face moistened with melting snow) outside the Manchester (N.H.) *Union Leader* in 1972 (Shogan 2001) or since Clinton declared himself "the Comeback Kid" after finishing second in the 1992 New Hampshire primary (Barilleaux and Adkins 1993).

Whether the media are miscast or not, presidential campaigns continue to be geared around the media, and television news content continues to be highly influential throughout the presidential nomination and election process, even in New Hampshire, the first and most important primary state (Farnsworth and Lichter 1999, 2002, 2003, 2006b). In fact, the accelerated campaign schedule may have made campaigns even more media-dominated. Certainly the candidates in 2008 engaged in heavy and expensive media campaigning during the primary and general election periods (Boatright 2009; Norrander 2009). This is not a new development. In 2004 Kerry and Dean spent tens of millions of dollars on campaign advertising during the primaries alone (Burden 2005). In 2000, McCain came close to becoming his own cable channel on his Straight Talk Express campaign bus (Corrado 2001; Sabato and Scott 2002; Stanley 2001).

Thus, the same law of unintended consequences that often applies to government policies may also apply to media influence in elections. Despite well-intentioned proposals to reduce this influence in politics, it remains and may even have *grown* in the wake of recent attempts to reform campaigns to make them *less* influenced by the news media.

Another possible reform to reduce the news media's influence—returning authority for the presidential nomination process back to the political party bosses—may be a cure worse than the disease. Primary voters have been decisive in the selection of presidential nominees for both major political parties starting with the 1972 nomination contests. Four years earlier,

Democratic Party bosses had nominated Vice President Hubert Humphrey rather than a candidate opposed to the Vietnam War, an act that triggered massive youth rioting in Chicago. The many political controversies of 1968, and Humphrey's subsequent loss to Richard M. Nixon, led to major reforms in the nomination process that gave rank-and-file partisan voters effective control over both the Democratic and Republican presidential nominations in 1972 and over every presidential campaign since then (Ceaser 1979; Maisel 2002; Polsby 1983; Polsby and Wildavsky 2000). Reducing media influence in presidential nominations by reducing the citizen influence in them would be a terrible idea from the standpoint of political participation, particularly when nearly half the country's adults don't vote in presidential elections as it is.

Reducing the Mediation, at Least Some of the Time

Technological developments increase the opportunities for candidates to send campaign news, information, and messages directly to citizens. Today's candidates can far more easily communicate directly with more voters than was possible when reporters functioned as a presidential campaign's only real gatekeeper in the electoral process. Technological advancements likewise offer candidates the opportunity to reach voters through a wider range of online and offline media channels, including channels that allow candidates to communicate in a less-mediated way with citizens.

One of the most notable improvements in the campaign environment in recent years is an increase in opportunities for the candidates to be heard in their own words and at greater length than the brief sound bite that is the norm in television news coverage. The rise of cable talk shows and online content has dramatically expanded the opportunities for candidates to speak without mediation. Even on ABC, CBS, and NBC substantial opportunities for unmediated discourse sometimes can be found in the morning shows and the evening comedy hours and talk shows. This is a particularly important change for campaign discourse.

Our content analysis that has shown that the unmediated campaign—be it through speeches, websites, talk-show content, or even political advertising—can be and often is far more substantial, far more issue-based, and far less negative in orientation than the campaign described in network news accounts. Viewership patterns demonstrate the popularity of these formats, and the opportunity for less-mediated communication by campaigns seems likely to grow, given the public interest.

This should be a naturally occurring development in future elections, and one that should be applauded. These unmediated and less-mediated avenues should not replace the network news, but the less-mediated communication channels seem likely to provide a healthy diet of issues and substance that can supplement and perhaps reduce the consumption of the high-fat, high-cholesterol offerings provided by today's network newscasts, the purveyors of fast-food journalism. The more visible these formats become, the more they can illustrate a news media credibility gap between what the candidates actually say and what network news reporters tell us the candidates are saying. Growing public awareness of this gap should help push the media in the direction of higher quality and more representative reporting. Of course, the pressure for more evenhanded coverage should be directed at both the networks and Fox News.

Greater opportunities for unmediated discourse may improve the performance of television in the future, but our current findings do not identify any such trends in the content of network newscasts. One glimmer of hope was CBS's decision to devote part of its *Evening News* program to the recorded unmediated messages of presidential candidates during a recent presidential election cycle. Although these presentations represented a tiny fraction of the network's broadcast time during the two-month period before the general elections, they at least provide a model that might be built upon in the future.

Many of our suggestions earlier in this chapter are designed to improve television news, not replace it. Our proposals in this realm include hour-long newscasts every weeknight (or, failing that, once a week); the use of the additional time for more substantive, issue-based reporting; extended interview sessions; and free airtime and perhaps even several mini-debates focusing on different issues. With more time for the evening news, there would be less need for candidates to try to reach voters through eight-second sound bites, less pressure to squeeze in as much commentary as possible through heavily reporter-mediated stories, and less of a demand for the barrage of negative commentaries that are the hallmarks of today's television and cable news programs.

It is our belief that television newscasts should change in ways that make them simultaneously more useful to democracy, more appealing to viewers, and more profitable to the corporate giants that control ABC, CBS, and NBC. The evidence of poor performance and declining market share for the network newscasts is overwhelming. From within the media industry often come calls for change, but these changes do not often occur, and when they do, they usually turn out to be temporary. Despite promises to improve and sometimes efforts in that direction, the networks often end up slipping back soon into the same tired, unproductive routines of the past.

If the first step on the road to recovery is recognizing that you have a problem, the media industry is now ready for the second step. The path back to higher-quality reporting has already been blazed by PBS, CNN, and the print press, and the less-mediated commentary of candidates and campaigns themselves also helps mark the way. But as the PEJ content analysis demonstrates, too many media outlets offered news content during the 2008 election cycle that resembled network news rather than reportage from the higher-quality venues.

An Internet Revolution?

More than a decade into the Internet age, many Americans regularly go online for political news and information (Pew 2008c). But not all do. When compared to other media genres, the Internet lagged behind cable news and remained just ahead of newspapers as a leading consumer media choice for information about the 2008 presidential election (see table 1.1 in chapter 1). Many media scholars and practitioners nevertheless have high hopes for a new form of democratic communication in the age of cyberjournalism (Drudge 2000; Hall 2001). Others are troubled by what they imagine to be the dystopias of unaccountable cybergossips and personalized "daily me" news diets that we consume alone (Seib 2001; Sunstein 2001). But the quantitative evidence so far suggests that neither the hopes nor the fears have yet come to pass (Davis 1999; Davis and Owen 1998; Farnsworth and Owen 2004; Margolis and Resnick 2000; Owen 2002).

For the moment, the most frequent users of the Web are those same highly informed citizens who already are very interested and very active in politics. Likewise, the dominant sources used in cyberspace are the websites of the mainstream media, whose offline successes contribute to the online attention they receive. The online offerings of the Big Three broadcasts networks seem to be having even more of a problem with market share than the networks' offline flagship newscasts. CNN is more popular online than the online news offerings of CBS, NBC, and ABC (Pew 2008c).

There is certainly an opportunity for important changes in media and politics as the Internet continues to develop and expand its reach still further (Gillmor 2004). In the same way that viewers have voted with their television remote controls for news sources that offer better election coverage than the networks, citizens can search out precisely the information they desire without having to wait for it to appear on a newscast or in print (Cornfield 2000; Glass 1996; Rash 1997). They can select more-substantive sources online and ignore those that offer junk-food journalism, if they have the time to do so and the means to distinguish among various online offerings. This individual-level control over what information a citizen attends to—and what is ignored—may offer the opportunity for a rejuvenated democracy of citizens who insist on more-responsive media sources and even more-responsive candidates and elected officials (Grossman 1995; Hall 2001). Of course, the online world may also be a place to get less-reliable information to the citizens more quickly.

Our content analysis of campaign websites in the 1996 campaign suggests that these forums, like candidate-interview programs, candidate speeches, and even candidate advertising, are excellent places for candidates to conduct campaigns that are more positive and issue-based than they are presented in the mainstream media, especially on the network evening newscasts. Of course, just because candidates can be more positive and issue-based in their online messages does not mean they will be, as 2004's results indicate.

Television can get into the act as well, through more issue-oriented web-sites and news presentations on air. As the volume of Internet users grows, and as the influence of less-mediated forms of campaign news and informa-tion expands, the mass media may be under even greater pressure to abandon the status quo coverage that focuses on horse-race politics, largely ignores issues, casts politics in a negative light, and rarely gives candidates more than a few seconds to speak to the American people in a nightly newscast. While those who see the Internet as a revolutionary new development in American politics may find themselves disappointed, the Web clearly can provide some relief for citizens seeking accurate representations of what candidates stand for. This medium can also help candidates find a more direct route to citizens than the network newscasts. In this way, competition from the expanded, less-mediated formats could indirectly nudge the quality of other media con-tent upward.

Final Thoughts

In the end, we find ourselves astonished, above all, that the mass media have been able to do so little with so much. On virtually every measure we have considered in this analysis of presidential campaign coverage—from volume, to horse race, to content, to tone, to issues, to sound bites—the Big Three net-work news programs—and the other media outlets that follow their leads—have been weighed in the balance and found wanting. They have repeatedly been compared unfavorably to some other news outlets and, most dramati-cally, even to the candidates' campaigns themselves. To make matters worse, on several measures the mass media seem to be doing worse—or at least no better—with each passing presidential election.

We hope the content analysis in this book offers ammunition to the many serious journalists in a variety of media formats who have been trying, in some cases for decades now, to push the mainstream media in the direction of greater substance and of higher-quality content in general. The mass media need as many internal agitators for quality as possible, and it is our hope that the results here can allow the activists to agitate with renewed vigor. Simply put, the content analysis and survey information presented here demonstrate that television newscasts need massive overhauls if they hope to remain influential sources of news and information for America's media consumers. Declining revenues, vanishing news consumers, and technological advancements suggest that time may be running out for many traditional news outlets.

The future is never certain, but the evidence here suggests that television news is not likely to thrive if it retains an approach to presidential election news marked by reduced news volume, coverage dominated by the horse race, and a corrosive negativity that can undermine efforts to keep a sense of civic society alive in this country. As the CMPA content analysis, the PEJ content analysis, and the viewer surveys indicate, the news media have lost their way for the past several presidential elections and are on a course to irrelevance. Changing course seems long overdue.

Perhaps the television networks will retain their renewed sense of mission found in fall 2001, when the networks devoted extraordinary resources to the extremely effective coverage of the terrorist attacks (Farnsworth and Lichter 2006a; Media Monitor 2001). Perhaps they will not. Who may replace the networks if they fail to adjust their coverage of presidential elections is subject to debate. Despite their growing pains and the questionable news practices associated with them, the new news media delivery systems do at least provide a laboratory for innovation and a natural experiment in the redefinition and presentation of election news. Print, CNN, PBS, and many online media outlets have proven to be effective competitors and should be even more competitive as Internet use expands in the coming years.

The Web may offer the greatest new opportunity to revitalize print journalism. The Internet gives newspapers the chance to take greater advantage of their most powerful assets: huge, well-trained newsrooms. It also removes what for decades has been their greatest disadvantage, the once-a-day news cycle. Perhaps the coming years will be marked by the resurgence of once-dominant newspaper companies in cyberspace. It would be ironic if network television, which came to prominence and dominance over print because of its technological advantages, falls victim to still newer technology wielded in cyberspace by the more informative and substantive print press. Newspapers, once practically left for dead beside technology's high-speed highway, may turn out to be the once and future king of the media world if a viable business model emerges for online revenue for newspapers.

An even greater irony, suggested by citizen surveys and by the CMPA content analysis, is that the future of campaign discourse may be far less mediated than the past heyday of network news. The most popular, most informative, and most effective campaign discourse is actually the less-mediated campaign discourse of debates and interview shows, as well as the unmediated campaign discourse of the campaign speeches and websites. The candidate-interview shows on cable television are positive developments, as is the unmediated communication potential offered by cyberspace. As information sources, these less-mediated and unmediated information outlets seem likely to grow in influence as more people venture online and turn to cable to answer their own questions about issue-based politics.

It is impossible to predict what new amalgam will eventually emerge from these competing voices. But to appropriate another Marxist metaphor, without substantive improvement from its performance in recent presidential elections, the broadcast network model that dominated election news in the latter half of the last century may simply wither away in the next one. If these thirty-minute newscasts continue their decline, they will do so for very capitalist reasons. Other news media outlets, and the unmediated campaign information sources themselves, are providing great competition for these horse-race-dominated, issue-starved, negatively oriented programs. Network television evening news shows, as America has known them since the 1960s, must evolve or will likely die, like the dinosaurs before them.

Appendix A

Campaign Information Items Used in the Content Analysis

THE SIX PRESIDENTIAL ELECTION STUDIES included more than twenty-five thousand campaign information items analyzed by the Center for Media and Public Affairs (CMPA) at George Mason University. These items include network evening news segments on ABC, CBS, and NBC in the following presidential election cycles: 1987–1988, 1991–1992, 1995–1996, 1999–2000, 2003–2004, and 2007–2008. Depending on the year, the content analysis draws from other news media, including PBS news programs; CNN programs; Fox News programs; and campaign news stories from daily newspapers, among them the *New York Times*, the *Washington Post*, the *Wall Street Journal*, and others newspapers and magazines. In 1996, candidate speeches, advertising, interviews, and websites were also contained in this content analysis and compared to the news coverage during that year.

The 2008 portion of this analysis includes findings drawn from a content analysis of 18,836 campaign news stories from broadcast, print, radio, online, and cable news outlets during 2008 by the Project for Excellence in Journalism. PEJ analyzed the news reports using procedures very similar to those employed by CMPA. Of course they are not responsible for our interpretations of their data.

Details for the individual campaign cycles follow.

2007–2008

CMPA

The CMPA 2007–2008 presidential campaign content analysis examines a total of 2,266 network news campaign stories. Because of the unusually early start to the 2008 nomination process (the Iowa caucuses were held on January 3 and the New Hampshire primary on January 8), we ended our preseason period on December 15, 2007, rather than the usual break point of December 31. There were 651 stories on the Big Three network evening news programs during the part of the preseason we analyzed (January 1 through December 15, 2007), 932 stories during the heavily contested portion of the primary season (December 16, 2007, through March 22, 2008), and 683 stories during the fall campaign (from the opening of the nominating conventions on August 23, 2008, through election eve on November 3, 2008).

In addition, the CMPA content analysis includes 514 news stories from the first half hour of Fox News's *Special Report with Brit Hume* during the general election campaign period.

PEJ

This 2008 portion of our study also includes findings drawn from a content analysis of 18,836 campaign news stories during 2008 by the Project for Excellence in Journalism. The broadcast news portion of this study includes 3,977 stories from the first thirty minutes of the morning shows and the entire thirty-minute evening news shows on ABC, CBS, and NBC, as well as the PBS *NewsHour*. The PBS analysis rotated daily between the first thirty minutes and the last thirty minutes of the hour-long newscast.

The 9,202 cable news stories analyzed by PEJ were drawn from CNN, MSNBC, and Fox News channels. Some material was drawn from daytime offerings and some from the early-evening and prime-time reports. The cable sample includes both news-oriented programs, like CNN's *Situation Room*, and more opinion-oriented programming, like Fox's *O'Reilly Factor* and MSNBC's *Countdown with Keith Olbermann*.

The 2,919 stories on radio programs include news reports on National Public Radio and a sampling of talk radio from both conservatives, such as Rush Limbaugh and Sean Hannity, and liberals, such as Ed Schultz and Randi Rhodes. The 1,264 online stories PEJ examined came from sites that created their own material for their websites (like CNN.com and MSNBC.com) and sites that provided material either entirely or largely generated by others (like Yahoo! News, AOL News, and Google News).

Finally, the newspaper portion of the PEJ study includes 1,474 front-page stories from both major papers and smaller news outlets. The *New York Times* was coded every day, and four other major papers—the *Wall Street Journal, Washington Post, Los Angeles Times,* and *USA Today*—were coded roughly every other day. A sample drawn from sixteen regional and local newspapers was also coded, with the papers selected for the analysis changing from day to day.

2003–2004

The 2003–2004 CMPA presidential campaign content analysis examines a total of 1,047 network news campaign stories. There were 187 stories on the Big Three network evening news programs during the preseason (January 1 through December 31, 2003), 356 stories during the primary season (January 1 through March 1, 2004), and 504 stories during the fall campaign (between September 7 and November 1, 2004).

In addition, the CMPA content analysis includes 560 sound bites from Fox News's *Special Report with Brit Hume* during the general election campaign period.

1999–2000

The 1999–2000 presidential campaign content analysis examines a total of 1,524 items. There were 294 stories on the Big Three network evening news programs during the preseason (January 1 through December 31, 1999), 550 stories during the primary season (January 1 through March 7, 2000), and 462 stories during the fall campaign (between September 4 and November 6, 2000).

In addition, the content analysis for this election cycle includes 218 news items from the *NewsHour* on PBS during the general election campaign period.

1995–1996

The 1995–1996 presidential campaign content analysis examines a total of 7,928 items. There were 485 stories on the Big Three network evening news programs during the preseason (January 1 through December 31, 1995), 699 stories during the primary season (January 1 through March 10, 1996), and 483 stories during the fall campaign (between September 2 and November 5, 1996).

The 699 network news stories during the primary period and the 483 news stories during the fall campaign were part of a total primary season and general election season campaign news analysis of 4,325 campaign news stories and editorials from the Big Three, PBS's *MacNeil-Lehrer*, the *New York Times*, the *Wall Street Journal*, and a local newspaper sample compiled from fifteen local newspapers. An additional 1,103 news stories and editorials from three leading New Hampshire media outlets—the *Concord Monitor*, the Manchester *Union-Leader*, and WMUR-TV (6 P.M. broadcast)—were analyzed from the period of January 20 to February 20, 1996 (the month before the crucial New Hampshire primary).

The 1996 content analysis paid particular attention to candidate discourse. The 1996 primary and general election campaign content analysis was also applied to 1,171 files posted on the Bill Clinton, Bob Dole, and Ross Perot campaign websites at the close of the campaign; 396 television commercials; 270 campaign stump speeches; 164 television interview segments; fifty-four free candidate airtime speeches during the fall; and fifty candidate exchanges during the presidential debates.

1991–1992

The 1991–1992 presidential campaign content analysis examines a total of 4,434 news items. There were 211 stories on the Big Three network evening news programs during the preseason (January 1 through December 31, 1991), 424 stories during the primary season (January 1 through March 17, 1992), and 772 stories during the fall campaign (between September 7 and November 3, 1992).

Also analyzed during the fall campaign period are 124 speeches and a total of 2,903 stories from CNN's *PrimeNews*, PBS's *NewsHour*, the *New York Times*, the *Washington Post*, and the *Wall Street Journal*.

1987–1988

The 1987–1988 presidential election campaign cycle content analysis examines a total of 8,550 news items. On the Big Three network evening news programs there were 379 preseason stories (February 1 through December 31, 1987), 597 primary season stories (January 1 through March 15, 1988), and 589 stories during the general election campaign (September 8 through November 8, 1988).

Those 589 stories were part of a total of 7,575 campaign news stories and editorials examined during the general election campaign from PBS, CNN, the *New York Times*, the *Washington Post*, the *Christian Science Monitor*, the *Wall Street Journal*, the *Los Angeles Times*, *Newsweek*, *Time*, *U.S. News & World Report*, the *National Journal*, the *New York Daily News*, the *Chicago Tribune*, the *Houston Chronicle*, and the *Sacramento Bee*. The 1987–1988 content analysis was provided by Bruce Buchanan (1991, 1995), and his analysis parameters were used by the Center for Media and Public Affairs (CMPA) in subsequent years.

Appendix B

Internet Resources on the News Media and Presidential Elections

Campaign Legal Center
(A public interest–advocacy organization focusing on campaign finance reform issues)
http://www.campaignlegalcenter.org/

Center for Responsive Politics
(A frequently cited Washington research organization that tracks the influence of money on politics)
http://www.opensecrets.org

CNN
(A key source of political and campaign news used by many viewers in the United States and around the world)
http://www.cnn.com/ELECTION/2008/

Columbia Journalism Review ("Campaign Desk")
(An important real-time critique of news coverage)
http://www.cjr.org/campaign_desk/

Cook Political Report
(A frequently updated source for handicapping upcoming campaigns)
http://www.cookpolitical.com/

George Mason University, Center for Media and Public Affairs
(A frequently cited research center that has examined decades of U.S. news coverage—and a key source for the information contained in this book)
http://www.cmpa.com/index.htm

Harvard University, Kennedy School of Government
Joan Shorenstein Center on the Press, Politics, and Public Policy
(A key research effort examining media and politics)
http://www.hks.harvard.edu/presspol/index.html

Media Tenor International
(Experts in U.S. and international news–content analysis—and a key source for the information contained in this book)
http://www.mediatenor.com/

New York Times Election 2008 Reports
(An archive of the highly influential newspaper's campaign news coverage)
http://elections.nytimes.com/2008/index.html?scp=2&sq=Election%20
2008&st=Search

PBS Election 2008 Election Reports
(An archive of the television network's unusually issue-based campaign coverage)
http://www.pbs.org/vote2008/

Pew Research Center for the People and the Press
(One of the most wide-ranging sources for public opinion, with a particular focus on the public involvement in politics and public evaluations of the news media)
http://people-press.org/

Poynter Institute
(A highly respected source of analysis and criticism of media content)
http://www.poynter.org

Project for Excellence in Journalism
(Experts in U.S. news content analysis—and a key source for the information contained in this book)
http://www.journalism.org/

Project Vote Smart
(A nonprofit organization that provides information about candidates for
office around the country)
http://www.vote-smart.org/index.htm

University of Virginia, Center for Politics
(A key source of national-campaign news)
http://www.centerforpolitics.org/

University of Wisconsin–Madison, Advertising Project
(A key source for information about campaign advertising around the
country)
http://wiscadproject.wisc.edu/

U.S. Federal Election Commission
(The U.S. government's searchable database of campaign contributions and
expenditures)
http://www.fec.gov

References

Abramson, Paul R., John H. Aldrich, and David W. Rhode. 2002. *Change and continuity in the 2000 elections*. Washington, D.C.: CQ Press.

———. 2010. *Change and continuity in the 2008 elections*. Washington, D.C.: CQ Press.

Adams, William C. 1987. As New Hampshire goes . . . In *Media and momentum: The New Hampshire primary and nomination politics*, ed. Gary R. Orren and Nelson W. Polsby. Chatham, N.J.: Chatham House.

Adams, William C., Dennis J. Smith, Allison Salzman, Ralph Crossen, Scot Hieber, Tom Naccarato, William Valentine, and Nina Weisbroth. 1994. Before and after the day after: The unexpected results of a televised drama. In *Media power in politics*, ed. Doris Graber. 3d ed. Washington, D.C.: CQ Press.

Adatto, Kiku. 1990. Sound bite democracy. Research paper, Kennedy School Press Politics Center, Harvard University.

Ahrens, Frank. 2002. In TV's numbers game, youth trumps ratings. *Washington Post*, March 13.

Aitken, Jonathan. 1993. *Nixon: A life*. Washington, D.C.: Regnery.

Allen, Mike. 2003. Bush cites 9/11 on all manner of questions. *Washington Post*, September 11.

———. 2007. Senator soothing: Hillary Clinton can be warm, casual. *Politico*, January 23. http://www.politico.com/news/stories/0107/2421.html (accessed January 23, 2007).

Alliance for Better Campaigns. 1999. *Money shouldn't be all that talks: Reinventing political campaigns on television*. Washington, D.C.: Alliance for Better Campaigns.

———. 2001. *Gouging democracy: How the television industry profiteered on campaign 2000*. Washington, D.C.: Alliance for Better Campaigns.

Alter, Jonathan. 1988. How the media blew it. *Newsweek*, November 28.

———. 1992. Go ahead, blame the media. *Newsweek*, November 2.

Alterman, Eric. 2003. *What liberal media?* New York: Basic Books.

Arterton, Christopher. 1984. *Media politics.* Lexington, Mass.: Lexington Books.

AuCoin, Don. 2000. Low ratings mark slim convention coverage. *Boston Globe*, August 5.

Auletta, Ken. 2004. Fortress Bush: How the White House keeps the press under control. *The New Yorker*, February 19.

Baker, Ross K. 1993. Sorting out and suiting up: The presidential nominations. In *The election of 1992: Reports and interpretations*, ed. Gerald M. Pomper. Chatham, N.J.: Chatham House.

Balz, Dan. 2007. Hillary Clinton opens presidential bid. *Washington Post*, January 21.

———. 2010. Can Sarah Palin transform celebrity into real political power? *Washington Post*, February 14.

Balz, Dan, and Jon Cohen. 2006. Independent voters favor the Democrats by 2 to 1 in poll. *Washington Post*, October 24.

———. 2007. Confidence in Bush leadership at all-time low, poll finds. *Washington Post*, January 22.

———. 2009. Deep divisions on health care. *Washington Post*, November 17.

Barilleaux, Ryan J., and Randall E. Adkins. 1993. The nominations: Process and patterns. In *The elections of 1992*, ed. Michael Nelson. Washington, D.C.: CQ Press.

Barstow, David. 2010. Tea Party lights fuse for rebellion on right. *New York Times*, February 15.

Barstow, David, and Don Van Natta, Jr. 2001. How Bush took Florida: Mining the overseas absentee vote. *New York Times*, July 15.

Bartels, Larry M. 1988. *Presidential primaries and the dynamics of public choice.* Princeton, N.J.: Princeton University.

———. 1993. Messages received: The political impact of media exposure. *American Political Science Review* 87:267–85.

Bennett, W. Lance. 2005. *News: The politics of illusion.* 6th ed. New York: Pearson/Longman.

Bernstein, Carl, and Bob Woodward. 1974. *All the president's men.* New York: Warner.

Boatright, Robert G. 2009. Campaign finance in the 2008 election. In *The American elections of 2008*, ed. Janet M. Box-Steffensmeier and Steven E. Schier. Lanham, Md.: Rowman & Littlefield.

Bode, Ken. 1992. Pull the plug. *Quill* (March): 10–13.

Boot, William. 1989. Campaign '88: TV overdoses on the inside dope. *Columbia Journalism Review* 27 (5) (January–February): 23–29.

Bosman, Julie. 2010. Edwards admits he fathered girl with mistress. *New York Times*, January 21.

Bozell, L. Brent, and Brent H. Baker. 1990. *And that's the way it wasn't.* Alexandria, Va.: Media Research Center.

Braestrup, Peter. 1983. *Big story.* New Haven, Conn.: Yale University Press.

Broder, David. 1990. Five ways to put some sanity back in elections. *Washington Post*, January 14.

Broh, C. Anthony. 1980. Horse race journalism. *Public Opinion Quarterly* 44:514–29.

Buchanan, Bruce. 1991. *Electing a president: The Markle Commission research on campaign '88.* Austin: University of Texas Press.

———. 1995. A tale of two campaigns or why '92's voters forced a presidential campaign better than '88's and how it could happen again. *Political Psychology* 16 (2): 297–318.

Buckley, C. 2000. Talk the vote. *TV Guide*, November 25.

Bugliosi, Vincent. 2001. *The betrayal of America: How the Supreme Court undermined the Constitution and chose our president.* New York: Avalon/Nation Books.

Buhr, Tami. 2001. What voters know about candidates and how they learn it: The 1996 New Hampshire Republican primary as a case study. In *In pursuit of the White House 2000: How we choose our presidential nominees,* ed. William G. Mayer. New York: Chatham House/Seven Bridges.

Bumiller, Elisabeth. 2004. Lawyer for Bush quits over links to Kerry's foes. *New York Times,* August 26.

Burden, Barry C. 2005. The nominations: Technology, money and transferable momentum. In *The elections of 2004,* ed. Michael Nelson. Washington, D.C.: CQ Press.

Burger, Timothy J. 2002. In the driver's seat: The Bush DUI. In *Overtime: The election 2000 thriller,* ed. Larry Sabato. New York: Longman.

Burns, James MacGregor, and Susan Dunn. 2001. *The three Roosevelts: Patrician leaders who transformed America.* New York: Atlantic Monthly Press.

Butterfield, Fox. 1990. Dukakis says race was harmed by TV. *New York Times,* April 22.

Campbell, David E. 2009. Public opinion and the 2008 presidential election. In *The American elections of 2008,* ed. Janet M. Box-Steffensmeier and Steven E. Schier. Lanham, Md.: Rowman & Littlefield.

Campbell, James E. 1992. Forecasting the presidential vote in the states. *American Journal of Political Science* 36 (2): 386–407.

———. 2001. The referendum that didn't happen: The forecasts of the 2000 presidential election. *Political Science and Politics* 34 (1): 33–8.

Cantril, Hadley, Hazel Gaudet, and Herta Herzog. 1940. *The invasion from Mars.* Princeton, N.J.: Princeton University Press.

Cappella, Joseph N., and Kathleen Hall Jamieson. 1997. *Spiral of cynicism: The press and the public good.* New York: Oxford University Press.

Ceaser, James W. 1979. *Presidential selection: Theory and development.* Princeton, N.J.: Princeton University Press.

Ceaser, James, and Andrew Busch. 1993. *Upside down and inside out: The 1992 elections and American politics.* Lanham, Md.: Rowman & Littlefield.

———. 1997. *Losing to win: The 1996 elections and American politics.* Lanham, Md.: Rowman & Littlefield.

———. 2001. *The perfect tie: The true story of the 2000 presidential election.* Lanham, Md.: Rowman & Littlefield.

———. 2005. *Red over blue.* Lanham, Md.: Rowman & Littlefield.

Ceaser, James, Andrew Busch, and John J. Pitney, Jr. 2009. *Epic journey: The 2008 elections and American politics.* Lanham, Md.: Rowman & Littlefield.

Cillizza, Chris, and Dan Balz. 2007. On the electronic campaign trail, politicians realize the importance of Web video. *Washington Post,* January 22.

Clancey, Maura, and Michael J. Robinson. 1985. General election coverage. In *The mass media in campaign '84,* ed. Michael J. Robinson and Austin Ranney. Washington, D.C.: American Enterprise Institute Press.

Cohen, Jon, and Jennifer Agiesta. 2008. Skepticism of Palin growing, poll finds. *Washington Post,* October 1.

Cook, Timothy E. 2005. *Governing with the news: The news media as a political institution.* 2d ed. Chicago: University of Chicago Press.

Cornfield, Mike. 2000. The Internet and democratic participation. *National Civic Review* 89 (3): 235–41.

Corrado, Anthony. 2001. Financing the 2000 elections. In *The election of 2000,* ed. Gerald M. Pomper. New York: Chatham House/Seven Bridges.

Craig, Stephen C. 1993. *The malevolent leaders.* Boulder, Colo.: Westview.

———. 1996. The angry voter: Politics and popular discontent in the 1990s. In *broken contract? Changing relationships between Americans and their government,* ed. Stephen C. Craig. Boulder, Colo.: Westview.

Cronin, Thomas E., and Michael A. Genovese. 1998. *The paradoxes of the American presidency.* New York: Oxford University Press.

Crotty, William J. 2009. The Bush legacy and the 2008 presidential election: Context and imprint. In *Winning the presidency, 2008,* ed. William J. Crotty. Boulder, Colo.: Paradigm.

D'Alessio, Dave, and Mike Allen. 2000. Media bias in presidential elections: A meta-analysis. *Journal of Communcation* 50 (4): 133–56.

Dautrich, Kenneth, and Thomas H. Hartley. 1999. *How the news media fail American voters: Causes, consequences, and remedies.* New York: Columbia University Press.

Davis, Richard. 1999. *The Web of politics: The Internet's impact on the American political system.* New York: Oxford University Press.

Davis, Richard, and Diana Owen. 1998. *New media and American politics.* New York: Oxford University Press.

Deakin, James. 1983. *Straight stuff: The reporters, the White House, and the truth.* New York: William Morrow.

De Moraes, Lisa. 2002. Rukeyser may have new show up his sleeve. *Washington Post,* April 2.

Denton, Robert E. 2009. Identity politics and the 2008 presidential campaign. In *The 2008 presidential campaign: A communication perspective,* ed. Robert E. Denton. Lanham, Md.: Rowman & Littlefield.

Dimock, Michael. 2004. Bush and public opinion. In *Considering the Bush presidency,* ed. Gary Gregg II and Mark J. Rozell. New York: Oxford.

Dionne, E. J. 1992. GOP accuses media of bias against Bush. *Washington Post,* August 13.

Downie, Leonard, Jr., and Robert G. Kaiser. 2002. *The news about the news: American journalism in peril.* New York: Knopf.

Drew, Dan, and David Weaver. 1991. Voter learning in the 1988 presidential election: Did the debates and the media matter? *Journalism Quarterly* 68 (Spring–Summer): 27–37.

Drudge, Matt. 2000. *Drudge manifesto.* New York: New American Library.

Duncan, Dayton. 1991. *Grass roots: One year in the life of the New Hampshire presidential primary.* New York: Viking.

Easton, David, and Jack Dennis. 1969. *Children in the political system: Origins of political legitimacy.* New York: McGraw-Hill.

Easton, Nina J., Michael Kranish, Patrick Healy, Glen Johnson, Anne E. Kornblut, and Brian Mooney. 2004. On the trail of Kerry's failed dream. *Boston Globe* (Sunday Magazine), November 14.

Edelman, Murray. 1985. *The symbolic uses of politics.* Urbana: University of Illinois Press.

Edwards, George C. III. 2003. *On deaf ears: The limits of the bully pulpit.* New Haven, Conn.: Yale University Press.

———. 2004. Riding high in the polls: George W. Bush and public opinion. In *The George W. Bush presidency: Appraisals and prospects,* ed. Colin Campbell and Bert A. Rockman. Washington, D.C.: CQ Press.

Egan, Timothy. 2004. Wounds opened anew as Vietnam resurfaces. *New York Times,* August 26.

Eggerton, John. 2004. Howard Dean: Scream never happened. *Broadcasting & Cable,* June 14.

Entman, Robert M. 2005. *Projections of power: Framing news, public opinion, and U.S. foreign policy.* Chicago: University of Chicago Press.

Epstein, Edward J. 1975. *News from nowhere.* Chicago: University of Chicago Press.

Etheridge, Eric. 2009. Muslim again? *New York Times* [online blog], June 3. http://opinionator.blogs.nytimes.com/2009/06/03/muslim-again/?scp=1&sq=Obama%20Muslim%20again&st=cse (accessed March 5, 2010).

Fair, Ray. 1978. The effects of economic events on votes for president. *Review of Economics and Statistics* 40:159–73.

Fallows, James. 2004. Blind into Baghdad. *The Atlantic,* January/February.

Farnsworth, Stephen J. 1997. *Political support in a frustrated America.* Ph.D. diss., Georgetown University.

———. 1999a. Federal frustration, state satisfaction? Voters and decentralized governmental power. *Publius* 29 (3): 75–88.

———. 1999b. Loving and loathing Virginia: Feelings about federalism in the Old Dominion. *Virginia Social Science Journal* 34:15–38.

———. 2000. Political support and citizen frustration: Testing three linkage theories. *Virginia Social Science Journal* 35: 69–84.

———. 2001. Patterns of political support: Examining Congress and the presidency. *Congress and the Presidency* 28 (1): 45–61.

———. 2009. *Spinner in chief: How presidents sell their policies and themselves.* Boulder, Colo.: Paradigm.

Farnsworth, Stephen J., and S. Robert Lichter. 1999. No small town poll: Public attention to network coverage of the 1992 New Hampshire primary. *Harvard International Journal of Press/politics* 4 (3): 51–61.

———. 2002. The 1996 New Hampshire Republican primary and network news. *Politics and Policy* 30 (1): 70–88.

———. 2003. The 2000 New Hampshire Democratic primary and network news. *American Behavioral Scientist* 46 (5): 588–99.

———. 2004. Increasing candidate-centered televised discourse: Evaluating local news coverage of campaign 2000. *Harvard International Journal of Press/Politics* 9 (2): 76–93.

———. 2005a. Local television news and campaign 2000: Assessing efforts to increase substantive content. *Politics & Policy* 33 (3): 496–520.

———. 2005b. The *Nightly news nightmare* revisited: Network television's coverage of the 2004 presidential election. Paper delivered at the Annual Meeting of the American Political Science Association. Washington, D.C.

———. 2006a. *The mediated presidency: Television news and presidential governance.* Lanham, Md.: Rowman & Littlefield.

———. 2006b. The 2004 New Hampshire Democratic primary and network news. *Harvard International Journal of Press/Politics* 11 (1): 53–63.

———. 2008. How television covers the presidential nomination process. In *The making of the presidential candidates, 2008*, ed. William G. Mayer. Lanham, Md.: Rowman & Littlefield.

Farnsworth, Stephen J., and Diana M. Owen. 2004. Internet use and the 2000 presidential election. *Electoral Studies* 23 (3): 415–29.

Fiedler, Tom. 2002. Introduction: The return of Key Largo. In *Overtime: The election 2000 thriller*, ed. Larry Sabato. New York: Longman.

Finnegan, Michael. 2004. Film and election politics cross in "Fahrenheit 9/11." *Los Angeles Times.* June 11.

Fishkin, James S. 1991. *Democracy and deliberation: New directions for democratic reform.* New Haven, Conn.: Yale University Press.

———. 1995. *The voice of the people: Public opinion and democracy.* New Haven, Conn.: Yale University Press.

Fitzwater, Marlin. 1995. *Call the briefing! Bush and Reagan, Sam and Helen: A decade with presidents and the press.* New York: Times Books/Random House.

Franken, Al. 1999. *Rush Limbaugh is a big fat idiot: And other observations.* New York: Delacourte.

Frankovic, Kathleen A., and Monika L. McDermott. 2001. Public opinion in the 2000 election: The ambivalent electorate. In *The election of 2000*, ed. Gerald M. Pomper. New York: Chatham House.

Frantzich, Stephen E. 2009. E-politics and the 2008 presidential campaign: Has the Internet "arrived"? In *Winning the presidency, 2008*, ed. William J. Crotty. Boulder, Colo.: Paradigm.

Gans, Herbert J. 1979. *Deciding what's news.* New York: Pantheon.

Gellman, Irwin F. 1999. *The contender: Richard Nixon, the Congress years.* New York: Free Press.

Georges, Christopher. 1993. Perot and con: Ross's teledemocracy is supposed to bypass special interests and take the money out of politics; it won't. *Washington Monthly* 25 (June): 38–43.

Gergen, David. 2000. *Eyewitness to power: The essence of leadership.* New York: Simon & Schuster.

Germond, Jack W., and Jules Witcover. 1989. *Whose broad stripes and bright stars? The trivial pursuit of the presidency, 1988.* New York: Warner.

———. 1993. *Mad as hell: Revolt at the ballot box, 1992.* New York: Warner.

Gillmor, Dan. 2004. *We the media: Grassroots journalism by the people, for the people.* Sebastopol, Calif.: O'Reilly Media.

Gillon, Steven M. 2002. Election of 1992. In *History of American presidential elections, 1789–2001.* Vol. 11, ed. Arthur M. Schlesinger, Jr., and Fred L. Israel. Philadelphia: Chelsea House.

Ginsberg, Benjamin. 1986. *The captive public: How mass opinion promotes state power.* New York: Basic.

Gitlin, Todd. 1980. *The whole world is watching: Mass media and the making and unmaking of the new left.* Berkeley: University of California Press.

Glass, Andrew. 1996. On-line elections: The Internet's impact on the political process. *Harvard International Journal of Press/Politics* 1 (4): 140–46.

Gold, Victor. 1994. George Bush speaks out. *Washingtonian*, February.

Goldberg, Bernard. 2002. *Bias: A CBS insider exposes how the media distort the news.* Washington, D.C.: Regnery.

Goldberg, Robert, and Gerald J. Goldberg. 1995. *Citizen Turner.* New York: Harcourt Brace.

Goldfarb, Zachary. 2007. Mobilized online, thousands gather to hear Obama. *Washington Post*, February 3.

Goodwin, Doris Kearns. 1994. *No ordinary time.* New York: Simon & Schuster.

Graber, Doris. 1987. Kind words and harsh pictures. In *Elections in America*, ed. K. Lehmann-Schlozman. Boston: Allen and Unwin.

———. 1988. *Processing the news.* 2d ed. New York: Longman.

———. 2006. *Mass media and American politics.* 7th ed. Washington, D.C.: CQ Press.

Graf, Joseph. 2008. New media: The cutting edge of campaign communications. In *Campaigns on the cutting edge*, ed. Richard J. Semiatin. Washington: CQ Press.

Greenberg, David. 2003. Calling a lie a lie. *Columbia Journalism Review* September/ October.

Gregg, Gary L. 2004. Dignified authenticity: George W. Bush and the symbolic presidency. In *Considering the Bush presidency*, ed. Gary Gregg II and Mark J. Rozell. New York: Oxford University Press.

Greenfield, Jeff. 2001. *Oh waiter! One order of crow! Inside the strangest presidential election finish in American history.* New York: Putnam.

Gronbeck, Bruce E. 2009. The Web, campaign 07–08 and engaged citizens. In *The 2008 presidential campaign: A communication perspective*, Robert E. Denton, Jr., ed. Lanham, Md.: Rowman & Littlefield.

Grossman, Lawrence K. 1995. *The electronic republic: Reshaping democracy in the information age.* New York: Penguin.

Halberstam, David. 1979. *The powers that be.* New York: Knopf.

Haldeman, H. R. 1994. *The Haldeman diaries: Inside the Nixon White House.* New York: Putnam.

Hall, Jim. 2001. *Online journalism: A critical primer.* London: Pluto.

Hallin, Daniel C. 1984. The media, the war in Vietnam, and political support: A critique of the thesis of an oppositional media. *Journal of Politics* 46 (1): 2–24.

Halperin, Mark, and John F. Harris. 2007. *The way to win: Taking the White House in 2008*. New York: Random House.

Harris, John F., and Jonathan Martin. 2009. The George W. Bush and Bill Clinton legacies in the 2008 elections. In *The American elections of 2008*, ed. Janet M. Box-Steffensmeier and Steven E. Schier. Lanham, Md.: Rowman & Littlefield.

Hart, Roderick P. 1994. *Seducing America: How television charms the modern voter.* New York: Oxford University Press.

Harwood Group. 1991. *Citizens and politics: A view from Main Street America.* Dayton, Ohio: Kettering Foundation.

———. 1993. *College students talk politics.* Dayton, Ohio: Kettering Foundation.

Healy, Patrick. 2007. To '08 hopefuls, media technology can be friend or foe. *New York Times*, January 31.

Herman, Edward S., and Noam Chomsky. 1988. *Manufacturing consent: The political economy of the mass media.* New York: Pantheon.

Hershey, Marjorie Randon. 1989. The campaign and the media. In *The election of 1988: Reports and interpretations*, ed. Gerald M. Pomper. Chatham, N.J.: Chatham House.

———. 2001. The campaign and the media. In *The election of 2000*, ed. Gerald M. Pomper. New York: Chatham House.

Hertsgaard, Mark. 1989. *On bended knee: The press and the Reagan presidency.* New York: Schocken.

Hess, Stephen. 2000a. Critical information not covered by the media. *USA Today*, September 25.

———. 2000b. Viewers seek fairness in TV political News. *USA Today*, October 23.

Hetherington, Marc. 2001. Declining trust and a shrinking policy agenda: Why media scholars should care. In *Communication in U.S. elections: New agendas*, ed. Roderick P. Hart and Daron R. Shaw. Lanham, Md.: Rowman & Littlefield.

Hertherington, Marc, and Suzanne Globetti. 2006. The presidency and political trust. In *The presidency and the political System.* 8th ed, ed. Michael Nelson. Washington, D.C.: CQ Press.

Hibbing, John R., and Elizabeth Theiss-Morse. 1995. *Congress as public enemy: Public attitudes toward American political institutions.* Cambridge: Cambridge University Press.

Hofstetter, C. Richard. 1976. *Bias in the news.* Columbus: Ohio State University Press.

Hollihan, Thomas A. 2001. *Uncivil wars: Political campaigns in a media age.* Boston: Bedford/St. Martin's.

Homaday, Ann. 2007. Throwing her hat on the Web. *Washington Post*, January 21.

Hulse, Carl. 2006. Senator from Virginia addresses Jewish ancestry. *New York Times*, September 20.

Hunt, A. 1985. Media bias is in the eye of the beholder. *Wall Street Journal*, July 23.

Iyengar, Shanto. 1991. *Is anyone responsible? How television frames political issues.* Chicago: University of Chicago Press.

Iyengar, Shanto, and Kyu Hahn. 2009. Red media, blue media: Evidence of ideological selectivity in media use. *Journal of Communication* 59 (1): 19–39.

Iyengar, Shanto, and Donald R. Kinder. 1987. *News that matters*. Chicago: University of Chicago Press.

Iyengar, Shanto, Helmut Norpoth, and Kyu S. Hahn. 2004. Consumer demand for election news: The horserace sells. *Journal of Politics* 66 (1): 157–75.

Jacobson, Gary C. 2001. Congress: Elections and stalemate. In *The elections of 2000*, ed. Michael Nelson. Washington, D.C.: CQ Press.

Jamieson, Kathleen Hall. 1996. *Packaging the presidency*. 3d ed. New York: Oxford University Press.

———. 2000. *Everything you think you know about politics and why you're wrong*. New York: Basic.

Jamieson, Kathleen Hall, and Paul Waldman. 2002. The morning after: The effect of the network call for Bush. *Political Communication* 19 (1): 113–18.

Janowitz, Morris. 1983. *The reconstruction of patriotism: Education for civic consciousness*. Chicago: University of Chicago Press.

Johnson, Peter. 2004. Kerry, Stewart, talk pop, politics. *USA Today*, August 25.

Jones, Jeffrey P. 2001. Forums for citizenship in popular culture. In *Politics, discourse, and American society: New agendas*, ed. Roderick P. Hart and Bartholomew H. Sparrow. Lanham, Md.: Rowman & Littlefield.

———. 2010. *Entertaining politics: Satiric television and political engagement*. Lanham, Md.: Rowman & Littlefield. Second edition.

Just, Marion R., Ann N. Crigler, Dean E. Alger, and Timothy E. Cook. 1996. *Crosstalk*. Chicago: University of Chicago Press.

Karabell, Zachary. 2000. *The last campaign: How Harry Truman won the 1948 election*. New York: Knopf.

Kellner, Douglas. 2002. Presidential politics: The movie. *American Behavioral Scientist* 46 (4): 467–86.

———. 2003. *From 9/11 to terror war: The dangers of the Bush legacy*. Lanham, Md.: Rowman & Littlefield.

Kerbel, Matthew Robert. 1995. *Remote and controlled: Media politics in a cynical age*. Boulder, Colo.: Westview.

———. 1998. *Edited for television: CNN, ABC, and American presidential elections*. 2d ed. Boulder, Colo.: Westview.

———. 2001. The media: Old frames in a time of transition. In *The elections of 2000*, ed. Michael Nelson. Washington, D.C.: CQ Press.

Kerbel, Matthew R., Sumaiya Apee, and Marc Howard Ross. 2000. PBS ain't so different: Public broadcasting, election frames, and democratic empowerment. *Harvard International Journal of Press/Politics* 5 (4): 8–29.

Key, V. O. 1966. *The responsible electorate*. Cambridge: Belknap Press of Harvard University Press.

Kinsley, Michael. 1992. Ask a silly question. *New Republic*, July 6.

Kirkpatrick, David D. 2006. Two ex-acquaintances of Senator Allen said he used slurs. *New York Times*, September 26.

Klain, Ronald A., and Jeremy B. Bash. 2002. The labor of Sisyphus: The Gore recount perspective. In *Overtime: The election 2000 thriller*, ed. Larry Sabato. New York: Longman.

Klapper, Joseph. 1960. *The effects of mass media*. Glencoe, Ill.: Free Press.

Klein, Joe. 2002. *The natural: The misunderstood presidency of Bill Clinton*. New York: Doubleday.

Kloer, P. 2000. Networks suffer convention deficit disorder. *Atlanta Journal-Constitution*, August 3.

Kovach, Bill, and Tom Rosenstiel. 1999. *Warp speed: America in the age of mixed media*. New York: Century Foundation Press.

Kumar, Martha Joynt. 2003a. The contemporary presidency: Communications operations in the White House of President George W. Bush: Making news on his terms. *Presidential Studies Quarterly* 33 (2): 366–93.

———. 2003b. Source material: The White House and the press: News organizations as a presidential resource and as a source of pressure. *Presidential Studies Quarterly* 33 (3): 669–83.

Kurtz, Howard. 1992a. The pundits, eating crow after Clinton comeback. *Washington Post*, March 18.

———. 1992b. Networks adapt to changed campaign role. *Washington Post*, June 21.

———. 1992c. When the media are on a roll, the candidate rides a wave. *Washington Post*, July 25.

———. 1992d. The talk show campaign: TV interviews emerge as preferred forum. *Washington Post*, October 28.

———. 1994. *Media circus: The trouble with America's newspapers*. New York: Times Books/Random House.

———. 1996a. Bob Dole's pollbearers. *Washington Post*, September 10.

———. 1996b. A big story, but only behind the scenes. *Washington Post*, November 13.

———. 1998. *Spin cycle: Inside the Clinton propaganda Machine*. New York: Free Press.

———. 2000a. Will the "slow" candidate win the big race? *Washington Post*, October 26.

———. 2000b. Is the press helping Bush? *Washington Post*, November 6.

———. 2001. Election coverage burned to a crisp. *Washington Post*, February 15.

———. 2002a. At ABC, a shaken news dynasty. *Washington Post*, March 6.

———. 2002b. Troubled times for network evening news. *Washington Post*, March 10.

———. 2005. Network fires four in wake of probe. *Washington Post*, January 11.

———. 2007a. Campaign allegations a source of vexation. *Washington Post*, January 22.

———. 2007b. Headmaster disputes claim that Obama attended Islamic school. *Washington Post*, January 23.

Larson, Stephanie G. 2001. Poll coverage of the 2000 presidential campaign on the network news. Paper delivered at the annual meeting of the American Political Science Association, San Francisco.

Laufer, Peter. 1995. *Inside talk radio: America's voice or just hot air?* Secaucus, N.J.: Carol.

Lawrence, Regina G. 2001. Defining events: Problem definition in the media arena. In *Politics, discourse, and American society: New agendas*, ed. Roderick P. Hart and Bartholomew H. Sparrow. Lanham, Md.: Rowman & Littlefield.

Lazarsfeld, Paul F., Bernard Berelson, and Hazel Gaudet. 1948. *The people's choice.* New York: Columbia University Press.

Leibovich, Mark. 2010. Palin, visible and vocal, is positioned for a variety of roles. *New York Times*, February 5.

Lengle, James I. 1981. *Representation and presidential primaries: The Democratic Party in the post-reform era.* Westport, Conn.: Greenwood.

———. 1987. Democratic Party reforms: The past as prologue to the 1988 campaign. *Journal of Law and Politics* 4:223–73.

Lengle, James I., Diana Owen, and Molly W. Sonner. 1995. Divisive primaries and Democratic electoral prospects. *Journal of Politics* 57:370–83.

Lesher, Stephan. 1982. *Media unbound: The impact of television journalism upon the public.* Boston: Houghton Mifflin.

Lewis, David A., and Roger P. Rose. 2002. The president, the press and the war-making power: An analysis of media coverage prior to the Persian Gulf War. *Presidential Studies Quarterly* 32 (3): 559–71.

Lewis-Beck, Michael S., and Tom W. Rice. 1992. *Forecasting elections.* Washington, D.C.: CQ Press.

Lewis-Beck, Michael S., and Charles Tien. 2001. Modeling the future: Lessons from the Gore forecast. *Political Science and Politics* 34 (1): 21–3.

Lichter, S. Robert. 1996. Consistently liberal: But does it matter? *Forbes Media Critic* (Fall): 26–39.

———. 2001. A plague on both parties: Substance and fairness in TV election news. *Harvard International Journal of Press/Politics* 6 (3): 8–30.

Lichter, S. Robert, Daniel Amundson, and Richard Noyes. 1988. *The video campaign.* Washington, D.C.: American Enterprise Institute.

———. 1989. Election '88: Media coverage. *Public Opinion* 11 (5): 18–19.

Lichter, S. Robert, and Richard E. Noyes. 1995. *Good intentions make bad news: Why Americans hate campaign journalism.* 2d ed. Lanham, Md.: Rowman & Littlefield.

———. 1998. *Why elections are bad news.* New York: Markle Foundation.

Lichter, S. Robert, Stanley Rothman, and Linda S. Lichter. 1990. *The media elite.* New York: Hastings House.

Lowi, Theodore J. 1985. *The personal president: Power invested, promise unfulfilled.* Ithaca, N.Y.: Cornell University Press.

Lowi, Theodore J., Benjamin Ginsberg, and Kenneth Shepsle. 2002. *American government: Power and purpose.* 7th ed. New York: Norton.

Maisel, L. Sandy. 2002. *Parties and elections in America: The electoral process.* 3d ed. Lanham, Md.: Rowman & Littlefield.

Margolis, Michael, and David Resnick. 2000. *Politics as usual: The cyberspace revolution.* Thousand Oaks, Calif.: Sage.

Massing, Michael. 2004. Now they tell us. *New York Review of Books*, February 26.

Mast, Gerald. 1971. *A short history of the movies.* Indianapolis: Pegasus.

Mayer, William G. 1987. The New Hampshire primary: A historical overview. In *Media and momentum: The New Hampshire primary and nomination politics*, ed. Gary R. Orren and Nelson W. Polsby. Chatham, N.J.: Chatham House.

————. 1996. Forecasting presidential nominations. In *In pursuit of the White House: How we choose our presidential nominees,* ed. William G. Mayer. Chatham, N.J.: Chatham House.

————. 1997. The presidential nominations. In *The elections of 1996: Reports and interpretations.* Chatham, N.J.: Chatham House.

————. 2001. The presidential nominations. In *The elections of 2000: Reports and interpretations.* Chatham, N.J.: Chatham House.

————. 2004. The basic dynamics of the contemporary nomination process: An expanded view. In *The making of the presidential candidates 2004,* ed. William G. Mayer. Lanham, Md.: Rowman & Littlefield.

McChesney, Robert W. 1999. *Rich media, poor democracy: Communication politics in dubious times.* New York: New Press.

————. 2004. *The problem of the media: U.S. communication politics in the 21st century.* New York: Monthly Review Press.

McCombs, Maxwell E., and Donald L. Shaw. 1977. *The Emergence of American Political Issues: The Agenda-Setting Functions of the Press.* St. Paul, MN: West Publishing.

————. 1993. The evolution of agenda-setting research: Twenty-five years in the marketplace of ideas. *Journal of Communication* 43 (2): 58.

McGinniss, Joe. 1969. *The selling of the president, 1968.* New York: Trident.

McKinley, Jesse. 2010. California ex-governor announces encore run. *New York Times,* March 2.

McLeod, Jack M., Gerald M. Kosicki, and Douglas M. McLeod. 1994. The Expanding Boundaries of political communication effects. In *Media effects: advances in theory and research,* ed. Jennings Bryant and Dolf Zillmann. Hillsdale, N.J.: Lawrence Erlbaum.

McLuhan, Marshall. 1964. *Understanding media: The extensions of man.* New York: Mentor.

McQuail, Denis. 2000. The influence and effects of mass media. In *Media power in politics,* ed. Doris Graber. 4th ed. Washington, D.C.: CQ Press.

McWilliams, Wilson C. 1993. The meaning of the election. In *The election of 1992: Reports and interpretations,* ed. Gerald M. Pomper. Chatham, N.J.: Chatham House.

Media Monitor. 2000. *Campaign 2000 final.* Washington, D.C.: Center for Media and Public Affairs.

————. 2001. *News in a time of terror.* Washington, D.C.: Center for Media and Public Affairs.

Meyer, Philip. 1993. The media reformation: Giving the agenda back to the people. In *The elections of 1992,* ed. Michael Nelson. Washington, D.C.: CQ Press.

Meyrowitz, Joshua. 1985. *No sense of place: The impact of electronic media on social behavior.* New York: Oxford University Press.

Milbank, Dana, and Mike Allen. 2004. Many gaps in Bush's Guard records. *Washington Post,* February 14.

Milbank, Dana, and Walter Pincus. 2003. Cheney defends U.S. actions in bid to revive public support. *Washington Post,* September 15.

Milbank, Dana, and Jim VandeHei. 2004. From Bush, unprecedented negativity. *Washington Post,* May 31.

Mindich, David T. Z. 2005. *Tuned out: Why Americans under 40 don't follow the news.* New York: Oxford University Press.

Mnookin, Seth. 2001. It happened one night. *Brill's Content* (February): 94–98, 150–53.

Moore, Frazier. 2010. Football, dramas, comedy make CBS most watched. The Associated Press, January 20. http://www.washingtonpost.com/wp-dyn/content/article/2010/01/20/AR2010012002268.html (accessed February 1, 2010).

Morris, Dick. 1997. *Behind the Oval Office: Winning the presidency in the nineties.* New York: Random House.

Mudd, Roger. 1987. Television network news in campaigns. In *Political persuasion in presidential campaigns,* ed. L. P. Devlin. New Brunswick, N.J.: Transaction.

Mueller, John E. 1973. *War, presidents, and public opinion.* New York: John Wiley & Sons.

Murray, Shailagh, Michael D. Shear, and Paul Kane. 2010. 2009 Democratic agenda severely weakened by Republicans' united opposition. *Washington Post,* January 24.

Mutz, Diana. 1992. Mass media and the depoliticization of personal experience. *American Journal of Political Science* 36 (2): 483–508.

———. 2006. *Hearing the other side: Deliberative vs. participatory democracy.* New York: Cambridge University Press.

Nader, Ralph. 2002. *Crashing the party: Taking on the corporate government in an age of surrender.* New York: St. Martin's.

Nagourney, Adam. 2004. Kerry might pay price for failing to strike back quickly. *New York Times,* August 21.

Nagourney, Adam, and Janet Elder. 2004. Bush's rating falls to its lowest point, new survey finds. *New York Times,* June 29.

Nagourney, Adam, and Megan Thee-Brennan. 2010. Poll finds edge for Obama over G.O.P. among the public. *New York Times,* February 11.

Nelson, Michael. 2001. The post-election election: Politics by other means. In *The elections of 2000,* ed. Michael Nelson. Washington, D.C.: CQ Press.

Neuman, W. Russell. 1986. *The paradox of mass politics: Knowledge and opinion in the American electorate.* Cambridge, Mass.: Harvard University Press.

Neustadt, Richard E. 1990. *Presidential power and the modern presidents: The politics of leadership from Roosevelt to Reagan.* New York: Free Press.

Nie, Norman H., Sidney Verba, and John R. Petrocik. 1979. *The changing American voter.* Cambridge, Mass.: Harvard University Press.

Nielsen Company. 2010. Television news ratings, week of January 18. http://en-us.nielsen.com/rankings/insights/rankings/television (accessed February 1, 2010).

Nincic, Miroslav. 1997. Loss aversion and the domestic context of military intervention. *Political Research Quarterly* 50 (1): 97–120.

Norrander, Barbara. 2009. Democratic marathon, Republican Sprint: The 2008 presidential nominations. In *The American elections of 2008,* ed. Janet M. Box-Steffensmeier and Steven E. Schier. Lanham, Md.: Rowman & Littlefield.

Norris, Pippa. 1996. Does television erode social capital? A reply to Putnam. *Political Science and Politics* 29 (3): 474–80.

———. 2001. A failing grade? The news media and campaign 2000. *Harvard International Journal of Press/Politics* 6 (2): 3–9.

Noyes, Richard, S. Robert Lichter, and Daniel Amundson. 1993. Was TV election news better this time? *Journal of Political Science* 21 (1): 3–25.

Orkent, Daniel. 2004. Weapons of mass destruction? Or mass distraction? *New York Times*, May 30.

Orren, Gary R., and Nelson W. Polsby, eds. 1987. *Media and momentum*. Chatham, N.J.: Chatham House.

Owen, Diana. 1995. The debate challenge: Candidate strategies in the new media age. In *Presidential campaign discourse: Strategic communication problems*, ed. Kathleen E. Kendall. Albany: State University of New York Press.

———. 1996. Who's talking? Who's listening? The new politics of talk radio shows. In *Broken contract? Changing relationships between Americans and their government*, ed. Stephen Craig. Boulder, Colo.: Westview.

———. 1997. The press' performance. In *Toward the millennium: The elections of 1996*, ed. Larry Sabato. Boston: Allyn & Bacon.

———. 2000. Popular politics and the Clinton/Lewinsky Affair: The implications for leadership. *Political Psychology* 21 (1): 161–77.

———. 2002. Media mayhem: Performance of the press in election 2000. In *Overtime: The election 2000 thriller*, ed. Larry Sabato. New York: Longman.

———. 2009. The campaign and the media. In *The American elections of 2008*, ed. Janet M. Box-Steffensmeier and Steven E. Schier. Lanham, Md.: Rowman & Littlefield.

Page, Benjamin I., Robert Y. Shapiro, and Glenn R. Dempsey. 1987. What moves public opinion. *American Political Science Review* 81 (1): 23–43.

Paletz, David L. 2002. *The media in American politics: Contents and consequences*. 2d ed. New York: Longman.

Paletz, David L., and Robert M. Entman. 1981. *Media power politics*. New York: Free Press.

Palmer, Niall A. 1997. *The New Hampshire primary and the American electoral process*. Westport, Conn.: Praeger.

Papai, Lacy, and Lori Robinson. 2000. Campaign reform. *American Journalism Review*, September.

Parmat, Herbert S. 2002. Election of 1988. In *History of American presidential elections, 1789–2001*. Vol. 11, ed. Arthur M. Schlesinger, Jr., and Fred L. Israel. Philadelphia: Chelsea House.

Patterson, Thomas E. 1980. *The mass media election: How Americans choose their president*. New York: Praeger.

———. 1994. *Out of order*. New York: Vintage.

———. 2000. Doing well and doing good. Research paper, Kennedy School Press Politics Center, Harvard University.

Patterson, Thomas E., and Robert McClure. 1976. *The unseeing eye*. New York: Putnam.

Perlstein, Rick. 2001. *Before the storm: Barry Goldwater and the unmaking of the American consensus*. New York: Hill & Wang.

Perret, Geoffrey. 2001. *Jack: A life like no other*. New York: Random House.

Pew Research Center for the People and the Press (cited in text as Pew). 1996. Survey. September 25–29.

———. 2000a. Voters unmoved by media characterizations of Bush and Gore. July 27.

———. 2000b. Media seen as fair, but tilting to Gore. October 15.

———. 2000c. Campaign 2000 highly rated. November 16.

———. 2000d. Internet election news audience seeks convenience, familiar names. December 3.

———. 2004a. Cable and Internet loom large in fragmented political news universe. January 11.

———. 2004b. News audiences increasingly politicized. June 8.

———. 2004c. Voters liked campaign 2004, but too much "mud-slinging." November 11.

———. 2008a. The Internet's broader role in campaign 2008. January 11.

———. 2008b. Key news audiences now blend online and traditional sources. August 17.

———. 2008c. High marks for the campaign, a high bar for Obama. November 13.

———. 2009. Press accuracy rating hits two decade low. September 13.

———. 2010. Understanding the participatory news consumer. March.

Polsby, Nelson. 1983. *Consequences of party reform.* Oxford: Oxford University Press.

Polsby, Nelson, and Aaron Wildavsky. 2000. *Presidential elections: Strategies and structures of American politics.* 10th ed. New York: Chatham House/Seven Bridges.

Pomper, Gerald M. 1989. The presidential election. In *The election of 1988*, ed. Gerald M. Pomper. Chatham, N.J.: Chatham House.

———. 2001. The presidential election. In *The election of 2000*, ed. Gerald M. Pomper. New York: Chatham House/Seven Bridges.

———. 2005. The presidential election: The ills of American politics after 9/11. In *The elections of 2004*, ed. Gerald M. Pomper. Washington, D.C.: CQ Press.

Postman, Neil. 1985. *Amusing ourselves to death.* New York: Penguin.

Publius (James Madison). 1788. The Federalist, vol. 51. *Independent Journal* (February 6, 1788).

Putnam, Robert D. 1995a. Bowling alone: America's declining social capital. *Journal of Democracy* 6 (January): 65–78.

———. 1995b. Tuning in, tuning out: The strange disappearance of social capital in America. *Political Science and Politics* 28 (4): 664–83.

———. 2000. *Bowling alone.* New York: Simon & Schuster.

Quirk, Paul J., and Jon K. Dalager. 1993. The election: A new Democrat and a new kind of presidential campaign. In *The elections of 1992*, ed. Michael Nelson. Washington, D.C.: CQ Press.

Ranney, Austin. 1983. *Channels of power.* New York: Basic.

Rash, Wayne, Jr. 1997. *Politics on the Nets.* New York: Freeman.

Rasmussen, Jim. 2004. Shame on the Swift Boat Veterans for Bush. *Wall Street Journal*, August 10.

Reich, Robert. 1998. *Locked in the cabinet.* New York: Vintage.

Rich, Frank. 2004. Paar to Leno, J.F.K. to J.F.K. *New York Times*, February 8 (2): 1.

Rimer, Sara, Ralph Blumenthal, and Raymond Bonner. 2004. Portrait of George W. Bush in '72: Unanchored in a turbulent time. *New York Times,* September 20.

Risen, James. 2006. *State of war: The secret history of the CIA and the Bush administration.* New York: Free Press.

Robinson, Michael J. 1976. Public affairs television and the growth of political malaise: The case of "The selling of the pentagon." *American Political Science Review* 70:409–32.

———. 1985. Where's the beef? Media and media elites in 1984. In *The American elections of 1984,* ed. Austin Ranney. Durham, N.C.: Duke University Press.

Robinson, Michael J., and Margaret A. Sheehan. 1983. *Over the wire and on TV.* New York: Russell Sage Foundation.

Roig-Franzia, Manuel, and Lois Romano. 2004. Few can offer confirmation of Bush's Guard service. *Washington Post,* February 15.

Rosen, Jay. 1992. Campaign issues: Discourse. *Columbia Journalism Review,* November–December: 34–35.

Rosenstiel, Tom. 1994. *Strange bedfellows: How television and the presidential candidates changed American politics, 1992.* New York: Hyperion.

Rosenstiel, Tom, and Bill Kovach. 2002. Why we need "Nightline." *Washington Post,* March 6.

Rueter, Theodore. 1988. Reflections on the New Hampshire primary. *Political Science and Politics* 21 (Spring): 273–77.

Rusher, William A. 1988. *The coming battle for the media.* New York: William Morrow.

Russert, Timothy J. 1990. For '92, the networks have to do better. *New York Times,* March 4.

Rutenberg, Jim. 2004a. CBS news concludes it was misled on Guard memos, network officials say. *New York Times,* September 20.

———. 2004b. Broadcast group to pre-empt programs for anti-Kerry film. *New York Times,* October 11.

Rutenberg, Jim, and Kate Zernike. 2004. CBS apologized for report on Bush Guard service. *New York Times,* September 21.

Ryan, Michael, and Douglas Kellner. 1988. *Camera politica: The politics and ideology of contemporary Hollywood film.* Bloomington: University of Indiana Press.

Sabato, Larry J. 2000. *Feeding frenzy: Attack journalism and American politics.* Baltimore: Lanahan.

———. 2002. The perfect storm: The election of the Century. In *Overtime: The election 2000 thriller,* ed. Larry Sabato. New York: Longman.

Sabato, Larry J., and Joshua J. Scott. 2002. The long road to a cliffhanger: Primaries and conventions. In *Overtime: The election 2000 thriller,* ed. Larry Sabato. New York: Longman.

Sabato, Larry J., Mark Stencel, and S. Robert Lichter. 2000. *Peepshow: Media and politics in an age of scandal.* Lanham, Md.: Rowman & Littlefield.

Samuelson, Robert J. 2005. Our entitlement paralysis. *Washington Post,* December 28.

Sanford, Bruce. 1999. *Don't shoot the messenger: How our growing hatred of the media threatens free speech for all of us.* New York: Free Press.

Schechter, Danny. 2003. *Media wars: News at a time of terror.* Lanham, Md.: Rowman & Littlefield.

Schneider, William, and I. A. Lewis. 1985. Views on the news. *Public Opinion* 8 (4): 6–11.

Schudson, Michael. 1978. *Discovering the news.* New York: Basic.

Seelye, Katharine Q. 2004. Both sides' commercials create a brew of negativity, at a boil. *New York Times,* September 22.

Seelye, Katharine Q., and Ralph Blumenthal. 2004. Documents suggest Guard gave Bush special treatment. *New York Times,* September 9.

Seib, Philip. 2001. *Going live: Getting the news right in a real-time, online world.* Lanham, Md.: Rowman & Littlefield.

Shear, Michael D. 2010. Better focus, faster response part of Obama communications plan. *Washington Post,* February 15.

Shogan, Robert. 2001. *Bad news: Where the press goes wrong in the making of the president.* Chicago: I. R. Dee.

Sigelman, Lee, and David Bullock. 1991. Candidates, issues, horse races, and hoopla: Presidential campaign coverage, 1888–1988. *American Politics Quarterly* 19 (1): 5–32.

Simien, Evelyn M. 2009. Clinton and Obama: The impact of race and sex on the 2008 Democratic presidential primaries. In *Winning the presidency, 2008,* ed. William J. Crotty. Boulder, Colo.: Paradigm.

Simon, Adam. 2001. A unified method for analyzing media framing. In *Communication in U.S. elections: New agendas,* ed. Roderick P. Hart and Daron R. Shaw. Lanham, Md.: Rowman & Littlefield.

Simon, Roger. 2001. *Divided we stand: How Al Gore beat George Bush and lost the presidency.* New York: Crown.

Skocpol, Theda. 1997. *Boomerang: Health care reform and the turn against government.* New York: Norton.

Smith, Culver H. 1977. *The press, politics, and patronage.* Athens: University of Georgia Press.

Smith, Ted. J., III, S. Robert Lichter, and Louis Harris and Associates. 1997. *What the people want from the press.* Washington, D.C.: Center for Media and Public Affairs.

Sparrow, Bartholomew. 1999. *Uncertain guardians: The news media as a political institution.* Baltimore, Md.: Johns Hopkins University Press.

Spitzer, Robert J. 2009. "Hot" and "not so hot" buttons in the 2008 presidential election: From Wasilla to Wall Street. In *Winning the presidency, 2008,* ed. William J. Crotty. Boulder, Colo.: Paradigm.

Sprague, Stuart. 1984. The New Hampshire primary. *Presidential Studies Quarterly* 14 (Winter): 127–31.

Stanley, Harold W. 1997. The nominations: Republican doldrums, Democratic revival. In *The elections of 1996,* ed. Michael Nelson. Washington, D.C.: CQ Press.

———. 2001. The nominations: Return of the party leaders. In *The elections of 2000,* ed. Michael Nelson. Washington, D.C.: CQ Press.

Stelter, Brian. 2010. Politicians as news analysts raise questions on their goal. *New York Times,* February 14.

Stephanopoulos, George. 1999. *All too human: A political education.* Boston: Little, Brown.

Stout, David. 2006. Senator said he meant no insult by remark. *New York Times*, August 16.

Sunstein, Cass R. 2001. *Republic.com*. Princeton, N.J.: Princeton University Press.

Sunstein, Cass R., and Richard A. Epstein. 2001. *The vote: Bush, Gore, and the Supreme Court*. Chicago: University of Chicago Press.

Tapper, Jake. 2001. *Down and dirty: The plot to steal the presidency*. Boston: Little, Brown.

———. 2002. Down and dirty, revisited: A postscript on Florida and the news media. In *Overtime: The election 2000 thriller*, ed. Larry Sabato. New York: Longman.

Taylor, Paul. 2000. The new political theater. *Mother Jones* (November–December): 30–33.

———. 2002. *The case for free air time*. Washington, D.C.: Alliance for better campaigns.

Terwilliger, George J., III. 2002. A campout for Lawyers: The Bush recount perspective. In *Overtime: The election 2000 thriller*, ed. Larry Sabato. New York: Longman.

Toner, Robin. 2006. In bruising Virginia senate fight, women may make the difference. *New York Times*, November 3.

Trippi, Joe. 2004. *The revolution will not be televised: Democracy, the Internet, and the overthrow of everything*. New York: HarperCollins.

Vavreck, Lynn. 2001. Voter uncertainty and candidate contact: New influences on voter behavior. In *Communication in U.S. elections: New agendas*, ed. Roderick P. Hart and Daron R. Shaw. Lanham, Md.: Rowman & Littlefield.

Veblen, Eric. 1975. *The Manchester union leader in New Hampshire elections*. Hanover, N.H.: University Press of New England.

Wade, Steven M. 2002. election of 1972. In *History of American presidential elections, 1789–2001*. Vol. 10, ed. Arthur M. Schlesinger, Jr., Fred L. Israel, and William P. Hanson. Philadelphia: Chelsea House.

Washington Post. 2001. *Deadlock: The inside story of America's closest election*. New York: PublicAffairs.

Wayne, Stephen J. 2001. *The road to the White House, 2000: The politics of presidential elections*. Boston: Bedford/St. Martin's.

———. 2003. *Is this any way to run a democratic election?* 2d ed. Boston: Houghton Mifflin.

West, Darrell M. 2005. *Air wars: Television advertising in election campaigns, 1952–2004*. 4th ed. Washington, D.C.: CQ Press.

West, Darrell M., and Burdett A. Loomis. 1999. *The sound of money: How political interests get what they want*. New York: Norton.

White, Theodore H. 1961. *The making of the president, 1960*. New York: Atheneum House.

———. 1978. *In search of history*. New York: Warner.

Wilgoren, Jodi. 2004. Truth be told, the Vietnam crossfire hurts Kerry more. *New York Times*, September 24.

Wlezien, Christopher. 2001. On forecasting the presidential vote. *Political Science and Politics* 34 (1): 25–31.

Woodward, Bob. 1994. *The agenda: Inside the Clinton White House.* New York: Pocket Books.

———. 1999. *Shadow: Five presidents and the legacy of Watergate.* New York: Simon & Schuster.

———. 2006. *State of denial: Bush at war, part three.* New York: Simon & Schuster.

Woodward, Bob, and Carl Bernstein. 1976. *The final days.* New York: Simon & Schuster.

Wright, Robin. 2004. Iraq occupation erodes Bush Doctrine. *Washington Post,* June 28.

Zernike, Kate, and Jim Rutenberg. 2004. Friendly fire: The birth of an attack on Kerry. *New York Times,* August 20.

Index

About the Authors

Stephen J. Farnsworth, Ph.D., teaches courses in political communication and journalism at George Mason University, where he is assistant professor of communication. He is also a former daily newspaper journalist.

S. Robert Lichter, Ph.D., is professor of communication at George Mason University, where he directs the Center for Media and Public Affairs, a non-profit, nonpartisan media research organization.